D1593547

Experience of God and the Rationality of Theistic Belief

A volume in the series

Cornell Studies in the Philosophy of Religion

EDITED BY WILLIAM P. ALSTON

A full list of titles in the series appears at the end of the book.

Jerome I. Gellman

Experience of God and the Rationality of Theistic Belief

Cornell University Press, Ithaca and London

Copyright © 1997 by Cornell University

All rights reserved. Except for brief quotations in a review, this book, or parts thereof, must not be reproduced in any form without permission in writing from the publisher. For information, address Cornell University Press, Sage House, 512 East State Street, Ithaca, New York 14850.

First published 1997 by Cornell University Press

Library of Congress Cataloging-in-Publication Data

Gellman, Jerome I.
   Experience of God and the rationality of theistic belief / Jerome
I. Gellman.
     p.   cm. — (Cornell studies in the philosophy of religion)
   Includes bibliographical references and index.
   ISBN 0-8014-3320-7 (cloth : alk. paper)
   1. God—Proof, Empirical.   2. Theism.   3. Experience (Religion)
I. Title II. Series.
   BL473.G44 1997
   212'.1—DC20   96-41524

Printed in the United States of America

This book is printed on Lyons Falls Turin Book,
a paper that is totally chlorine-free and acid-free.

Cloth printing   10 9 8 7 6 5 4 3 2 1

SSH
CIR

R0125972817

SOCIAL SCIENCES DIVISION
CHICAGO PUBLIC LIBRARY
400 SOUTH STATE STREET
CHICAGO, IL 60605

To Edie

Contents

Preface

This book was written from the conviction that in an impressive number of instances God has been and continues to be known in experience. This conviction came about in part because of my own mystic-like experiences, which I deem to be far dimmer and poorer than what others seem to have known. I realized that there are those who would dismiss all apparent experiences of God as "subjective." Yet others would claim to be able to discover alleged psychological, or other, facts about subjects who seemed to experience God which would explain away what had happened. Then there would be those who would dismiss such experiences as credible only if one accepted a certain amount of religious doctrine, the latter being dubious, or worse, in their eyes. Still others might invoke religious doctrine to deny that experiences of God really did take place, or took place as often as it seemed to me they did. And others would have different objections. In pondering all these objections I found myself thoroughly convinced that even were we to grant that some supposed experiences of God could be dismissed, and were we to set religious doctrine aside altogether, the attempt at a general dismissal of experiences of God could not succeed. This book was undertaken to clarify and defend that conviction.

I owe a debt of gratitude to a number of people in connection with this book. For the style of the argument I am indebted to Richard Swinburne and his "principle of credulity." For the clarification of several of the epistemological issues involved in the topic of experience of God I am grateful for the writings of William Alston. And for the philosophical spirit of this work I owe much to Alvin Plantinga, my teacher back in the old glory days of the Wayne State University philosophy department. From Plantinga I learned a degree of rigor, clarity, and courage in philosophical argumentation in general, and in philosophy of religion in particular, which has served as a model I have tried to emulate, with what success I cannot say.

In addition I thank William Alston for his most helpful comments on the manuscript. Also, early on Ira Schnall read the first three chapters and raised several points that forced me to think more carefully than I had about the epistemological commitments into which I was getting myself. And David Widerker's criticisms were most appreciated in the writing of Chapter 7.

I thank as well the members of the theology seminar of the Shalom Hartman Institute in Jerusalem, especially Yitzhak Benbaji, Eliezer Malchiel, and Avi Ravitsky, who challenged the ideas in this book with admirable tenacity and thereby brought me to a higher level of effort at clarity and detail than I might otherwise have undertaken.

On a more personal note, I am thankful for Rabbi Shalom Noah Brozovsky, the Slonimer Rebbe. Although he would not agree with some of the things I have written here, without his spiritual teaching I doubt this work would have been written.

And finally, I am grateful to my wife, Edie, for her loving patience and understanding—always. To her I dedicate this book.

I pray my book not be as a stumbling block to the reader.
So may it be Thy will.

JEROME (YEHUDA) GELLMAN

Beer-sheva, Israel

Experience of God
and the Rationality of
Theistic Belief

Introduction

I

This work is a sustained argument for the rationality of belief in God based on the evidence that across various religions down through history people seem to have experienced God.[1]

If we confine ourselves to rationality in light of evidence, a belief may be said to be *externally* rational when in light of the evidence it *would* be rational to accept it; and it is *internally* rational, relative to a person, when actually held by that person in a rational way relative to the evidence. A belief can be externally rational, then, even if nobody holds it, as long as it would be rational to hold it. And a belief that is externally rational may be held in an internally irrational way by any given person.

We are interested in arguing for the external rationality of belief in God on the basis of the available evidence of apparent experiences of God, considered within the total relevant available evidence. We are not concerned to defend the internal rationality of the belief of any believer in God. A given believer may form a belief that fails to be internally rational, even if externally rational in light of the evidence available to her. She may misperceive the evidence or reason incorrectly from the evidence to the

---

[1] As we use the term here, that someone has an "experience" of God entails that God exists and that the experience is *of* God, in the sense of God's being an actual being which the person experiences. When we wish to leave open the entailment to God's existence we will write of "seeming," or "alleged" experiences of God, or the like. Even though by our usage every *experience* of God is truly and really of God, sometimes we will write of "true" or "real" or "actual" experiences of God when wishing to emphasize that if a person has an experience of God, then God is an actual object of the experience, and so exists.

conclusion. We are here setting aside the entire issue of the internal rationality of the belief in God of actual believers.

We may distinguish four grades of external rationality, as follows:

> The belief *that p* possesses *universal strong* (external) rationality when in light of the total relevant evidence, on *any* reasonable application of the canons of rationality it is rational to believe that p and not rational to believe that not-p.

> The belief *that p* possesses *strong* (external) rationality when in light of the total relevant evidence, there exists *some* reasonable application of the canons of rationality on which it is rational to believe that p and not rational to believe that not-p.

> The belief *that p* possesses *universal weak* (external) rationality when in light of the total relevant evidence, on *any* reasonable application of the canons of rationality it is rational to believe that p and also rational to believe that not-p.

> The belief *that p* possesses *weak* (external) rationality when in light of the total relevant evidence, there exists *some* reasonable application of the canons of rationality on which it is rational to believe that p and also rational to believe that not-p.

If a belief possesses universal strong rationality it also possesses strong rationality. But a belief may possess strong rationality and not universal strong rationality, because all applications of the canons of reasoning to the same evidence need not yield uniform results. This is because principles of rationality often call for judgments about matters not rigorously provided for in those principles. For example, sometimes we are required to draw a conclusion, "everything else being equal." But whether everything else *is* equal may be a matter of judgment for which there are no rigorous procedures. If *any* reasonable judgment on the matter would draw the same conclusion, then belief in that conclusion possesses universal strong rationality. But if some reasonable judgments would draw that conclusion while others wouldn't, then the belief would have strong rationality but not universal strong rationality.

In this work we will be arguing for the strong (external) rationality of belief in God from apparent experiences of God and in light of our total relevant evidence. We will not be arguing for its *universal* strong rationality. And that is because we concede that at various junctures of our argument a person could make reasonable applications of our principles different from the ones we make which would block our conclusion in the end, or would greatly weaken it. One reason that happens is because principles we appeal to contain an "everything else being equal" clause, which requires a judgment not provided for by canons of rationality. We are concerned to argue, then, only that the applications we make of our principles at those junctures are reasonable applications of canons of rationality.

At the same time, the principles of rationality we shall be employing show not only that it is reasonable or justified to believe that God exists. They also show that it is *not* reasonable or justified to believe that God does *not* exist. All told, then, we will be arguing that the canons of rationality have at least some reasonable application to the facts concerning what are apparently experiences of God on which it is rational to believe that God exists and not rational to believe that God does not exist. Thus, we are arguing for the strong (external) rationality of belief in God.

We have no interest in claiming that belief in God is rational *only* if based on evidence, let alone only if based on considerations of experience of God. We ourselves have argued elsewhere that belief in God can be proper in the absence of any evidence, being a "rock-bottom" belief,[2] and Alvin Plantinga has argued convincingly that belief in God can be what he calls "properly basic" and as such perfectly rational in the absence of evidential justification.[3]

So we are not claiming that a believer in God, to be rational, must base her belief on evidence or even think that her belief is somehow rationally defensible on evidential grounds, even if she herself does not quite know how that would go. We recognize that in certain circumstances a believer who just "finds herself" believing in God without any justifying evidence, *could* be perfectly rational in doing so.

Nonetheless, the evidential endeavor has great importance. For one thing, there may be many believers for whom belief in God is not rock-bottom or basic, and for whom, in their present cognitive state, belief in God is rational or justified only if based on evidence. Second, we argue that belief in God is *strongly* rational "for everyone" in light of the evidence. This implies that (on at least some applications of canons of rationality) "for everyone" it is externally rational to believe in God and that "for everyone" it is not externally rational not to believe in God. But justifying a belief in God as a rock-bottom or basic belief that has no

---

[2] See Jerome I. Gellman, "Religious Diversity and the Epistemic Justification of Religious Belief," *Faith and Philosophy* (1993): 345–64.

[3] See Alvin Plantinga, "Is Belief in God Rational?" in *Rationality and Religious Belief*, ed. C. F. Delaney (Notre Dame: University of Notre Dame Press, 1979), pp. 7–27, and Plantinga, "Is Belief in God Properly Basic?" *Noûs* 15 (1981): 41–53.

justifying evidence would imply only that it was rational for the person in question to believe in God (when the belief was held in a certain way), and at most that it was not rational for that person not to believe in God.

And finally, philosophers of religion should address the needs of "evidentialists," people who just find themselves believing that belief in God requires evidential support in order to be rational, as well as the needs of those who have no firm opinion about whether or not belief in God requires evidential support. Our enterprise is designed to show that when left to evidence, belief in God is (externally) strongly rational. This is not meant to imply that only on evidence is belief in God rational or quite in order.

Our argument will be based upon the claim that purportedly God has been experienced over the course of history by a great number of adherents in several of the world's major religions. This is testified to by the Bible and other religious texts, and by numerous reports and descriptions of people's experiences. When we say that God has purportedly been experienced we do not mean to refer exclusively or even mainly to purported *revelations* from God, taking "revelation" in the narrow sense of an experience in which it seems that God has revealed some truths or commands or His will for humankind or for an entire nation, or the like. Judging from the history of purported experiences of God, they are typically of God's very presence or of God's acting toward the subject of the experience in some way or other, or of God's revealing His will as that pertains solely to the particular person undergoing the experience. Revelations, in the present narrow sense, are not typical of alleged experiences of God. For this reason, our main focus will not be on alleged experiences of such revelations.[4]

We shall deal with the topic of revelation only in connection with the protestation that revelations between religions tend to be mutually inconsistent, and that for this reason at least this type of alleged experience of God is an unreliable basis on which to argue. We shall reply in Chapter 4

[4] There are other senses of "revelation" besides one involving propositional content or commands, ones for which the above would have to be revised. For example, on what George Lindbeck calls the "experiential-expressive" model of understanding the relationship between religion and experience, it could turn out that most apparent experiences of God are revelations, in the sense of being the type of experience which grounds religious doctrine and behavior as "expressive" of that experience. See George Lindbeck, *The Nature of Doctrine: Religion and Theology in a Postliberal Age* (Philadelphia: Westminster Press, 1984), chapters 1 and 2. See also Keith Ward, *Religion and Revelation* (Oxford: Clarendon Press, 1994), for a concept of revelation involving less than the revealing of specific propositional content.

that there is much less inconsistency between alleged revelations than might be supposed, and so there is less reason than might be supposed to have to choose between them. Hence, over all, the issue of revelation does not impugn the reliability of alleged experiences of God.

In what follows we present only an argument scheme rather than an argument, since the claim that God is reported to be experienced is only stated and sparsely illustrated in this work, not documented. There are many sourcebooks from which the reader can learn of the widespread apparent phenomenon of experience of God across various religions. Our aim is to concentrate with care and in depth upon the philosophical argument predicated on the claim that God is apparently experienced. The bibliography at the end of this work includes studies which flesh out our argument scheme.

II

From the claim about purported experiences of God, we will be drawing the conclusion that God *really is* experienced across various of the world's religions. But although we are interested in affirming that God is truly experienced in various religions, nothing in our argument is meant to imply what we might call "hard pluralism," that (somehow) all religions are equally valid.[5] On the one hand, it *is* perfectly consistent with what we argue that all religions are *equally* graced with God's living presence, and equally bring their adherents to a realization of God. Also, it is consistent with our argument to claim that all religions are but human attempts, some better, some worse, to relate in an appropriate way toward God, and that none of them has any particular Divine sanction, or at least no more than any other religion.[6]

On the other hand, it is *also* perfectly consistent with the argument of this work to be what we might call a "soft pluralist," and argue, believe, or have faith that one religion has a fuller understanding of these matters than do others, or that God has a special relationship with one people, or that God, although *appearing* to all, has revealed His will only to some and not to others.

A Christian, for example, could accept our conclusion that God is experienced by adherents of various religions and adopt Karl Rahner's doctrine

---

[5] The terms "hard" and "soft" pluralism are borrowed from Ward, *Religion and Revelation*, pp. 317–18.

[6] This is the position of John Hick. See John Hick, *An Interpretation of Religion: Human Responses to the Transcendent* (London: Macmillan, 1989).

of anonymous Christianity, that "Christianity does not simply confront the member of an extra-Christian religion as a mere non-Christian but as someone who can and must be regarded in this or that respect as an anonymous Christian."[7] Hence, a Moslem could be thought to experience God as an anonymous Christian.

Or a devout Jew could agree with our argument and accept the view of Rabbi Abraham Isaac Kook (1865–1935) that *individuals* in religions other than Judaism can reach spiritual heights of knowledge of God, but that only the Jewish people enjoys such spiritual grace as a nation. Then she could believe, in consistency with the argument of this book, that while God is experienced by devotees of religions other than Judaism, an experience of God on a national level is reserved for the Jews alone.[8]

Or one could believe that there is a kind of "Divine Sense" placed in the heart and mind of every human being by which every person is aware of God's presence, and that this awareness is *somewhat* corrupted or dulled in others but not in those who adhered to one's own religion.[9] And so on.

Thus our argument leaves the status of any particular religion entirely open as regards to its truth, in itself or relative to other religions.

The conclusion that God really is experienced across various of the world's religions clashes, though, with particularistic religious doctrines which maintain that God could be known only by adherents of one's own religion. A devout Christian of a certain pious inclination might believe that God would appear only to devout Christians, and a devout Jew might hold that God reveals Himself only to members of the Chosen People. Such particularistic doctrines might be invoked to deny that God is experienced in religions other than one's own. If such doctrines were purportedly based on evidence independent of that provided by the particularist theology, then the evidence would have to be produced in order to counter the argument of this book that the evidence shows that God really is experienced by adherents of several of the world's religions.

Rather than being grounded in evidence, however, particularistic doctrines might reflect a religious world-view that constitutes the most funda-

[7] Karl Rahner, *Theological Investigations*, vol. 5 (Baltimore: Helicon Press, 1966), p. 131.

[8] See Abraham Isaac Kook, *The Essential Writings of Abraham Isaac Kook*, ed. and trans. Ben Zion Bokser (Amity, N.Y.: Amity House, 1988), pp. 31 and 168, and *Kook, A. Y.: Selected Letters*, trans. and annotated Tzvi Feldman (Ma'aleh Adumim, Israel: Ma'aliot 1986), pp. 115–18. Rabbi Kook also maintains that the awareness of God of a non-Jew is dimmer than that of a Jew.

[9] This would be different from what is apparently the doctrine of John Calvin that the Divine Sense has been *totally* corrupted for all humans but restored inside Christianity by an act of grace.

mental way a person has of confronting reality. The question of how such fundamental world-views function evidentially and how they confront independent evidence is a deep and large question which we are not capable of dealing with here (or maybe anywhere, for that matter). In any event, in arguing that God is experienced by the adherents of more than one religion we do not mean to imply that it is irrational to maintain a particularistic doctrine. We do not deny the rationality of religious beliefs that include a particularistic doctrine on which basis our argument would be unacceptable. But such a position does not clash with our claim that experience of God shows that belief in God's existence is *strongly* rational. For it to be strongly rational it's enough that there exist *some* reasonable application of the canons of rationality on which, because of the apparent experience of God across religions, down through history, it is rational to believe that God exists and not rational to believe that God does not exist. And that, we wish to claim, there is.

One who acknowledges the possibility of experiences of God only in his own religion might be able to produce an argument similar to ours having a weaker evidential base and thus supporting its conclusion to a relatively weaker degree than does our argument. We acknowledge that there may be other applications of the canons of rationality, such as those taking into consideration particularistic doctrines, on which the evidence of there being alleged experiences of God would be much curtailed relative to the evidence we recognize in this study.

Analogously, our conclusion may be resisted or rejected in the name of a conviction that our whole enterprise is hopeless or frivolous on the grounds that God could not possibly be really and truly experienced by anyone. One might be convinced, for example, that God is "transcendent," beyond the reach of finite mortals. But that claim does not deserve to be taken seriously without further argument, in the face of what seem to be a large number of instances in which mere finite mortals *have* experienced God. Or, one might be convinced that God does not exist, and so regard the idea of God's being experienced to be unworthy of serious consideration. Such a view too, however, would be disproved by our argument that from the substantial evidence that God *seems* to be experienced across several of the world's religions it should be concluded that God is *actually* experienced, and so exists. Of course, such a view may itself appeal to evidence, including evidence that God does not exist. In this work we will not be able to treat exhaustively the charge that there is evidence against the existence of God, evidence that overcomes our argument in favor of God's existence. But in the final two chapters we address some of the more important charges of this kind, and find them to be without basis. Although we hope to make an important contribution toward a negative conclusion about there being evidence that God does not exist, a final verdict on whether or not our argument for God's existence is outweighed by counter-evidence will have to wait.

It is possible, however, that the belief that God could not possibly be experienced might be part of a basic world-view, analogous to a religious world-view, on which it turns out that God could not possibly be experienced. As in the case of particularistic religious outlooks, we decline to enter into the philosophical issue of how such a world-view figures in discussions of evidence. We will make do by acknowledging the possibility of such a view being rational, and at the same time stressing that this possibility does not damage our claim to be able to show that the belief in God is (externally) strongly rational. At most, that such views are rational shows that belief in God does not enjoy *universal* strong rationality.

For purposes of this work, in all of our references to "evidence" for or against the existence of God we mean to "bracket" the relevance of both in-principle particularistic religious doctrines as well as in-principle views that God could not possibly be experienced.

III

For the style of argument employed in this work we are indebted to Richard Swinburne. Swinburne has argued that alleged experiences of God support belief in the existence of God on the basis of a principle he calls the "principle of credulity," which states that "it is a principle of rationality that (in the absence of special considerations) if it seems (epistemically) to a subject that x is present, then probably x is present."[10] He applies this principle to alleged experiences of God to reach the conclusion that probably God is present and experienced, and so exists. We base our argument on what we take to be an improved version of the principle of credulity, and then set out to defend our conclusion against objections. Unlike Swinburne, however, we argue that alleged experiences of God are themselves sufficient to show the strong rationality of belief in God (in the absence of countervailing evidence, of course). Swinburne uses such experiences only as part of a cumulative case for the existence of God.

We think of ourselves as taking Swinburne's basic insight, in the form of the principle of credulity, and giving it its most expanded development and

[10] Richard Swinburne, *The Existence of God*, rev. ed. (Oxford: Clarendon Press, 1991), p. 254.

defense to date. In addition, during the writing of this work, Carolyn Franks Davis's defense of Swinburne's argument came to our attention and we have learned much from it. We have depended upon it especially for our discussion of reductionism, in Chapter 5.[11]

In addition to Swinburne, William Alston has defended the rationality of believing that God is actually experienced.[12] Alston's argument is that taking certain experiences to be *of God* is part of a "doxastic practice," and that it is rationally justified to engage in that practice. Alston's argument relies on an analysis of the notion of a practice and of the justification of engaging in practices. Our defense of the rationality of believing that God is experienced and so exists does not proceed by way of defending a practice in which thinking oneself to be experiencing God occurs. We wish to appeal more directly to the perceptual basis of that rationality. Another difference between Alston's approach and ours is that Alston's argument establishes only the weak rationality of belief in God, whereas we desire to establish its strong rationality. Despite these differences, we owe a great deal to Alston's work for clarifying for us some of the central epistemological issues involved in defending the claim that God is experienced. If we are indebted to Swinburne for the direction of our argument, we are equally indebted to Alston for central epistemological tools which help us to carry it through.

In Chapter 1 we attend to preliminary matters. We first clarify what is meant by an "experience" of God, including grading levels of a person's realization that she is having an experience of God. Then we tackle what is meant by "God," concentrating on its meaning in religious life, where alleged experiences of God tend to occur. We defend the position that "God" is a proper name, to be understood along the lines of a modified theory of proper names as rigid designators.

In Chapter 2 we present our argument from alleged experiences of God and the frequency and variability with which they occur. We defend and employ two principles of rational reasoning from appearance to reality, one of them a variant on Swinburne's principle of credulity, and the other marking the strength of numbers and variability for evidence.

Chapter 3 deals with a number of different objections that grow out of the fact that alleged experiences of God are almost always private affairs and relatively uncommon, compared especially to our perception of physi-

[11] See Caroline Franks Davis, *The Evidential Force of Religious Experience* (Oxford: Clarendon Press, 1989).

[12] See William P. Alston, *Perceiving God: The Epistemology of Religious Experience* (Ithaca: Cornell University Press, 1991).

cal objects. The objections take us into issues of the epistemological justification of particular perceptual judgments in general.

Chapter 4 addresses objections arising out of the facts of religious diversity. We consider three major problem areas. The first is that in different
religions in which it is claimed that *God* is experienced, God is claimed to
be experienced in different ways, ways sometimes incompatible with one
another or at least widely at variance. From this there arises what we call
the "Argument from Multiple Theisms." The second issue arises from the
purported experience in the world's religions of hordes of lesser deities.
This poses the "Argument from Multiple Deities." And the third problem
arises from the purported experience in different religions of beings, each
claimed to be experienced as absolutely perfect or as in some sense "ultimate," where the properties of at least some of them are allegedly incompatible with properties attributed to God on purported experiences of
Him. This we call the "Argument from Multiple Perfect Beings." We conclude that our argument survives each one of these objections.

Chapter 5 is an examination of so-called reductionist arguments against
taking purported experiences of God as indications of God's presence or
existence. The reductionist makes the factual claim that a person who is
supposedly experiencing God is usually in some special circumstance or
other (other than that of allegedly experiencing God, and what is entailed
thereby). We address this factual claim, both in the form that the special
circumstances are pathological and in the form that they are nonpathological but insidious nonetheless. We examine the "Truth Reductionist"
charge that such special circumstances show that a person is *not* experiencing God as well as the "Evidence Reductionist" claim that such special
circumstances show that the alleged experience is not *evidence* on behalf of
God's being experienced in fact.

Chapter 6 opens with a summary of the discussion up until that point,
and we note that none of the objections aimed at the "experience end" of
alleged experiences of God does damage to our argument in Chapter 2.
We then turn to a consideration of arguments or evidence against God's
existence, as counterarguments from the "object end" to our argument
from the apparent experience of God. We survey the major intellectual
reasons for religious unbelief in contemporary Western society, attempting
to show that they are by and large irrelevant to the question of God's
existence. And then we set out to examine the first of two arguments
which, judging from the philosophical literature, seem to be the strongest
ones against the existence of God. In the remainder of Chapter 6 we take

up the charge that the concept of God is internally self-inconsistent or logically incoherent.

Chapter 7 is given over to the Argument from Evil. We discuss two forms of that argument, one which claims that there is a logical contradiction between the existence of God and evil, and one which has it that God's existence is only improbable given the existence of evil.

Chapter 7 closes with a summary of what is accomplished in this work:

It follows from what is said up until Chapter 6 that if there is no evidence against the existence of God, then it is strongly rational, on our argument, to believe that God is experienced and thus exists. And while we cannot claim to establish here that there is no evidence against God's existence, enough is said to weaken the impression that our argument from experience of God faces a vast array of types of counterevidence. And we also dispose of the two most dangerous looking arguments against God's existence.

So we conclude that as far as we take the question, which we trust is quite far, there is no evidence that God does not exist, and so our argument stands unchallenged by counterevidence to God's existence from the "object end" of those experiences. But neither is our argument adequately challenged from the "experience end."

Hence, we conclude that as far as we have considered the question, on the basis of the apparent experience of God it is strongly rational to believe that God is experienced and thus that God exists.

[1]

"Experience of God"

We begin by explicating the meaning of the expression "experience of God."[1] We attend first to the meaning of "experience of" as applied to God, and then to the meaning of "God."

I

As we will be using the term, that a person has an "experience" of X, or "experiences" X, entails that X exists and that the person's experience is *of* X, an actual being or object which the person experiences. When we wish to cancel the entailment we will write of "putative" or "purported" or "alleged" or "apparent" experiences of X. Even though by our usage, therefore, every *experience* of God is really of God as an actual being, sometimes we will write of "true" or "real" experiences of God when wishing to emphasize that if a person has an experience of God, then God exists and is an actual object of the experience.

Apparent experiences of God can be dramatic affairs, such as conversion experiences, or be soft, calm, and composed, or be something in between. A person might have what seems to her to be an experience of God only rarely or once in a lifetime. Or, a person may seem to sense God quite

---

[1] Martin Buber has protested against the use of phrases like "experience of God," because it fails to capture the structure of "relatedness" that is disclosed between a person and God. We, however, intend the phrase to be wide enough to include what Buber was concerned to include. See Martin Buber, *I and Thou*, ed. and trans. Walter Kaufmann (New York: Charles Scribner's, 1970).

regularly or even seem to sense God's presence day by day as a familiar component of his wakeful consciousness.

Apparent experiences of God can range from an awareness of a most vivid and rich content to only a dim awareness of God's presence.

One will not be said to have an apparent "experience of God," as we are using this terminology, only because of having being aroused to contemplate the deeper side of life and brought to think of God. In Aldous Huxley's *Point Counterpoint* one of the characters believes that Beethoven's trios are a proof for the existence of God. We have heard the trios, and do not wish to deny that by listening to them one could come to have an awareness of what seems to be God's very presence. However, we must also be on guard against possibly confusing an experience in which, say, one is moved to deeply think about the meaning of life and (thus) about God, with one in which it seems that God is given as a very object of one's present experience.

Having an apparent experience of God, therefore, is analogous to having an apparent experience of a tree. One would not be said to have had an alleged experience of a tree if only having had a vivid idea of a tree come to mind, or because of a welling up inside of warm feelings when thinking about the tree in the yard. One would have had to have seemed to perceive the tree.

And the same principle works for experiencing God. An experience of God involves a subject's experiencing some phenomenal content which is *of* God. And an apparent or purported experience of God involves a subject's experiencing a phenomenal content which seems to be of God. Alleged experiences of God are typically of God's very presence or of God's acting toward the subject of the experience in some way or other. In a recent study of contemporary Christian believers, Johan Unger lists the following categories of reported experiences of God:[2]

1. Experiences of God's presence—either localized presence or omnipresence.

2. Experiences of God's action—either help, or enlightenment.

3. Experiences of God's call—to communion or service

4. Experiences of God's features—hand, face, etc.

5. Experiences of God as totality—the entire stimulus situation as God.

[2] In Johan Unger, *On Religious Experience: A Psychological Study* (Uppsala: Uppsala University Press, 1976), p. 98.

An apparent experience of God may involve sensory phenomenal content, as for example when God is apprehended "through" the perception of physical events or objects, or, as sometimes happens, when a person reports perceiving an extraordinary sensory content, such as a special sensory light, when experiencing God. But typically, an apparent experience of God consists of experiencing a nonsensory phenomenal content. An experience of such a sort is analogous to sense experience with regard to (A): its being a mode of experiential cognition, and (B): its having a phenomenal content analogous to the phenomenal content of sense-experience. We will therefore follow the usage of William Alston, and of John Baillie before him, and refer equally to the "experience" of God and to the "perception" of God.[3]

Readers who believe that only sensory experience should count as "perception" and who would therefore wish to deny that a nonsensory experience of God can be a "perception," may interpret this locution when used to describe an apparent experience of God to be meant to be taken only analogically with ordinary sense perception, as per (A) and (B).

We accept the "appearance theory of perception" for perception in general, as presented and argued for by William Alston and others.[4] We will not rehearse the arguments here, but we have been convinced by both Alston's argument that the leading competitor of the appearance theory (the "causal theory of perception") is flawed in principle, and by Alston's appeal to the intuitive rightness of the appearance theory. On the appearance theory of perception, a sensory experience itself displays an act-object structure. That implies that a sensory experience's seeming to be a perception *of something* is internal to the experience, belonging to the phenomenology of the experience itself.

On this theory, sensory perception does not consist merely of experiencing certain "qualities," which are then ascribed to some object or other. Perceiving a tree does not mean having an experience of certain qualities which is caused, in an appropriate way, by a tree. Rather, a sensory experience consists in something's appearing to the subject as such-and-such. The experience is constituted in an act-object form. It is part of the phenomenology of perception that it involves the (seeming) perception

---

[3] See William P. Alston, *Perceiving God: The Epistemology of Religious Experience* (Ithaca: Cornell University Press, 1991); and John Baillie, *The Sense of the Presence of God* (New York: Scribner's, 1962), p. 53.

[4] See William P. Alston, "Externalist Theories of Perception," *Philosophy and Phenomenological Research* 51 (1990): 73–97; Alston, *Perceiving God*, pp. 54–67; and P. Snowdon, "Perception, Vision, and Causation," *Proceedings of the Aristotelian Society* 81 (1980–81): 175–92.

of an object which appears to one. And when the perception is veridical the object of the perception is that object which *appeared* to the subject or was *presented* to the subject in the experience.

This does not mean that in order to count as a perception a subject must *take* the appearing object in a certain way. It means only that the object presents itself to the subject in some way or other. To say that a person *perceives* an object does not entail that she think about the object or make a judgment about it. Nor is perceiving an object only a matter of the object's *causing* the experience. Perception is a matter of an object's being present to one as such-and-such.

When a person only seems to perceive a certain object, O, but does not, the appropriate thing to say on this theory is that she had an experience with an act-object structure, which seemed to be an "of-O" experience, but was not.

By analogy, we adopt the appearance theory of perception for experiences of God. Thus, having an experience of God involves a phenomenal content displaying an act-object structure in which God appears to or is presented to a subject. It is not a matter of merely experiencing certain qualities that one then ascribes to God as the appropriate cause of their having been experienced.

And, to carry the analogy further, a subject need not *take* the appearing object to be God in order to be said to be experiencing or perceiving God. God need only be presented to the subject in some way or other. To say that a person *perceives* God does not entail that he think about God or make a judgment about Him. And there are surely differing degrees of realization that it is God that one is perceiving.

We have said that we accept the appearance theory of perception and will therefore talk about experience of God in the language of that theory. As far as we can tell, however, nothing in our argument for the strong rationality of believing that God is experienced and hence exists depends upon the truth of that theory. Thus a reader who supports another theory of perception may recast what we write into the vocabulary of his favorite theory without our argument being affected in a negative way.

II

We wish to develop further the analogy between sense perception and perception of God, as well as prepare some of the ground for our argument in the next chapter, by pointing out analogous grades of perceptual awareness in the two cases.

With sense perception, we may distinguish four grades of awareness or lack of awareness of X on the part of a subject, when "she is perceiving X" is true of her (where "X" is any way of referring to a specific object or kind of object).

Grade 1:

The person is fully aware of X *as* X. She *takes* what she is perceiving to be "X." For example, "She sees a tree" is true, and she is aware of the tree as a tree.

Grade 2:

The person is fully aware of X, but is not aware of X *as* X because she does not *take* what she perceives to be X. This can happen for various reasons, including that she does not have the concept "X," or believes that what is appearing to her is not X, or mistakes X for something else, or because X is not appearing in an X-like way.

Grade 3:

The person is only "subliminally" aware of X (whether or not *as* X). The subject is not fully aware of X, but X *registers* with the subject as indicated by the potential power of the perception of X to modify or influence the person's behavior. Evidence for a subliminal perception having occurred could include independent evidence that X was present to the subject, as well as evidence of behavioral changes best explained in that way.

Grade 4:

The person perceives X (whether or not *as* X) without being aware of X even subliminally. X is presented perceptually to the person, but the perception of X has no power to influence the subject's behavior. An example might be when you are engaged in deep discussion with a friend about what it means to say that "S experiences X." As you speak, an ant crawls up the front of your friend's shirt right in your line of vision. You, however, are so engrossed in arguing, that even though you perceive the ant, it fails to *register* with you. There is not created in you any predilection to modified behavior. We would want to say that you experienced or *perceived* the ant, because the ant was present to you perceptually. It was present to your senses in a way in which an ant crawling up the back of your friend's shirt was not. You *saw* the ant in front in a sense in which you did not even *see* the ant on your friend's back. To be sure, you were not *aware* that

you were seeing the ant. But you saw it nonetheless. The ant was present
to you in such a way that had you only consciously attended to your
present visual perception you would have had a conscious "of-ant" perceptual experience.

Now some readers may object to our including Grade 4, and maybe
Grade 3 as well, as *perceptions* of X on the grounds that in a perception of X
a subject must *take* X to be something or other or to have some qualities or
other. As we have said, we think otherwise. But nothing of importance
hangs on whether the word "perception" does or does not cover these two
kinds of cases. We could accommodate these worries about the word "perception" by recasting Grades 3 and 4 as follows:

Grade 3 Revised:
   There occur episodes in which an object, X, is present to a subject's
senses in such a way that X has the potential to influence the person's
behavior, even though the person is not aware of X.

Grade 4 Revised:
   There occur episodes in which an object, X, is present to a subject's
senses in such a way that X has no potential to influence the person's
behavior, but were the subject to consciously attend to what was present to
her senses, she would have a conscious experience of it.

So restated, we could then say that in Grades 3 and 4 the object was in a
sense-relation to the subject. In this way we would accommodate the feeling
that Grades 3 and 4 are not really perceptions.
   By analogy with ordinary sense-perception, in putative experiences of
God we may distinguish four grades of awareness or lack of awareness of
God on the part of a subject, when "She is perceiving God" is true of her.

Grade 1:
   The person is fully aware of God as God. She *takes* what she is experiencing to be God. In accordance with our previous remarks on ordinary
perception, a Grade 1 experience of God is not one in which only certain
"qualities" are perceived, which are then related to God, or then ascribed
to God as cause. It is not a matter of having an experience about which, as
it were, one then begins to ask of what, if anything, it is true. Rather, that
the experience is "of-God" is part of the phenomenology of the experience itself. There is an act-object structure to the experience, in which the

object appears with a bruteness of presence or objectivity. The bruteness is as much a phenomenal feature of a Grade 1 experience of God as it is of a Grade 1 experience of a tree.

Grade 2:

There is as much of an act-object structure to the experience as in Grade 1, in which God appears with a bruteness of presence or objectivity, but the person is not aware of God *as* God because she does not *take* what she perceives to be God. There are several ways in which this could happen. For one, a person may be perceiving God but misidentify what she is experiencing, identifying it as something other than God. For example, she might think she is experiencing a projection of her childhood image of her father, when really she is experiencing God. Or she might be convinced that she is experiencing the palpable beauty of a winter forest, when really experiencing God.

Or a person may not be sufficiently prepared for an experience of God, and so might fail to comprehend what she is experiencing. She might be aware of experiencing "something" but not able to identify it. Or she might be skeptical about the possibility of experiencing God altogether, or just not take the possibility seriously enough to be able to recognize that what she is experiencing is God, even though it is.

Or, a person may be aware of God, but not be aware of God *as* God because she may simply lack the concepts with which to formulate the thought that it is God.

A study discussed by Johan Unger shows how much more prevalent statistically are reports of experiencing God among persons belonging to organized churches, than among others.[5] A skeptic might attribute this to the suggestiveness of the church-going environment. But from a point of view recognizing these experiences as genuine, a good explanation for this phenomenon would be that the church people are in a better position to recognize a perception of God when it occurs than are others.

An alleged Grade 2 perception of God occurs in the biblical story of Samuel and Eli (Samuel I;3). Samuel, the Bible relates, had not yet known God, so when God calls to Samuel, Samuel runs to Eli, thinking that it was Eli who had called him. This happens three times. The first two times Eli simply sends Samuel back to bed. But by the third time Eli realizes that God is calling the lad and tells Samuel that it is God who has spoken. So the next time God calls, Samuel himself recognizes the call as divine.

[5] In Unger, *On Religious Experience*, pp. 45–55.

Grade 3:

The person is only "subliminally" aware of God (whether or not *as* God). The subject is not fully aware of God, but God "registers" with the subject as indicated by the potential power of the perception of God to modify the person's behavior.

From a point of view which recognizes perceptions of God, Grade 3 experiences might be invoked to help explain certain deep personal transformations, such as a person's marked change toward becoming a better or more spiritual person, explained as resulting from an intimate, subliminal awareness of God. In addition, from such a point of view Grade 3 experiences of God might help explain otherwise inexplicable acts of sudden, great unselfishness or heroism as responses to God when one does not realize that one is aware of God.

For all any of us knows, God may be appearing regularly in Grade 3 perceptions. This assumption could serve as the basis of a theistic psychology in which the subject is regarded as sometimes, at least, responding, unknowingly, to God, when she thinks she is responding to other stimuli or to other persons.

Of course, a Grade 3 experience of God could take place without any behavioral modifications in the subject. In a Grade 3 perception, the experience of God has the *potential* to influence the subject's behavior, but might not have any actual behavioral results.

Grade 4:

The person perceives God (whether or not *as* God) without being aware of God even subliminally. God is presented perceptually, but the perception of God has no power to influence the subject's behavior. She may be said to experience or perceive God because God is present to her in a nonsensory, perceptual way. Had she only been properly attentive, she could have had a conscious "of-God" experience.

From a point of view which recognizes perceptions of God, for all anyone knows God appears all the time to all creatures in Grade 4 experiences.

If some people object, as before, to our including Grades 3 and 4, in particular, as grades of *perception* of God, we can accommodate these worries by recasting Grades 3 and 4 as follows:

Grade 3, Revised:

God is present to a subject in a nonsensory way such that the episode has the potential to influence the person's behavior, even though the person is not aware of God.

Grade 4, Revised:
    God is present to a subject in a nonsensory way such that the episode has no potential to influence the person's behavior, but if the subject were to have consciously attended to what is present she would have a conscious perception of God.

Our argument from apparent experiences of God to God's actually being experienced will utilize apparent experiences of both the first and second grades. An apparent perception of God of the first grade is normally accessible to the consciousness of the experiencing person, and can be reported and conveyed by her to others. An apparent perception of the second grade is not readily accessible to the experiencing subject as an experience of *God*, but might be recognizable by others as an apparent experience of God, at least on occasion. So an experience of the second grade could be referred to in an argument of the sort we will present, even though in such cases it is false to assume that it seems to the subject that God is present.

Subsequent to establishing that God is experienced, based on apparent experiences of God of the first two grades, the way is then open to invoke subliminal perceptions of God of the third grade as explanatory of certain sorts of behavior, such as great spiritual growth and the like, which might be difficult to explain otherwise. Success in such explanatory endeavors, judged by what appears to be the best explanation of the phenomenon in question, would strengthen the initial argument that was based solely on the first two grades of awareness of God in perceptions of Him. And finally, depending on what is known about experiences of God and what is revealed about God in experiences of Him, and perhaps also on what might follow from theories about God, it might then be warranted to assert that God is always appearing to all of us, at least in perceptions of the fourth grade.

III

We now turn to the meaning of "God," and do so by considering its meaning in the religious life, where apparent experiences of God generally take place. In the dominant theological and mystical traditions, and among informed believers, "God" is regarded as an *absolutely perfect being*. The *generic* concept of God's being an absolutely perfect being, prior to particular ways of specifying the attributes upon which God's perfection is supervenient, is that God is possessed of a (positive) value such that no being could possibly possess a (positive) value greater than that. This can be explicated as: God possesses in every possible world the highest (positive) value that any possible being possesses in any possible world. A more modest explication would be that God *in fact* possesses the highest (positive) value that any possible being possesses in any possible world.[6] We will say, then, that the generic concept of an absolutely perfect being is that of a "maximally valuable being," leaving that phrase to wander freely between either of the two above explications.

It is, furthermore, part of the *generic* concept of an absolutely perfect being that every other being depends in some important way on this being for its existence, whereas the being itself depends upon nothing else for *its* existence. In different ways of delineating the attributes of a perfect being this concept can receive different interpretations, including thinking of a perfect being as the uncreated creator of all other beings, or as the sustaining ground of the existence of all other beings at every moment. The generic idea is, in any case, that an absolutely perfect being is ontologically independent whereas all others are ontologically utterly dependent upon it.

It follows that there could be at most one maximally valuable being. This is because there could not be two beings of each of which it were true that every other being ontologically depended upon it while it depended ontologically upon nothing else. Hence *a* maximally valuable being is *the* maximally valuable being.

God, when thought of as an absolutely perfect being, that is as a maximally valuable being, is commonly thought of as being omnipotent, omniscient, and wholly good.[7] When asking how these attributes enter into discourse about God, we do not rule out the possibility that a person could (allegedly) know by experience of God that God possessed these attributes. A person might be able to have an (alleged) experience in which God appears to be omnipotent, omniscient, or wholly good, or all of them together. Or, God could (allegedly) reveal to a person that He was omnipotent, omniscient, and wholly good.

More often, though, we believe that the "omni-attributes" enter into

---

[6] If it were argued that a being could have maximal possible value in any world only if it had it in every world, then the two explications would become equivalent.

[7] Other attributes are commonly attributed to God in virtue of His being an absolutely perfect being, such as His being eternal. For simplicity's sake throughout we will limit our attention to the three mentioned in the text.

discourse about God in a *secondary elaboration* upon the *generic* concept of an "absolutely perfect" or "maximally valuable" being.

This secondary elaboration can be thought of as being either *theologically* or *experientially* based, or both. When theologically based, the secondary elaboration results from pondering the *concept* of "absolute perfection" to see what it implies. When experientially based the secondary elaboration is explicative of alleged experiences of God in which He is disclosed to be an absolutely perfect being, taken together with experiences in which God is allegedly perceived as possessing (at least some) power, knowledge, and goodness. Then the attributes of omnipotence, omniscience, and omni-goodness are ascribed to God, because they are deemed to be elaborations true to what is disclosed about God in experiences of Him.[8]

We suggest that the elaboration of the generic concept of God's absolute perfection by way of the omni-attributes has a four-tiered structure. The first tier consists of asserting that God is absolutely perfect in the generic sense. The second tier consists of either the assertion that God's being perfect must mean that He possesses power, knowledge, and goodness, *or* consists of recognizing power, knowledge, and goodness, per se, in (alleged) experiences of God. The third tier involves thinking that God, since maximally valuable, must possess power, knowledge, and goodness, *individually*, in a perfect way or to a perfect degree. And the fourth tier has the assertion that God therefore must be able to "do everything," (be omnipotent), and "know everything," (be omniscient), and "do everything for the good," (be wholly good) in order for each of His power, knowledge, and goodness to be possessed by Him in a perfect way or to a perfect degree.

Whether this theological or experiential elaboration is compelling is discussed in Chapter 6. In the meantime we simply note that typically the attributes of omnipotence, omniscience, and omni-goodness seem to enter discourse about God in a secondary elaboration upon God's being thought of or experienced as an absolutely perfect or maximally valuable being.

We have said that God is regarded as an absolutely perfect being in the dominant theological and mystical traditions, and among informed be-

---

[8] This general approach to the omni-attributes as explications of absolute perfection is presented by Jerome I. Gellman in "The Paradox of Omnipotence, and Perfection," *Sophia* 14 (1975): 14, 31–39; and Gellman, "Omnipotence and Impeccability," *The New Scholasticism* 51 (1977): 151–61. A somewhat different form of this approach has been argued by George N. Schlesinger in "Divine Perfection," *Religious Studies* 21 (1985): 147–58; and Schlesinger, *New Perspectives on Old-Time Religion* (Oxford: Clarendon Press, 1988), pp. 4–34. We are not committed to Schlesinger's "Single–Divine–Attribute Doctrine," which has been much discussed in the philosophical literature. For more on this, see H. Scott Hestevold, "The Anselmian 'Single-Divine-Attribute Doctrine'," *Religious Studies* 29 (1993): 63–77.

lievers. But in a religious context, as opposed perhaps to purely philosophical uses of the name, we do not believe that "God" can be regarded as
synonymous with the phrase "an (or: the) absolutely perfect being." That
is because we regard the word "God" as used in a religious context to be
typically a proper name, meant to name some specific being one has in
mind, much as the name "John" is a proper name. And on each of the
currently leading philosophical theories about the meaning of proper
names, "God" would not be synonymous with the phrase, "a perfect being."⁹

Saul Kripke views proper names as being typically "rigid designators."¹⁰
A "rigid designator" refers to the same being or entity in every possible
world in which the being or entity exists, regardless of the differences in its
properties between worlds. The reference of a rigid designator is fixed by
an "initial baptism" in which the name comes to refer to a particular object. Subsequent references by the same term are meant to refer to that
very being which was named in the initial baptism, via a "referential
chain" leading back to the named object. It is the initial naming and subsequent referential chain which fix who or what is referred to by the rigid
designator. The naming is direct and successful without benefit of identifying descriptions.

For example, for Kripke the name "Aristotle" is a rigid designator referring to Aristotle, "our" Aristotle, in virtue of the name (actually a different, Greek name originally) having been pinned directly on that very person. It makes sense to imagine that Aristotle, that very person whom we
today call by that name, *could* have died at an early age and never studied
philosophy. In fact it even makes sense to think that someone could now
discover that Aristotle, our Aristotle, died at an early age and never studied
philosophy. This is because it makes sense to suppose that the name had
been given to him, our Aristotle, when it was, and that subsequently he,
our Aristotle, died at an early age and never studied philosophy. Instead,
the legend that he was a great philosopher grew up around *him*, our Aristotle. This is so even though the most central descriptions we think of
when thinking of Aristotle include that of his having been a philosopher,
since descriptions are not part of the semantic meaning of "Aristotle."

A second view of proper names, championed independently by Jerrold
Katz and Kent Bach, is that, unlike on Kripke's view, a proper name has

⁹ For an earlier attempt of the author to deal with the naming of God, see Jerome I.
Gellman, "Naming, and Naming God," *Religious Studies* 29 (1993): 193–216.
¹⁰ See Saul Kripke, *Naming and Necessity* (Oxford: Basil Blackwell, 1980).

meaning apart from the question of how it is used to refer.[11] To clarify their view and how it differs from Kripke's, let us attend to the distinction between the *semantic* and *pragmatic* aspects of language. Let the *semantic* properties of a sentence token, S, be those properties that S inherits from its sentence type. And let the *pragmatic* properties of a token, S, be those properties of S that belong to the token but which are not inherited from its type.[12]

For example, one understands the Spanish sentence, "Yo hablo Espanol," ("I speak Spanish") quite well even when it is not being *used* but merely presented, say, in a Spanish language learning list without reference to any person and any time. What one understands in that context is no more than that this sentence is used by a speaker to say of her/him self that she/he speaks Spanish. What is thereby understood is a property of the sentence type, since the sentence token is not being *used* by anyone at the time when it is read. The reader in understanding the sentence has grasped, therefore, the *semantic* properties of the type.

On the other hand, when hearing a token of that sentence as used, and understanding that it, the token, is presently being used by Bill to say of *himself* that *he* speaks Spanish, we grasp a fact about the token which is not inherited from the type. It is not a property of the type, after all, that it be used by Bill to say that he speaks Spanish. What we have then grasped is a *pragmatic* fact about the particular sentence token, a fact about how it is being employed in the present context.

According to Katz and Bach, then, the semantic sense of a proper name, "N," is given by the formula (using Katz's version of it): "The thing which is a bearer of 'N.'[13] Thus "Aristotle was a philosopher," means semantically, "The thing which is a bearer of 'Aristotle' was a philosopher," where exactly *which* "thing" which is a bearer of "Aristotle" one means to be talking about will be given by contextual indications. Katz calls this the "Pure Metalinguistic Description Theory," and Bach calls it the "Nominal Description Theory."

According to Kripke, the "meaning" of proper names is exhausted by the fact that they are rigid designators. The "meaning" of a name is the object to which it refers. It follows that if a proper name fails to refer, then any sentence in which it is used lacks truth value. There is a "hole" in the sentence, as it were, where the proper name appears.

---

[11] See Jerrold J. Katz, "Names without Bearers," *The Philosophical Review* 103 (1994): 1–39, and Kent Bach, *Thought and Reference* (Oxford: Clarendon Press, 1987).

[12] See Bach's *Thought and Reference*, where this conception of the distinction between the semantic and the pragmatic is developed.

[13] See Katz, "Names without Bearers," p. 5.

On the theory of Bach and Katz, if a proper name fails to refer then the sentence of which it is a part still has truth value. There is no semantic "hole" where the name is, since the semantic meaning of the proper name is given by mention of the name itself, and the name itself does exist.

Now whichever view one favors concerning the *semantics* of proper names, proper names may be considered, on Katz's and Bach's view no less than on Kripke's, to be rigid designators if we take "rigid designator" to be a concept belonging to *pragmatics*, a concept having to do with how proper names are used in practice, used, that is, in actual sentence tokens. So regarded, on both Kripke's view and on Katz's and Bach's view of the semantics we may assume that ordinarily proper names function pragmatically in the way Kripke proposes, regardless of how their semantics works out.

We take the notion of "rigid designator" to be a concept of pragmatics, then, having to do with how proper names are *used* in sentence tokens. On our conception a rigid designator need not actually succeed in referring. Were we to suddenly discover that there never really was a person who was the bearer of "Aristotle," for example, that would not change the fact that the name belonged all along to the pragmatic category of rigid designation. What makes it a rigid designator is the fact that it was *meant* to be used to refer in the way explained by Kripke. If the name does in fact refer, does originate in an actual object so named, then it is what we could call a "successful rigid designator." If not, then it is a "failed rigid designator." So we must amend slightly our earlier characterization of a "rigid designator" and now say that a "rigid designator" *purports* to refer to a being or entity in every possible world in which it exists, regardless of the differences in its properties between worlds.

Returning now to our explication of "God," when we affirm that in a religious context "God" is typically a proper name we mean to be making two affirmations. The first is that as used in religious contexts "God" typically either has no descriptive *semantic* content, or else has the semantic content assigned to it by the Nominal Description Theory. On the latter, "God exists" has the *semantic* content of "The thing which is a bearer of 'God' exists." And the second affirmation is that (with qualifications soon to follow) in those contexts "God" functions *pragmatically* as a rigid designator intended to refer to a particular being standing at the origin of a referential chain into which users of that name intend to join.

Put less rigorously, in affirming that "God" is a proper name we mean to affirm that the typical believer, when speaking of God, does not intend just to be speaking of "whatever it may be" that satisfies a certain description, such as "an absolutely perfect being." Rather, she has in mind a *particular reality*, named by the term "God," that very reality to which she refers via a referential chain leading back to its naming. The reality she has in mind, the particular being to which she means to refer, will be that very reality whom she believes was revealed to Abraham, Moses and the prophets, or who was revealed to them and also became incarnate in Jesus, or who was revealed to them and also sent the Angel Gabriel to Mohammed.[14] This means that at the origin of the name "God" (actually other terms referentially equivalent with it) there is believed to be an experience in which God is present. We believe, then, that the use of the name "God" in the religious life is predicated upon the belief in God's being actually experienced or present and thus nameable.[15]

The believer may think herself to have experiences of that very same being as well. Her use of "God" then will be intended to name the reality she herself allegedly knows by experience, whom she takes to be the very same reality referred to in the referential chain going back to Moses, or Jesus, or Mohammed.[16]

The intention of the typical believer, then, is to tie in to a referential chain that culminates (originates) in the (at least) past experience of a particular being, whose name is "God." This being's name was fixed then and continues to be called by that name now, or by referential equivalents, the reference secured by means of the referential chain reaching back to the initial fixing of the name.

IV

We wish now to introduce an important qualification into our endorsement of proper names as rigid designators. Typically an act of naming, including the naming of God, does not exist in isolation, but as part of what we may call a "naming game." A naming game determines what

[14] She may believe that the referential chain originates with or goes through these particular historical personages, but that belief is not crucial to the success of reference. Hence she may be wrong about that and still succeed in referring via the actual referential chain she hooks up with.

[15] A difference between rigid designators in general and the name of God shows up in the fact that in the Bible God is not given His name by those who know Him, but reveals His name to them. This difference, however, need not make a difference to the logic of rigid designation for the name of God.

[16] We remind the reader that this characterization of the use of the name "God" need not be thought to rest upon the assumption that God exists. What makes "God" a name is the *intention* to use it in the way described in the text. As before, we may distinguish successful names, where the object named exists, from failed names, where the referential chain leads back to nowhere.

constitutes a proper candidate for the receiving of a name within that game. The naming game is played by the initial giver of a name and subsequently by those who "pick the name up." An appreciation of the nature of naming games and how they affect the use of proper names is required to round out our views on names and the name "God."[17]

It is correct to say, as Kripke does, that when naming an object one does not usually have in mind a *definite* description by which one intends to fix the reference. But it is also correct to say that when naming we are generally aware, to one degree or another and in various degrees of explicitness or vagueness, what a proper naming-candidate must be like for the naming game being played. We illustrate this fact via some examples meant to appeal directly to our linguistic intuitions.

1. You are at the zoo with your children. You have all been giving funny-sounding names to individual animals all afternoon. Late in the afternoon, you sight what you and your kids think is a smallish animal off in the grass of the Australian display, and you dub it with the name "Kuzu," just for fun. On coming closer to the Australian pavilion you discover that what you *thought* was an animal was merely a pile of soiled rags bearing the configuration of a kind of funny-looking animal. You all grab the rags and playfully toss them up in the air before dutifully gathering them up and depositing them in the nearest bin. Upon discovering the pile of rags, you would not say that Kuzu, that is, "your" Kuzu, turned out to be a configuration of rags, or was the rags themselves. You would not consider "Kuzu" to have been the name of anything. You and your children had been fooled.

It's true that you and your children never made any *explicit* rule to the effect that you would be naming only animals. Nonetheless, that was the game you were playing, and it was implicitly understood that you were giving funny names to animals only. By virtue of the focus of the naming it was understood that only animals would get such names. Under the circumstances it is clear that you and your children would not wish to say that "Kuzu" named a bunch of rags. Rags held no interest for you, and there was no point or purpose or fun in giving a name to them. "Kuzu" just wasn't the name of anything, even though for a time you thought it was.

2. A child is born. The parents refer to it as "Sally" to one another and in the presence of others. They mean to be naming a human child. Later, it turns out that "Sally" was a baby monkey switched with their child by a

---

[17] This section includes material previously published in Jerome I. Gellman, "The Name of God," *Noûs* 29 (1995): 536–43.

malevolent nurse at the hospital. This species of monkey is such that its babies are hardly distinguishable from human ones until around a month old. When they find out, the parents no longer would call the monkey by the name "Sally," and no one else would be correct in doing so. A mistake was made in the giving of the name. The name went astray. To be sure, there was no definite description in mind when giving and using the name, but there was an assumed category of a proper candidate for naming. The object named had to be a human being.

3. When Aristotle was born, he was given the name "Aristotle" (or a Greek equivalent). As already noted, we can imagine all kinds of counterfactual conditions in which Aristotle, *our* Aristotle, would have been quite different than he in fact was. We can imagine finding out that we had been wrong all along concerning fundamental facts about the very person, Aristotle, *our* Aristotle. It is possible that we could find out that Aristotle, *our* Aristotle, was never a philosopher, had never been a pupil of Plato's, and had never tutored Alexander the Great. It is possible that we could find out that Aristotle was really a fisherman who never had thought of philosophy, and who died at the age of 17. All the rest was legend that grew up around *him*, our Aristotle. In that case, the name "Aristotle" would still have named *our* Aristotle.

But suppose, instead, it were discovered that there had never been such a *person*, Aristotle. Suppose, instead, that what was *thought* to be a person, was instead a great hoax. It was nothing but a series of persons inside a series of body-costumes made to look like one person. The people inside and the costumes were changed from time to time, as "Aristotle" was expected to grow bigger, and then age, and the people acted in accordance with what was supposed to be done in that period of time. So there never was any *person* "Aristotle" let alone any philosopher by that name. In such a case, we should plausibly conclude that the name "Aristotle" had never really succeeded in referring. In particular, the name "Aristotle" would not be the name of the *series* of persons and costumes, or of the series of hidden persons alone. This would be because while "Aristotle" was not fixed by any definite descriptions, it *was* meant to name an object belonging, at least, to the category of being a person.[18]

4. Consider Kripke's suggestion that we imagine that all of the things written in the Bible about Jonah were false. Imagine that the story of the

---

[18] This point is entirely independent of the claim that Aristotle, *our* Aristotle, could not have been other than a human being. This latter claim is a claim about the very person who is Aristotle. The thesis defended here is that in the usual usage, the term "Aristotle" could not have named anything other than a human being.

whale, and the rest was mere legend that was told about Jonah. Kripke uses this example to show that it would be coherent to suppose we were referring to Jonah, the same person referred to in the biblical story, even though we disavowed all of the descriptions that might fix the reference of "Jonah" for us. And this shows that "Jonah" is not equivalent in any way to any descriptions we believe true of the person so named.

Now notice how when we consider this example we implicitly sneak in to our imaginary story the fact that Jonah was a person. We think of the Bible story as being false of "him." But suppose that the person people thought they were naming "Jonah" was really a large piece of driftwood on the beach, which they glimpsed momentarily. Thinking it was a person, they dubbed it "Jonah" and made up the whole story about the whale having disgorged "him" onto the beach. But in that case there never *was* a "Jonah." We would not want to say that the *driftwood* was "Jonah," because at the very start "Jonah" was meant to be the name of a *person*. We (including the initial baptizer) were all fooled. There was no person for the story to be about. Consider how odd it would be to say, "People think that Jonah was swallowed by a whale, but the truth is that Jonah grew in a forest, was built into the stern of a ship, and bobbed ashore when the ship broke up in a storm."[19]

These examples illustrate that typically acts of conferring a name take place within a naming game" that sets (somewhat imprecisely at times, no doubt) the parameters for appropriate naming candidates, by determining what *kind* of being must be named. In the event that an act of naming goes beyond those parameters the initial baptism is undermined and defeated by the failure to conform to the game.

Since we consider "God" in the religious life to be a name, we posit that the reference to God by the name "God" ordinarily takes place within a naming game. That game determines the parameters for successful naming, beyond which the name does not refer, by fixing what *kind* of being "God" must name.[20]

---

[19] However, it would not be odd to say, "People think that 'Jonah' was swallowed by a whale, but the truth is that 'Jonah' grew in a forest, was built into the stern of a ship, and bobbed ashore when the ship broke up in a storm." The quotes around the name make the difference, and prove the point.

[20] In truth, there may not be any *one* game that is being played with the name "God" and its referential equivalents. In fact, different games may be played by different religions and different subgroups within a given religion. Nonetheless, despite these possibilities of divergent religious games, there would seem to exist sufficient similarity between and within

So what are the parameters for successful naming in the naming game in which God is named? What *kind* of being must "God" name? Another way to ask the same question is to ask what would have to be discovered in order to render the name "God" inappropriate and inapplicable, in the way in which the discovery of rags undermined the use of the name "Kuzu" at the zoo?

We have already said that being "an absolutely perfect being" was not part of the (semantic) meaning of "God." Can we now sneak that attribute back in as setting the conditions for successful reference within the naming game with "God?"

We think not, because surely for many unsophisticated, or otherwise rank and file believers, "God" simply names the being with whom they and their ancestors have intimacy, the being to whom they turn in time of trouble, and the one whom they worship. They may not ever get so far as to think of God as an "absolutely perfect" or "maximally valuable" being. They may have some ideas about God's exalted degree of power, goodness, and wisdom, to be sure, but we may assume that these are quite vague and not well thought out. Were they to come to acquire the idea of an "absolutely perfect being" and then come to discover that God, *their* God, was not such a being, it is hard to imagine that they would typically consider the name "God" to have become inappropriate or its application undermined by that discovery. They would continue to believe that God, their God, existed, though *He* was not absolutely perfect.

Consider next more sophisticated believers who do think of God as an absolutely perfect being. Suppose that *they* were to discover or come to believe that the very being whom they believe to have been known by Moses and Aaron, that they had been meaning to refer to as "God," was less than an absolutely perfect being. We should not be in a hurry to conclude that they would then feel it most appropriate to say that "God" did not refer, or that God did not exist. That is because just as the fact that we believe Aristotle to have been a philosopher does not determine the limits of successful reference with the name "Aristotle," so what they be-lieve *about* God need not determine the parameters for successful reference within the naming game in which "God" figures. It would all depend, we believe, upon what has been discovered or come to be believed about the very being hitherto called "God."

---

religions which speak of God to be able to determine, at least at some high level of gener-ality, something instructive about *the* naming game in which "God" is employed.

We can imagine cases in which believers, sophisticated ones included, discover or come to believe that they had been mistaken about the nature of the being they had intended to refer to by the name "God," as a result of which they would say that God did not exist or was not known to exist, rather than that they had discovered or come to believe something new *about God*. Suppose it were shown that what believers *thought* was an experience of God by them and/or others was really only the experience of a projection of a father image. In that case, it seems quite clear that the appropriate response would not be to say that it had been shown that *God* was a father image. Rather, what had been shown was that *God* did not exist or that they had never experienced anything to which the name "God" properly applied.[21] A father image lies outside the limits of the God-naming game no less than a pile of rags lies outside the limits of the animal-naming game at the zoo.

Or suppose that believers became convinced, perhaps from a consideration of great evils that befell them, that what they had been meaning to refer to all along with the name "God" was in fact a perfect devil, omnipotent, omniscient, and perfectly malevolent. The plausible reaction would not be to say that *God* was the Devil. Rather, the plausible response would be to say that they had been mistaken in thinking that they had ever been referring to God. This would be the case not because the name "God" was equivalent to or "fixed" by a definite description now precluded by the new discovery, but because the naming of God takes place within a certain naming game which determines the *type* of being to which "God" must refer. The Devil is not the *type* of being which qualifies as named, given the limits of possible named candidates.[22]

What then determines the *type* of being that must be referred to if "God" is to succeed in referring? What are the outer limits, as it were, of the naming game in which God is named?

In his book *The Examined Life*, Robert Nozick includes a chapter entitled "The Nature of God, the Nature of Faith."[23] In that chapter Nozick presents what he calls "the concept of God." Let us regiment Nozick's formulation, with some changes, and call it "(N)":

[21] See Richard B. Miller, "The Reference of 'God'," *Faith and Philosophy* 3 (1986): 3–15, where this is argued.

[22] See William P. Alston, "Referring to God," *International Journal for Philosophy of Religion* 24 (1988): 113–28, for a different view on this matter.

[23] See Robert Nozick, *The Examined Life: Philosophical Meditations* (New York: Simon and Schuster, 1989), pp. 46–54.

God is:

(1) the most perfect actual being,

(2) who is very high on the scale of perfection,

(3) whose perfection is vastly greater than that of the second most perfect actual being, and

(4) upon whom other beings in some important way are dependent.[24]

Nozick does not explain what it means to say that (N) gives "the concept of God." Since we consider "God" to be a proper name in the religious life, for us (N) does not give the semantic meaning of "God." Either "God" has no semantic meaning or only that ascribed to it by the Nominal Description Theory of names. We submit, however, that (N) well captures the conditions necessary for successful naming within the naming game in which God is named in religions. (N) tells us what *type* or *kind* of being may properly be called "God." Namely, (N) tells us that the one so named must *at least* fulfill the conditions of: having the most perfection of any being *there is*, possessing a very high degree of perfection (way above any other being in perfection), and having other beings dependent upon it in important ways.

We may summarize these conditions by stating that it is generally a necessary condition of successfully naming a being "God" that it name what we shall call a *"supremely valuable being,"* or simply a *"supreme being."*[25] This is not unlike its being a necessary condition of successfully naming something "Kuzu" that it be an animal. Being a *supreme being* sets the outer parameter of successful naming in the naming game with "God."

If X is an absolutely perfect being, then X is a supreme being. But if X is a supreme being it does not follow that X is an absolutely perfect being. Yet, if there exists a supreme being, X, and a perfect being, Y, then X and Y are the same being. This follows at least from the fact that no other being can approach the value of a supreme being. Hence, if a perfect being exists it must be the same as X.

If it were to be discovered that the being who lies at the inception of the referential chain of "God," for example the being believed to have appeared to Abraham, failed to fulfill the requirements of (N), failed to be a *supreme being*, then the natural conclusion would be that "God" had failed

---

[24] The original says that God is the one who is in some way most importantly connected to our universe, perhaps as its creator. It seems clear to us that this "connection" must be one of dependence, including ontological dependence.

[25] In what follows we will use these terms in this technical sense.

to refer. This would be similar to where you discover that "Kuzu" was not an animal at all, and that therefore "Kuzu" did not refer. That (N) gives the rules for the game of naming God explains why father images and the Devil could not be named "God," and also explains how God, in daily religious life, could continue to be God and not be an absolutely perfect being.

Being a supremely valuable being, however, is not a *sufficient* condition for something to be properly referred to by "God." "God" is not equivalent to the description *a supreme being*. Not just *any* supreme being would properly be called "God." What else would have to be the case? The being in question would have to be *the very being* who was experienced—who appeared, for example, to Father Abraham and to others—to whom the believer intended to refer, intending to hook up with that particular referential chain. If it turned out, for example, that *the very being* who had been appearing to believers all along was an imposter, and not a supreme being, but that there *was* a supreme being who never had appeared to anyone and whose existence was not even suspected, the latter would not suddenly become the bearer of the name "God." The name "God" is intended to refer to that *particular* being, who is supremely valuable, who is allegedly known by experience, and not to just any supremely valuable being, whoever that may be.

(N) leaves matters not quite well defined. It uses phrases like, "very high on the scale of perfection," "perfection vastly greater than that of the second most perfect actual being," and "upon whom other beings in some important way are dependent." But far from this being a valid criticism of (N), this stands in (N)'s favor. For it is to be expected of rank and file believers that their "concept of God" *be* quite vaguely defined. And sophisticated believers as well should not be expected to have thought out very carefully under what conditions the name "God" would fail to refer (short of there never having been anything at the object end of alleged experiences of God).

Hence, we conclude, "God" is a rigid designator which succeeds in referring only if it refers to a supremely valuable being.

We can now summarize our discussion of what the word "God" means. "God," we maintain, is a proper name, which:

(1) either has no semantic meaning or has only the meaning ascribed to it on the Nominal Description Theory;

(2) is a rigid designator intended to refer to a particular being allegedly known in experience by the person using the name or known in alleged experiences by others, the user of the name

intending to tie in to a referential chain going back to the naming of that being in those (alleged) experiences;

(3) succeeds in referring only if it refers to a "supremely valuable" being, as captured by (N);

(4) (putatively) refers to a being often thought of (in a generic way) as an absolutely perfect being;

(5) (putatively) refers to a being often thought of as omnipotent, omniscient, and wholly good, in a secondary elaboration of either the concept of an absolutely perfect being or of a (putative) experience of God as an absolutely perfect being.

V

It follows from our characterization of "God" that important metaphysical issues may be left undecided granted a uniformity of meaning and reference for that name. That is to say, two persons could be referring to the very same thing or entity, God, and be giving that name the same semantic meaning, even though they differed about important metaphysical beliefs *about* that very being, God.

For example, two persons could be referring to the very same entity, even though one of them may believe any of the following:

(1) God is separate from the world.

(2) God is outside time.

(3) God has no body.

(4) God is love.

while the other believed any of the following:

(1a) The world is included in the being of God.

(2a) God is in time.

(3a) God has a body.

(4a) God is justice.

All that need follow from the two holding opposing beliefs of these sorts is that they have differing beliefs about that very being, God, named equally by both of them. The commonality of reference will be secured by way of each of them tying in to the same referential chain reaching back to experiences of a being both of whom mean to be referring to by the name "God."

Supposing that God is actually experienced, the possible explanations of divergences in such beliefs about God are many. For example, different persons may have different ideas about what makes for perfection, agreeing that God is perfect. They may hold different theories about this matter, theories made possible perhaps because God just doesn't reveal enough about Himself for persons to know that many metaphysical truths about Him. Or, perhaps, some persons, or their traditions, have experienced God more fully and thus know more metaphysical truths about Him, while others are merely theorizing, without having had experiences which would verify their metaphysical views. Or maybe God just appears differently to different subjects or peoples. And so on.

On the other hand, it follows from our characterization of "God" that none of the following sentences could possibly be true:

(G1) "God is only a projection of a father image."

(G2) "God is only a reflection of the authority of society."

(G3) "God is evil."

In each case, the sentence could not be true because any object of which the predicate were true would not be correctly referred to by the name "God." And this is so because any object of which the predicate were true would not be characterized by (N). If "God" succeeded in referring in any of these sentences they would have to be false. Each of (G1)-(G3), therefore, suffers from a kind of incoherence.[26]

On the other hand, the truth of each of the following sentences is not ruled out by anything we have claimed about the meaning of "God":

(D1) "What people thought was God was really nothing but a projection of a father image."

(D2) "What people thought was God was really nothing but a reflection of the authority of society."

(D3) "What people thought was God was really an evil being."

The truth of each of these sentences is not ruled out by the meaning of "God," because in each case the predicate of the sentence is not being

[26] Alternatively we could say that people who talk this way are giving a new meaning to the term "God" relative to its typical religious use.

ascribed to *God*, but to what people thought was God, and which turns out, so it is claimed, not to be God. Each sentence (D1)-(D3) expresses a "disappearance theory" of God, akin to a "disappearance theory" of sensations being brain processes. On a "disappearance theory" of sensations being brain processes, it is not said that:

(B1) "Sensations *are* brain processes."

but rather that:

(B2) "What people thought were sensations are really nothing but brain processes."

We may doubt whether (B1) is as much as coherent. The concept of "sensation" precludes a sensation from being in the brain, or of travelling from place to place in the brain. A *sensation* could not be a brain process. But (B2) may be interpreted to mean that when people had certain experiences they *thought* that the object of their experience, *what* it was they were experiencing, was sensations, whereas in truth what they were really experiencing were brain processes. Whether expressing a truth or not, (B2) is at least coherent.

We could say something similar about "disappearance theories" of God. It may be said, for example, that when people have had certain experiences, they *thought* they were experiencing God, but in truth all they were really experiencing was a projected image of their own fathers instead. If the argument of this book is correct, no such disappearance theory of God is true, at least not always or generally. But at least its truth is not ruled out by the proper usage of the term "God."

This completes our account of the meaning of "God" in the religious life. In dealing with claims of experiences of God, it is the religious meaning of "God" which is most relevant, since typically such claims are made by persons who take themselves to have experienced the being referred to by the name "God" in their religious tradition. Hence, in what follows we shall be assuming the religious use of "God" in our deliberations on alleged experiences of God.

VI

It remains for us to say something about the ways in which an identification of God can be made, supposing that God is experienced. How does a person identify what he is experiencing as *God*, in particular, rather than some other object or being? Broadly speaking, identification of God can be made in one of two ways, what we shall call "recognition-identification" and "auto-identification."

Recognition-identification of God is analogous to sense-recognition of physical objects. So to understand this way of identifying God, let us first make some brief observations about how a person recognizes physical objects by sense perception.

Recognition-identification of physical objects is no doubt a combination of an instinctive *processing* and a *practice*. As an instinctive processing it is shared with other animals, and involves the processing of present and past images (in the human case: whether provided by one's own past experiences or by descriptions of other persons' experiences) by the brain to "decide" just what is confronting the organism at the present moment. This is a complex procedure which enables us to recognize one and the same object in widely different contexts, from different angles, under different lighting, and in different conditions of the sensing organism. As a rule, the organism that makes the identification is not aware of this processing, in virtue of which it is justified in taking what it experiences as the object it is.

As a *practice*, recognition-identification of physical objects involves what is more like a human "convention" of taking experiences, each of some object, and *gathering* them together as experiences of one object. The practice regards certain kinds of features of our experience as sufficient to justify gathering a present experience together with previous experiences, as experiences of one object, referred to by name or description. As a practice, recognition-identification goes beyond what is instinctively known, in the service of human pursuits, curiosity, and knowledge which are far richer than what is available to other animals.

Recognition-identification of a physical object does not require of a person making an identification that he be able to articulate the grounds on which the identification is made in order for him to know himself to be justified in making an identification (let alone in order for him to *be* justified in doing so). That is because on the processing end an organism (in this case, a person) is generally not aware of the complex processing taking place in the brain, and on the practice end the elements that go into an identification may be so complex and the procedures so habitual that the person may not be able to *say* much that is very informative about the grounds for recognition. In order to know that he is justified in making an identification of this sort, it's enough that a person just know *that* he is aware of the grounds. In fact he might not be able to say anything more than that. He may just have a "flash of recognition."

The ways a subject recognizes an object as the same as a previously experienced one, whether previously experienced by her or by others, are many and sundry. Especially weighty are factors having to do with what the object can be expected to be like when perceived. These include, first and foremost, similarity in phenomenal features, with wide possibilities for how similar they must be. Second, there are overall impressions, including the "flavor" of an object, and gestalt impressions—(either as perceptually known by the present perceiver or as reported). Third, there is identification based on the fact that given what is known about the object in question it could be expected to appear in the way it is presently appearing, even if the object has never before been actually perceived or reported to be perceived in quite this way. And fourth, there are judgments based on what nonperceptual or quasiperceptual effect the perception of the object can be expected to have on the subject ("You will know him by his commanding presence when he walks into the room").

Also important in recognition-identification are such factors as under what conditions an object can be expected to appear and not appear, at what times and location or range of locations the object can be expected to appear and not appear, and the relative plausibilities of what one is perceiving as being one particular object *rather than* some other.

In the practice of recognition-identification there is room for error. A person may be mistaken about *this* and *that* having similar perceptual features. For example, memory can be faulty. And *this* object might be distinct from *that* one in spite of phenomenal similarities. In addition, flavor and a gestalt can be misleading in their generality. One can be wrong about how an object can be expected to appear. And, finally, expectations can be defeated.

The practice of recognition-identification requires us to go only so far in taking care to make justified identifications. There is a point beyond which we are not required to go. For example, we make momentous identifications of individuals in some cases without having to bother to ask ourselves if they might not have phenomenal twins. The degree of care we must take is at least partly a function both of what would be at stake in taking more care and what would be at stake in not bothering to do so, both of these context-dependent matters. The practice of recognition-identification, then, is geared to practical needs and human limitations.

Finally, while the identification of an object by recognition is commonly made by the person who presently perceives the object, it is sometimes made by others who do not perceive the object but who are in a position to judge what the object is on the basis of what the perceiver is able to tell them about what she perceives. If the perceiver is justified in accepting their word for it, then the perceiver too shall be said to know by recognition–identification what has been perceived.

The recognition–identification of God as God should be understood by way of analogy with the recognition–identification of physical objects. Given that there is a (putative) nonsensory mode of perceptual cognition of God, we may assume there to be instinctive processing going on in the brain, analogous to what transpires in sensory processing for recognition. Whether we share this mode of (putative) cognition with other animals, we do not know. And by analogy with the practice of sensory recognition, (putatively) one can be aided in recognizing God by reference to the conditions under which God might be expected to appear and not appear (e.g., everything else being equal, God should not be expected to appear to one who does not open his heart to God), to what locations or range of locations God might be expected to appear and not appear at (e.g., God might be expected to appear, among other places, at places where God has appeared before and where people now go to seek God, such as a place of prayer), and to the relative plausibilities of what one is now perceiving being God *rather than* some other being.

Especially weighty for purposes of recognition–identification are specific phenomenal features similar to those experienced or reported in the past, the flavor, the overall perceptual gestalt, and the nonperceptual or quasiperceptual effect God may be expected to have on one.

As in sensory recognition, there is a point beyond which one is not ordinarily obliged to go (e.g., relative at least to some phenomenal content, can't God have a phenomenal twin?). And as in sensory recognition, the subject may not be able to *say* much in the way of describing the basis of identification. Pure "flashes of recognition" are to be expected. And aids to identification may lead a person into error. But, as in sensory recognition, these facts should not prohibit engagement in the practice.

And as with the general practice, a person who perceives God may know it is God he is perceiving only by accepting the judgment of others who are in a position to recognize by what has been told them about the object presently perceived that it is God.

As we envision recognition–identification of God, putatively at least, a being is experienced and gets the name "God" (really another name much earlier in the referential chain than "God"), either by "baptism" or by what we will call below, "auto-identification." Others then have experiences which, on the basis of what is said about this being they take to be experiences of this same being, "God". As time goes on and this being is more widely perceived, the fund of knowledge about it and about the conditions in which it is experienced and not experienced is enriched in various ways. A "network" of identifying features emerges. The network is the product of the ways by which the identification of God can be made.

The network may be presumed to have developed to be so rich that some later identifications may be made in ways entirely different from earlier ones. The network may have overlapping identifying features or may involve "family resemblances" between identifying marks sufficient to warrant identification. In this way, variegated means of identifying God are established entirely upon perceptual grounds together with independently warranted background knowledge.[27] The network can always be augmented by a personal experience in which God appears in a way hitherto unfamiliar, the identification based upon the retroactive reflection that God could have been expected to appear in this way. Also, the fund of identifications may be employed by a person other than the present perceiver, a person in a position to recognize God as the object of the experience, even if the present perceiver is in no such position.

A second means for identifying God is by what we are calling "auto-identification." In auto-identification an object identifies *itself* to the perceiver. Instead of the perceiver having to make a judgment of recognition, the perceiver is informed of the identity of the object by the object itself. If a person tells you who he is, and you are impressed by his sincerity and have no reason to doubt him, then you learn who he is without having to recognize him.

In the same way, God can be identified, at least putatively, because God *informs* a subject that He is God. And a subject can identify the one presently appearing as the same one who appeared to others when the subject is told as much by the being presently appearing to him.

The most obvious form of auto-identification occurs when an object identifies itself by speaking to the perceiver, or by otherwise expressing or conveying the thought. God could convey His identity to a person in some such way as this. But we should not be too hasty to suppose that this is the only means of auto-identification available to God. To be sure, it's hard to imagine what other ways of auto-identification would be like. However,

---

[27] In Chapter 4 we take up the issue of diverse networks for identifying God as they exist in different religious traditions.

mystical experiences of God are so strange to ordinary sense perception that we should not rule out the possibility that there is, in at least some mystical experiences, what amounts to an auto-identification of God by means nonmystics cannot begin to imagine. If there are such ways, then a person could identify God as God simply by *having* the experience she has, without having to *recognize* God as God.

Auto-identification of God is suggested by the biblical record, where Abraham does not *name* God, but is informed by God who He is. God is not "baptized" by Abraham, but gives His name. And subsequently others, including Isaac and Jacob, are informed by God who He is and that it is He who appeared to Abraham before them.

The ways of identifying God in experience, then, putatively, are recognition-identification and auto-identification. And of the two, the former is plausibly the more common.

VII

In order for "God" to refer, it must refer to a "supreme being," as the term has been explained earlier in this chapter. But of course this does not mean that in order to be able to identify God in experience one must be perceiving God *as* supreme or *as* absolutely perfect. It is sufficient that the means of identification conform with the network or be based upon retroactive reflection about how God could have been expected to appear in *this* way.

However, if God is to be known by experience, it seems plausible to suppose that at least sometimes God must be known as a supremely valuable being on the basis of experience. And putatively at least, this is so. Putatively, at least, God has been experienced to be great enough to have been known as a supreme being. And God has been allegedly experienced to be an absolutely perfect being. In addition there are experiences which phenomenally *indicate* that they are of a perfect being even if the perfection is not somehow given phenomenally in the experience. These include experiences having a phenomenal nature which on retroactive reflection could have been expected to have been a way that a perfect being would have appeared.

Some readers may doubt whether it is possible to be perceptually aware that a being is absolutely perfect or for an experience to phenomenally indicate the presence of such a being. It should be pointed out to them that a subject could know by experience that God was perfect if God auto-identified Himself to her as such. So that's a way of knowing it by experience. But aside from that possibility, such readers will have to contend with the fact that such experiences are reported to have taken place. Whether at this point in our presentation one is prepared to accept that this shows that a perfect being exists, it does count in favor of the existence of such experiences, phenomenally speaking.

Admittedly, occasional isolated reports don't add up to much, but the more a certain type of experience is reported the greater the likelihood that such types of experiences do occur. Reports of experiences of God's perfection are, after all, not isolated or very small in number. They represent apparent experiences from various religious and mystical traditions over time. Our issue in this section of this chapter is not whether the alleged experiences of perfection are truly experiences of a perfect being. The present issue is only whether there are experiences which seem to be perceptions of a perfect being and whether there are experiences which *seem* to indicate the presence of such a being. A correct judgment here should be based upon *looking* to see what human beings report to have seemed to experience.

Suppose there were disembodied minds who had never experienced physical motion and who doubted whether it was possible to have an experience which even *seemed* to be of motion. Then imagine that we, who have been experiencing motion all along, somehow began to communicate with them. We sincerely testify to them that we really have motion experiences, experiences which at least *seem* to be of moving objects. There is a point at which it would be unreasonable for them to continue to deny the possibility of someone's at least *seeming* to experience motion.

Likewise, the fact that subjects sincerely report experiencing that God is perfect is a reason for thinking that it is at least possible to *seem* to do so.

Behind possible resistance to the idea of an experience in which it seems that God is absolutely perfect may be lurking a pictorial way of thinking what such an experience would have to be like. One might be thinking that in such an experience one is somehow *picturing* an "infinite" array or an "endless" being. And of course it's hard to imagine what that would *look* like.

But that resistance construes the possibilities much too narrowly. Alleged experiences of God are not to be thought of as being somehow phenomenally like visual experiences or other sense experiences. Their typical nonsensory nature should be taken seriously. Furthermore, the alleged experience of God as perfect can be conceived of in various nonpictorial ways. Perhaps perfection can be given phenomenally as a *simple* quality, the quality of being without limitations, for example. The subject (allegedly) just

perceives a being who presents itself with the simple property of being
without limit. This would not require the subject to picture any infinite or
endless array.

Or a subject might (allegedly) experience what we might call God's
ongoing "amplification," perceived to *be* without limitations, but without
the actual "endlessness" of the amplification being perceived. An analogy
would be one's seeing an image reflected back and forth between two
facing mirrors in an ongoing series of receding images, getting smaller and
smaller as they go. One sees that and experiences the quality of "endlessness" without having actually to perceive an endless series of reflections.[28]

So we see little force behind the refusal to recognize what at least *seem* to
be experiences of God as an absolutely perfect being.

We have now clarified what we take to be the meaning of "God" in
typical religious contexts, and what we mean in the remainder of this work
by an "experience" of God. In religious contexts ordinarily "God" is a
name, used by a believer to refer to a specific "supreme being," one assumed to have been experienced in the past by others, and perhaps also by
the believer herself. And in an "experience" of God there is (typically) a
nonsensory phenomenal content which one experiences and which is putatively *of* God, although there are varying grades of awareness on the part
of a subject that it is God who is (putatively) experienced. With these
terms in hand we can turn in the next chapter to our argument for the
strong rationality of believing that *God* is actually *experienced* and so exists.

As noted earlier, our argument from apparent experiences of God to
prove God's actually being experienced is based both on experiences in
which a person is apparently fully aware of God as God, in which she takes
what she is experiencing to be God, and on experiences in which a person
is apparently fully aware of God, but is not aware of God *as* God because
she does not *take* what she perceives to be God. An apparent perception of
God of the first sort is normally accessible to the consciousness of the
experiencing person, and can be reported and conveyed by her to others.
An apparent perception of the second sort is not readily accessible to the
experiencing subject as an experience of *God*, but might be recognizable
by others as an apparent experience of God, at least on occasion. So, an
experience of the second grade could be referred to in an argument of the

---

[28] For an earlier defense by the author of the possibility of seeming to experience God as
perfect or infinite, see Jerome I. Gellman, "Experiencing God's Infinity," *American Philosophical Quarterly* 31 (1994): 53–61.

sort we will present, even though in such cases it is false to say that it seems to the subject herself that God is present.

Subsequent to our argument, it would be possible to invoke what we have called "subliminal" perceptions of God as the best explanation for certain sorts of behavior, such as great spiritual growth or great spiritual disturbance and the like, which might be difficult to explain otherwise. Success in such explanatory endeavors would strengthen our argument, which is based solely on the first two grades of awareness of God in perception. But we do not pursue that opening in this work.

[2]

The Argument

We are now in a position to present our argument for the strong rationality of the belief that God is really and truly experienced and hence exists, based on alleged experiences of God.

There are certain principles about how to connect experience with reality which we all implicitly recognize as authoritative. We all regularly appeal to these rules when attempting to rationally determine the connection between experience and reality in contexts other than the experience of God. In our argument here, these principles will simply be assumed to govern correctly the relevant, rational deliberations. Thus, the argument starts with these principles.

The principles to which we here are going to appeal do not only give conditions under which a certain kind of belief *that p* is weakly rational, under which conditions, that is, not only is the belief *that p* rational, but also the belief *that not-p* is rational. These principles yield strong rationality, showing that a belief *that p* is rational while a belief *that not-p* is not. At the same time, though, at least because of the clause "everything else being equal" which these principles contain, not every reasonable, proper application of them, even when considering the same evidence, need yield the same results. Reasonable, informed human beings could conceivably reach different conclusions from these same principles even though they all agreed on the principles and on the relevant evidence to which the principles were to be applied. They could reasonably differ over whether everything else *was* equal. Hence, we do not claim that *all* reasonable, proper applications of these principles would show, with regard to a belief *that p*, that it was rational and that the belief *that not-p* was not. So our principles do not serve to show that a belief possesses "universal" strong rationality.

The application of these principles to putative experiences of God will show that it is strongly rational to accept that God really is experienced, and hence that God exists, everything else being equal. The ensuing chapters are dedicated to various charges to the effect that not everything else *is* equal, and that our argument is therefore overridden or weakened. On the assumption that we have defeated these charges, and after having attended to the topic of alleged evidence against God's existence, we conclude that as far as we can see and as far as we have gone it is rational overall to accept that God really is experienced, and hence that God exists, and not rational to believe otherwise.

Our principles do not show that believing that God is experienced and thus exists possesses what we called "universal" strong rationality. We claim no more than that there is *a* reasonable, plausible, and proper application of these rules which requires this conclusion.

I

We begin our argument with the following principle, connecting experience to reality:

> If a person, S, has an experience, E, which seems (phenomenally) to be of a particular object, O (or of an object of kind, K), then *everything else being equal* the best explanation of S's having E is that S has experienced O (or an object of kind, K), rather than something else or nothing at all.

Let us call this principle, the principle of the "Best Explanation of Experience," or "BEE."

We clarify a number of features of BEE:

(1) BEE is meant to apply only to what can be judged by what is phenomenally present to S. This excludes cases where, for example, it seems that O is present to S only on the basis of S's hunch or inner conviction of some sort. This restriction coheres with our characterization of a putative experience of God as involving perceptually phenomenal content.

(2) In BEE it is required only *that* S seem to have an experience of a certain sort. It is not necessary that it seem *to S* that she is having an experience of that sort. S may not realize that what she is experiencing is O. S may describe an experience of hers to someone else who may then have good reason to assert that S seems to have had an experience of O while S herself did not realize that her experience was of O.

(3) In BEE we are thinking of perception along the lines of an Appearance Theory of Perception, as noted in Chapter 1. Recall that on this theory sensory perception does not consist merely of experiencing certain "qualities," caused by an object, the identity of which we set out to determine in order to know what object we have perceived. Rather, the experience is phenomenally constituted in the first place by an act-object form. Hence, in BEE we consider S to be having an "of-O" experience as given phenomenally. But we do not believe that anything in our argument hinges upon this way of thinking about perception, because, as we will argue below, the rational status of BEE does not depend upon the truth of any particular philosophical theory about perception.

(4) That S's experiencing O is the "best explanation" of what S has experienced is meant to entail that it is a perfectly good explanation and does not mean just that it beats all other explanations but might itself be rather weak.

(5) If S seems to experience O, then on BEE this creates a *presumption* that S has experienced O, and thus of O's existence. Thus on BEE an apparent experience of O is *evidence* for O's presence and existence. Since, however, BEE carries the condition, "everything else being equal," that the experience really is of O can be overturned or defeated by considerations stronger than the presumption the putative experience creates on it own behalf. So a putative experience of O is in itself neither self-validating nor neutral as to what it is really an experience of, if anything.

(6) The logic of the clause "everything else being equal" in BEE (and in the further principle to be introduced below) is such that the burden of proof is not upon the one who claims that everything else *is* equal, but on the one who would argue that everything else is *not* equal. Or to put it differently, everything else being equal, everything else *is* equal.

(7) The presumption which, according to BEE, a putative experience of O carries for its being a real experience of O, is independent of knowledge of a prior correlation between putative experiences of O and the actual presence of O being experienced, or of any other correlation which would imply that one. According to BEE it is rational in and of itself to take a putative experience of O as best explained as being really of O, everything else being equal. This includes the very first time a person seems to experience an object O. It is then already rational to assume, everything else being equal, that O is present to the subject as an object of experience.

(8) BEE relates to what is the best explanation of S's putative experience of O, choosing between saying either that S has experienced O or that S has experienced something other than O or that S has experienced nothing at all. Between the three, BEE affirms that the best (and good) expla-

nation is, everything else being equal, that S has experienced O. BEE does not relate directly to such questions as how it is that O was there to be experienced, or how it is that S came to be in a position or place to have an apparent experience of O or came to have the concepts necessary to form the belief (if she did form it) that it was O that was being experienced.

On the other hand, BEE has implications for explanations not covered by it directly. For example, it follows from BEE that any explanation of any of these other matters, such as how S came to be in a position to have an apparent experience of O which implied that S did *not* have a real experience of O, is to be rejected, everything else being equal, in favor of an explanation which did not have such an implication.

(9) According to BEE, that the best explanation of S's having the experience she has is that S has experienced O, is the best explanation *simpliciter*, and not only for S. Assuming we can trust S's report of his experience, S's experience counts as evidence for its authenticity for all others besides S.

Those familiar with the literature on the evidential value of putative experiences of God will recognize BEE as first cousin to a principle formulated by Richard Swinburne, the "Principle of Credulity" ("PC"). Swinburne writes, "It is a principle of rationality that (in the absence of special considerations) if it seems (epistemically) to a subject that x is present, then probably x is present."[1] In the "epistemic" sense of "seems," "It seems to S that O is present," means that S is inclined to believe that O is present on the basis of his present perception.[2]

BEE is indeed a variant of PC, and we are indebted to Swinburne for our principle and for the direction of our argument. At the same time, there are differences between BEE and PC. The main differences between them are that, first, PC applies only when it seems *to* S that O is present. BEE has no such limitation, as explained in number 2 above. And second, in PC Swinburne speaks of what is "probable" whereas in BEE we prefer to speak of the "best explanation" of what S is experiencing. The use of "probable" here can be misleading, suggesting a statistical form of argument. But these differences are relatively minor, and we consider our argument to be an expansion upon Swinburne's important insight.

[1] Richard Swinburne, *The Existence of God*, rev. ed. (Oxford: Clarendon Press, 1991), p. 254.
[2] Ibid., p. 245.

BEE implies that if a person seems to be seeing a tree in front of him, then the best (and good) explanation of that person's having that experience, everything else being equal, is that there is indeed a tree in front of him which he sees, rather than something else or nothing at all. And that means that everything else being equal it is rational to believe that the person is seeing a tree, and not rational to believe that he isn't. And BEE implies that if a person seems to see a flying saucer, then the best explanation of that fact, everything else being equal, is that there is a flying saucer which he sees. So it is rational, everything else being equal, to believe that he does and not rational to believe that he does not. This latter example illustrates that in any given case, admitting that S seems to see O and accepting BEE does not commit one to accepting that S really does see O, since the clause "everything else being equal" may point us in precisely the opposite direction. But it does illustrate that unless everything else is not equal an experience counts in favor of its own objectivity.

We claim that BEE is a principle of rationality widely recognized as governing our everyday rational discourse connecting experience to reality. As such its rationality is independent of its being shown to be so by philosophical argumentation. A clear indication of its status in our thinking is that when a person has had a putative experience of something and we do not wish to accept what would follow were the experience to be veridical, we feel obligated to come up with a *reason* for thinking that the experience should not be accepted at face value. We do not deem ourselves free simply to ignore the experiential claim. But that is tantamount to recognizing that a putative experience counts in favor of its own veracity and that unless we have a better reason to reject it, then the experience should be accepted as being *of* reality.

Richard Swinburne suggests that philosophers who wish to reject PC "do not seem to be aware of the skeptical bog in which failure to accept the Principle of Credulity for other experiences will land them."[3] Presumably Swinburne means to argue that unless we assume PC we could never be justified in believing in the existence of an external world, such as, say, trees and flowers. In particular, we could not base such a belief on an inductive correlation between seemings and reality if the only access we have to the physical world is, presumably, the seemings. Hence we must be willing to accept PC prior to the building up of inductive correlations between seemings and reality, and in fact these correlations are

[3] Ibid., p. 254.

established by employing PC. Swinburne's defense of PC would hold for BEE as well.

We do not wish to rest the defense of BEE on its indispensability for defeating skepticism, however. The issue of how our knowledge of an external world gets established is quite controversial, and any particular theory on that is likely to be less obvious and less sure than that BEE is an acceptable principle of rational reasoning. As we have said, people generally employ it regularly in their cognitive enterprises, and it is a central element of their rational thinking.

Any epistemological theory should be able to account for the correctness of the employment of BEE. This accounting should be a requirement of any theory of perception. Hence, we are content to leave as open questions which epistemological theory is correct and how BEE is to be accommodated in the correct theory. BEE could be a principle within a foundationalist doctrine[4] or could be at the service of a coherentist understanding, say, as part of a policy of "inference to the best explanation."[5] In any case, the acceptability of BEE should not depend upon the success of any of these high-level philosophical enterprises.[6]

II

Having presented and explained BEE, we now present the first part of our argument, the application of BEE to alleged experiences of God:

We maintain that BEE applies just as much to putative experiences of

[4] BEE-like principles appear in this way in John L. Pollock, *Knowledge and Justification* (Princeton: Princeton University Press, 1974).

[5] See in this connection, Peter Lipton, *Inference to the Best Explanation* (New York: Routledge, and Kegan Paul, 1991), chapter 4, especially pp. 72–73.

To be precise, a coherentist treatment would not be of BEE alone, but of BEE in the context of the principle of Strength of Number Greatness, introduced later in this chapter.

[6] We have advanced BEE as a principle that takes us from "seemings" to beliefs. We could just as easily have formulated BEE directly about perceptual beliefs alone and have omitted "seemings" altogether. For instance, BEE could have been cast in something like the following way:

> If a person S's experience causes in S a perceptual belief that a particular object O (or an object of kind, K) is present, then *everything else being equal* the best explanation of S's having that perceptual belief is that S has experienced O (or an object of kind, K), rather than something else or nothing at all.

Our argument for the rationality of belief in the existence of God would not be affected by such a formulation. (Strictly speaking, though, this formulation captures the spirit of BEE only for those cases where the subject of the experience herself forms the belief. BEE also covers cases where others form the belief based on the subject's perception.)

God as to putative perceptions of a material object. No matter which epistemological theory we may favor, it is intuitively plausible to maintain that, everything else being equal, that a person has an apparent experience of God is best explained (and well explained) by saying that the person experienced God, rather than something else or nothing at all.

Whether BEE, along with the principle introduced later in this chapter, confers *as much* rationality upon belief in God as it does on belief in physical objects is another matter. The question of the relative rationality of the two beliefs on the basis of experience is separate from an acknowledgment of the fact that when a person seems to experience God, that creates the presumption, everything else being equal, that God is experienced by him. In the coming chapter we examine the relative rationality of believing in God and in physical objects on experience. We need not reach a verdict on that issue, however, in order to be justified in asserting the very *applicability* of BEE to alleged experiences of God.

There is no doubt that very many people throughout history have had experiences, each of which *seems* on a phenomenal basis to be an experience of God. The traditions of Judaism, Christianity, and Islam are saturated by the sense their adherents have of the presence and reality of God. There exists, furthermore, a most impressive array of first-hand reports of vivid experiences of various sorts each of which is best described as a putative experience of God. Such reports are more common in some religious traditions than in others and in some denominations more than others within the same religious tradition, yet they are a pervasive feature of them all.[7] That God exists is not just an "idea" of these religions, but is believed to be disclosed in a living awareness of God, more vividly among great spiritual souls, less vividly among less spiritually endowed adherents. In line with our stated aims, we will not take the time to document that fact. It is well documented in the Bible, in other religious texts, and in various collections and studies of religious experience.[8]

In the contemporary world as well, many people of diverse cultural backgrounds and religious (and some of nonreligious) persuasions likewise seem to have had experiences of God, or do have such experiences regularly.[9]

---

[7] It is rare to find a first-person report of an experience of God in traditional Jewish texts. Nonetheless, there are many Jewish texts describing experiences of God which texts should be taken as reflecting an event that occurred in the life of the writer.

[8] The bibliography includes references to some of these studies.

[9] See Timothy Beardsworth, *A Sense of Presence* (Oxford: Oxford University Press, 1977) and Johan Unger, *On Religious Experience: A Psychological Study* (Uppsala: Uppsala University Press, 1976) for some studies of contemporary religious experiences.

Now consider just one such apparent experience of God, "G." From BEE it follows that, everything else being equal, the best (and good) explanation of G is that God is being experienced, rather than nothing or something else instead. Hence, everything else being equal, BEE renders it rational to believe that God is experienced and exists, and not rational to believe that God is not experienced, or that God doesn't exist.

G can be a type of experience we have called a "Grade 1" perception of God, in which it seems to the subject that God *as* God is present. It would follow from BEE that if in G it seemed to a subject, S, that God was (phenomenally) present to her then the best explanation of that, everything else being equal, is that S was indeed experiencing God.

Or G could be a Grade 2 perception of God in which S is aware of God in some way or other, but in which it did not seem *to* S that God was present or being experienced. This could be, for example, because S lacks the conceptual equipment to make the relevant judgments. Based upon previous perceptions of God, the genuineness of which was attested to by BEE, persons other than S could be in a position to judge rationally that S was aware of God even if S herself wasn't aware that it was God. They could make this judgment on the basis of what S reports of the phenomenal content of her experience together with their knowledge of what has been disclosed in previous experiences of God. S's experience would thus seem to *others* to be an experience of God, and on BEE, everything else being equal, the best explanation of S's experience would be that S was experiencing God.

III

Up to this point, we have been focusing upon the evidential value of a single apparent perception of God, arguing that it is strongly rational to believe that *it* was an experience of God, and thus that God exists. But we are not limited in our argument to the evidential value provided by a single apparent experience or even to a small number of them.

This brings us to a second principle governing the rationality of reasoning from experience to reality:

If a person, S, has an experience, E, which seems (phenomenally) to be of a particular object, O (or of an object of kind, K), then our belief that S's having experienced O (or an object of kind K) is the best explanation (everything else being equal) of E, is strengthened in proportion to the number of purported experiences of O there are and in proportion to the variability of circumstances in which such experiences occur.

Let us call this the principle of "Strength in Number Greatness," or, STING. According to STING, the presumption created by BEE that a seeming experience of an object, O, is a true experience of O, is strengthened the more "sightings" of O there are, and the more variable the circumstances under which O is sighted. That means that the presumption created together by *many* experiences of O in varied circumstances is stronger than the presumption created by any individual perception of O. And for that reason any counterargument to the presumption of truth is going to have to be stronger than it would have to have been had an experience been backed by a single experience or by a very few.

In addition, the more *varied* the conditions in which O is sighted the more difficult it will be to find a general reason against the presumption of truth, since any such reason will have to be found in all the varied circumstances in which the experience takes place.

STING is first cousin to a line of reasoning endorsed by C. D. Broad:

> When there is a nucleus of agreement between the experiences of men in different places, times, and traditions, and when they all tend to put much the same kind of interpretation on the cognitive content of these experiences, it is reasonable to ascribe this agreement to their all being in contact with a certain objective aspect of reality *unless* there be some positive reason to think otherwise.[10]

Now as we have already noted, the traditions of Judaism, Christianity, and Islam are permeated by the sense their adherents have of God's presence. There exists a most impressive array of first-hand reports about vivid experiences of various sorts best described as putative experiences of God. And in contemporary times, many people of diverse cultural backgrounds and religious (and some of nonreligious) persuasions likewise seem to have had experiences of God, or have such experiences regularly.

Considering the large number of such putative perceptions of God, STING strengthens the belief that the best explanation, everything else being equal, of a person's seeming to experience God is that he really is experiencing God.

Furthermore, given the richly *varied* circumstances in which such experiences take place, the conclusion is strengthened further by STING. The

[10] C. D. Broad, *Religion, Philosophy, and Psychical Research* (London: Routledge and Kegan Paul, 1953).

experience of God is reported by widely different cultures and religions over a wide span of time and by individuals of greatly differing temperament, education, social status, and immediate personal circumstances. This diversity makes it all the more difficult to come up with some wholesale considerations which would defeat the evidential value of such experiences as a class. It also makes it more difficult to come up with counterconsiderations against the genuineness of a specific experience, backed as it is by a large number of similar experiences for which there might not be any counterconsiderations.[11]

Hence, the overall conclusion is that each individual experience allegedly of God that has occurred has a strong presumption in its favor of being in fact an experience of God, everything else being equal. Thus BEE and STING show that it is rationally wellgrounded, if all else is indeed equal, to believe that God exists and not rational to believe that God does not exist.

IV

With an argument using a variant of BEE and of STING, which we will include under the names "BEE" and "STING," it can be shown that it is strongly rational to believe that God is an absolutely perfect being. The variant of BEE is this:

> If a person, S, has an experience, E, in which it seems (phenomenally) that a particular object, O (or an object of kind, K) has a property P, then *everything else being equal*, the best explanation of S's having E is that S has (truly) experienced O (or an object of kind, K) possessing P.[12]

Along with it we endorse the analogous variant of STING. From these two principles it follows that putative experiences of God as absolutely perfect ground the strong rationality of believing that God is absolutely perfect, everything else being equal.

This second argument for God's absolute perfection, however, is not as

[11] In Chapter 5 we take up the "reductionist argument," which charges that alleged experiences of God can best be explained by reference to various pathological or nonpathological special circumstances of subjects claiming to have had such experiences. We show that this objection fails.

[12] This principle applies both when it seems *of* O, acknowledged to exist, *that* it has P, and when what seems is that: "an-object-O-has-P." That is, "an object O" can be read either inside or outside the scope of "seems."

well supported as the first, concerning God's very existence, since judging from the literature the number of experiences of God as perfect is considerably smaller than the total number of experiences of God. So while BEE and STING support the strong rationality of believing that God is perfect, the support they give is not as impressive as their support for God's very existence.

We do not mean to suggest that putative experiences of God as perfect must face the tribunal of rationality in isolation from other putative experiences of God. After all, the many putative experiences of God in which He is not perceived to be absolutely perfect support the conclusion that there is such a being as God which in turn supports the conclusion that in putative experiences of God as perfect it is a real being, God, who is being perceived. The provided support rules out a number of ways of possibly disqualifying the experiences of God as perfect as unveridical. Hence, putative experiences of God as perfect receive rational support from other experiences of God.

It still seems, though, that the argument that God is absolutely perfect is less well supported than is the argument to God's existence. From this it does not follow, of course, that the argument for God's being absolutely perfect is not well supported. And judging by the literature, experiences of God as absolutely perfect are of sufficient number and variation to present a well supported case, everything else being equal, for the strong rationality of believing that God is absolutely perfect.

In the chapters that follow, our main focus will be on the first argument, for God's very existence, rather than on the second, for God's absolute pefection, although we will have occasion to address the second argument as well. Unless otherwise stated, our discussion of the first argument is meant to apply in an analogous way also to the second argument.

The remainder of this book is dedicated to a defense of our argument. One kind of charge defended against is that BEE is not an acceptable principle when applied to supposed perceptions of God. Another is that while BEE may be applicable to the case of God, there are other equally convincing principles which, if considered along with the fact that so many people *fail* to experience God, neutralizes our employment of BEE and STING.

A third kind of charge we defend against focuses on the clause in BEE and STING which allows a conclusion to be drawn only "everything else being equal." We look at various reasons that might be raised to claim that everything else is *not* equal. These reasons have to do, respectively, with the world's diversity of religions and with the alleged conditions of people who seem to perceive God, (these conditions alleged to be pathological in nature or else nonpathological but damaging nonetheless to the claim that it is rational to believe that they are perceiving God).

Finally, we address some of the main issues involved in the charge that there is sufficient evidence against God's existence for it to be the case that relative to our total evidence, and not only relative to our argument from BEE and STING, it is *not* strongly rational to believe that God is experienced and thus that God exists.

On Not Experiencing God—
Objections to the Argument

In this chapter we wish to consider objections to our argument, each of which is built in one way or another around the absence of the experience of God or the failure to experience God. The first objection, stated by Michael Martin, charges that the result of applying BEE to putative experiences of God is neutralized or outweighed by an equally valid principle applying to instances where people have tried to experience God and have failed. The second objection comes from William Rowe who rejects BEE as a valid principle when applied to putative experiences of God, arguing that the failure of persons other than the subject of a putative experience of God to have such an experience counts against the validity of a putative experience of God. And the third objection charges that the frequency with which putative experiences of God occur is too meager to establish the rationality of belief in God on the basis of experience. We consider each objection in turn.

I

Michael Martin has objected to Richard Swinburne's claim that the Principle of Credulity can be applied to alleged experiences of God to show that God exists. Martin's objection, if correct, would be telling against our argument as well. In presenting Martin's argument, we will be pretending that Martin addressed himself directly to BEE, and we recast his argument accordingly. We beg the reader to keep this in mind.

Recall BEE:

> If a person, S, has an experience, E, which seems (phenomenally)
> to be of a particular object, O (or of an object of kind, K), then
> *everything else being equal* the best explanation of S's having E is that
> S has experienced O (or an object of kind, K), rather than some-
> thing else or nothing at all.

Martin's argument (recast) is founded on the claim that a principle
equally legitimate and equally convincing would mark the connection between what seems to be absent and what really is absent, as follows:

> If a person, S, has an experience, E, which seems (phenomenally)
> to be of the absence of a particular object, O (or of an object of
> kind, K), then *everything else being equal* the best explanation of S's
> having E is that S has experienced the absence of O (or of an
> object of kind, K).[1]

Let us call this "negative" version of BEE, "BEEN."

Martin argues for parity between BEE and BEEN by example. He says,
"The experience of a chair is a good ground for believing that the chair is
present. [And] the experience of the absence of a chair is a good ground
for supposing that a chair is absent."[2]

Martin next notes that "many people have tried to experience God and
have failed." Therefore, the application of BEEN to their experiences
should count for God's being absent no less than the application of BEE to
experiences of God counts for the presence of God because if God exists
then He exists everywhere. If God is perceived to be absent anywhere,
then God is absent everywhere, and does not exist. Hence the application
of BEEN yields the conclusion that God does not exist no less than BEE
yields the result that God does exist.

Thus does Martin wish to argue that putative experiences of God's absence, (God's nonexistence) neutralize or overweigh whatever evidential
value there may be in putative experiences of God's presence, (God's existence).

An obvious reply to Martin would be to argue that BEEN is not applicable to the case of God. Let us call this the "Nonapplicability Reply."
The Nonapplicability Reply begins by noting the distinction to be made
between:

---

[1] See Michael Martin, *Atheism: A Philosophical Justification* (Philadelphia: Temple University
Press, 1990), p. 170, the "negative principle of credulity," "(NPC)."

[2] Ibid.

(A) S observes the absence of O.

and

(B) S fails to observe the presence of O after searching thoroughly for O.

In some cases (A) and (B) are equivalent, for all practical purposes. If a chair were reported present in an average furnished room and S searched the room thoroughly for a chair and found none, we may say not only that S "failed to find" a chair, but also that S "discovered there was no chair" in the room. We may even say that S "saw that there was no chair" in the room. In this situation it would be quite natural to assert that S had observed the absence of a chair. (We would be able to say this especially if S were able to scan the room for a chair in one sweep and failed to see any chair.) In a case such as this, (A) and (B) coincide.

But in other cases (A) and (B) diverge. Consider where S conducts a search for a reported mouse in the same furnished household room, but fails to observe a mouse. This would not count for the same as S observing that the mouse was absent. And the reason for this is that from what we know of mice, they are quite successful in hiding in difficult-to-reveal places and in moving around quickly and silently from place to place, only to reappear when least expected. Hence, that S has failed to come up with a mouse may give some ground for *inferring* that there is no mouse, depending on how well and how long S has searched and perhaps on S's success record in the past in uncovering mice or some similar objects. But S's failure to see a mouse in the room would not be tantamount to S's having *observed* that there was no mouse in the room.[3] In this situation (A) and (B) diverge.

The Nonapplicability Reply against Martin continues by asking how we know, in any given case, whether or not (A) is tantamount to (B). How can we tell in a particular instance whether failing to experience O, after searching thoroughly, is tantamount or not to experiencing its absence?

Suppose some biologists report sighting an animal never before seen. Others look for it and fail to find it. Have the latter experienced the *absence* of the animal or have they merely failed to find it? There are cases where we won't be able to determine this because not enough will be known about the animal being reported. We may not know what sizes it comes in.

---

[3] No doubt when S sees no chair in the room some inferences are involved, but they are sufficiently implicit for it to be natural to say that S "sees that there is no chair" in the room.

We might not know whether it is sluggish or swift, cunning or dull, shy or daring. We may not know its mode of locomotion or habits of appearing, by day, by night, by full moon, and so on. As the object is sighted more often we will presumably learn more that will be relevant to coming to know the difference between experiencing its absence and failing to experience its presence. For example, if those who claim to have sighted the animal profess to have sighted that it is stable and doesn't move around much, that it appears quite regularly in a certain area, and so forth, then the conditions for experiencing its absence will have improved. But if those who have seen it report on how elusive it is, and so on, then it will be harder to identify genuine instances of observing its absence.

This illustration shows that knowing whether we have experienced the absence of something or merely have failed to experience its presence is parasitic upon experiences of its presence, or at the least of the presence of objects similar to it in relevant ways. It is only by taking putative experiences of an object at face value, everything else being equal, that we learn enough about the object in question to make out the distinction between (A) and (B), if at all.

How, then, do we in fact *know* when we fail to see a mouse that it is not the same as seeing that there is no mouse there? And how do we in fact *know* when we fail to see a chair, in most ordinary cases, that it's tantamount to seeing that there is no chair there? The answer is that we know these things by relying upon BEE and STING. It is because of our taking many and varied alleged experiences of mice and of chairs (and of other, similar, objects as well), respectively, as true experiences of mice and chairs (and of those other objects) that we come to know about their habits of coming and going. It is on the basis of BEE that we know, for example, that chairs stay put and do not hide. That is why if we scan an ordinary room and see no chairs, that counts as seeing that there is no chair. And it is on the basis of BEE that we know about mice moving around quietly and not being easily detectable. So that's how we know that if someone searches an ordinary room, with an ordinary amount of furniture and bookcases, the fact that he does not see the mouse is not tantamount to his seeing that there is no mouse there.

So we are beholden to BEE to give us knowledge about the presence of O in general, before we can even begin to formulate applications of BEEN. That is because BEEN applies to cases where a subject has "an experience which seems to be of the absence" of O. But we can identify such cases only by depending on BEE. Were we not to grant epistemic priority to BEE we would never be able to tell in any case whether our failure to observe O was or was not the same as observing the absence of O. We could not as much as make the distinction between (A) and (B). So BEE has a logical priority to BEEN.[4]

Now suppose it happens that from the very start most people who sight O report sighting it only sporadically. Few report regular sightings. Perhaps some report rough conditions that from their experience seem, normally, to be *necessary* for sighting O. But none have any idea what sufficient conditions for O's being observable might be like. O is reported to make an impression of being quite elusive. In the main, sightings are reported from time to time, but without any discernible pattern that would make reliable prediction possible. And let us suppose that from sightings of O not enough is known to compare O to other known objects from which we could make informed predictions about O on the basis of relevant similarities to their behavior.

In such circumstances, the Nonapplicability Reply concludes that there would not be enough information available to apply BEEN. And that is because applying BEEN requires S's putative observation that O is absent. But in the described circumstances there would not be enough to go on to distinguish between (A) "S observes the absence of O" and (B) "S fails to observe the presence of O after searching thoroughly for O." In the described circumstances, when a person, S, does not see O after a thorough search we may not know enough to be able to say whether S is observing the absence of O or only has failed to observe the presence of O. Not

[4] BEE might be thought not to have logical priority to BEEN in cases where O has never been observed but where we have a well-confirmed theory from which it follows that O will be observable at place p at time t. Then if we look for O at p at t and fail to observe it, that would be tantamount to observing that O was absent. Hence, we will have observed the absence of O without ever having had observed O. For example, suppose we have never observed a planet in sector 112 of the sky, but our astronomical knowledge predicts that there is a hitherto unseen planet which will appear there at time t. At t we look carefully at sector 112 and the planet does not appear. We have observed that there is no planet there even though we never observed a planet there. But this suggestion does not really work. It is hard to imagine that any well-confirmed theory could predict that O would appear at p at t without having to depend upon the observation of the presence of some objects or other to which O is assumed to bear a resemblance in the relevant way for our observations. Hence, although we do not necessarily have to have used BEE on O itself before we can be said to be able to observe O's absence, we do have to have used BEE on some objects thought to be like O in relevant respects. We could never have made a prediction that a planet would appear in sector 112 at t unless we had made observations of planets, or the like, before this.

In addition, in the case where we will be wanting to insist on the priority of BEE to BEEN, that of alleged experiences of God, there are no independently well-confirmed theories about God which would help us predict that God will be observed at place p at time t.

enough will be known about O to make this distinction. We could not (yet) apply BEEN.

But consider now a weaker analog of BEEN, BEEN.A:

> If a person, S, has searched thoroughly for O (or for an object of kind, K) and has failed to observe O (or an object of kind, K), then *everything else being equal* the best explanation of S's failure to observe O (or object of kind, K) is that O (or an object of kind, K) is absent.

BEEN.A applies where BEEN itself doesn't. The question arises: would BEEN.A apply in our hypothetical case?[5] No. BEEN.A would not apply there any more than BEEN does. And the reason still is that we would not know enough of what would count as searching *thoroughly* for O, for we would not have enough knowledge of when or where or how O could be expected to appear were it to be present.

But in our hypothetical case, BEE would apply. Positive sightings of O would count, everything else being equal, in favor of O being present. And if there were an impressive number of sightings in different circumstances then STING would strengthen the results of applying BEE.

The moral of the story is that BEEN, and its weaker analog BEEN.A, are not on a par with BEE. Sometimes BEE will apply where BEEN and BEEN.A do not.

The Nonapplicability Reply concludes by applying the above findings to putative experiences of God. Such putative experiences have been and continue to be reported in diverse circumstances. BEE and STING support the conclusion, therefore, that these are truly experiences of God, everything else being equal. But from what we know of these reports, relying on BEE and STING, the experience of God comes only to some individuals and not to others. And to those to whom it does comes it does so, in the main, only sporadically, though some saintly souls report a life lived constantly in the presence of God. In addition, judging from those who have had such experiences we are not able to say what conditions are *sufficient* to experience God. From what is disclosed about God in such experiences everything points to the fact that God cannot be coerced into appearing. In fact, judging from the reports of some of the world's greatest

---

[5] Even if it would apply, we should note that BEEN.A is evidentially weaker than BEEN. That's why we quickly give up the search for a chair in a room where someone has failed to find one, yet sometimes set mouse traps even where a thorough search has failed to find a mouse.

mystics, sometimes God is experienced only when one does not "try" to experience Him. God makes the impression of being quite elusive.

It may be that God can be expected to appear, among other places, where He has appeared previously and where people now sincerely seek His presence, as in a house of prayer. But that expectation is a very mild one, judging by what we know from BEE and STING, from which principles, we have argued, our perceptual knowledge of God must be built up.

It is true that there exist mystical traditions which teach a path to the experience of God, a path of arduous training and self-deprivation. But typically these traditions do not look upon such techniques as guarantees of having such experiences. And in any case the vast majority of reported putative perceptions of God occur outside of organized mystical traditions.

Finally, God appears to be so unlike any other known object that there is no basis upon which to make even educated guesses about when God will or will not appear by reference to them.

In light of all of these considerations, the conclusion which emerges is that based on putative experiences of God supported by BEE and STING, we just do not know enough about the sufficient conditions under which God appears and does not appear to be able to determine with any assurance when we should say that "S has experienced God's absence," and when we should say instead "S has failed to experience God." Thus BEEN cannot be applied in the case of God, since BEEN applies solely to putative instances of experiencing God's absence.

Similarly, BEEN.A is not effective in the case of putative experiences of God. That is because not enough is known about the conditions under which God appears for us to be able to give sufficient meaning to the notion of "thoroughly searching" for Him, meaning that would confer good evidential weight upon the *failure* to find Him. On the basis of experiences of God attested to by BEE and STING, we do not know enough about what one must do in order to thoroughly search for God in order for us to know that such a search has failed rather than simply not having been thorough enough. So when Martin affirms that "many people have tried to experience God and have failed," if he means to be referring to searching thoroughly for God, then Martin's argument fails.

But perhaps Martin means to be referring to something less than a "thorough search" for God. Perhaps he means that lots of people have "made an effort," some effort, to experience God and have failed. But if so, what does Martin think people do when they try to experience God? He does not tell us.

Perhaps we can point to what might amount to making an effort to experience God which would not count as searching thoroughly for Him. Recall that one guise under which God is experienced, in various degrees of clarity and fullness, is that of a "maximally valuable being" or "absolutely perfect being." In this type of experience, a value perception lies at the very heart of recognizing God as God, a value perception the subject must be capable of acknowledging. Acknowledging God as a maximally valuable being involves acknowledging that it be fit and proper for God to be the center of one's entire value orientation. And this acknowledgment requires a de-emphasis of one's own self and what is of earthly importance to one as the focuses of one's value orientation. This is why persons who experience God are often profoundly shaken and greatly transformed in the way they subsequently assess the value of various aspects of their life.

Indeed it is a widely held teaching in the world's religions that in seeking God one should labor hard to erase one's self-centered and selfish stance in the world, to abandon one's own self as one's value center, so that God can become the value center of one's life. And typically, the mystic "path" is shaped and formed precisely by such a goal.[6]

In light of this, it may be proposed that a strong, determined effort to decenter oneself as one's value center should count, at least, as "trying" to experience God. If so, then where God had been sought in this way and not found, perhaps a weaker form of BEEN.A, reformulated for cases of "trying" to experience O, would yield at least *some* evidence that God was absent, to a degree our Nonapplicability Reply has been interested to deny.

This suggestion is not successful, however. A determined effort at de-centering the self coupled with the failure to have experienced God cannot count as evidence of the absence of God, since from what is known about God from alleged experiences of Him, He cannot be coerced to appear. God's hand cannot be forced. Decentering of the self only conduces to having an experience of God from the side of the subject, making the subject a proper vessel for receiving God's self-disclosure. Hence, that one has tried to decenter oneself and failed to experience God counts no more against God's existence than does just going to where there is some light and failing to see a mouse counts against there being a mouse in the vicinity.

In addition, it is very difficult to say when a true effort to perceive God by an attempt at self-decentering has taken place. It is notoriously difficult,

---

[6] We do not mean to suggest that decentering one's own self as one's value center in favor of God must be an all-or-nothing proposition. There are, surely, grades of ability to perceive God as the value center. But typically there seems to be required a minimal ability of detachment from self-centeredness in order to know God in an experiential way.

after all, to determine a person's authentic stance in the world. The dangers of self-deception and bad faith are everywhere. Existentialist philosophers and theologians, chief amongst them Kierkegaard, have made us keenly aware of the potential dangers from self-deception in regards to faith in God. It is therefore extremely difficult for a person, and surely others looking in on him, to determine when he really has made an authentic, non-compromising effort at a decentering of the self. Hence, it would be extremely difficult in any given case to establish that one had truly tried hard to decenter oneself and hence had to that extent tried to perceive God, but had failed. By the nature of the case, therefore, there is a built-in asymmetry between establishing that one had observed God and establishing that one had failed to observe God after having undertaken these steps to find God.

The Nonapplicability Reply concludes, therefore, that neither BEEN nor BEEN.A are useful in the case of God, because we don't know enough to be able to say when a person has experienced God's absence and we don't know enough to be able to say when a person has searched thoroughly for God, or even has made a really genuine effort to perceive God. Thus BEEN and BEEN.A are not effective in neutralizing or overweighing the positive reasons provided by BEE for thinking that God is truly experienced. Martin has not given us an adequate reason to doubt the success of our argument from BEE.

II

Whereas Martin accepted Swinburne's Principle of Credulity and tried to neutralize it with another principle and other evidence, William Rowe has rejected Swinburne's Principle of Credulity as a proper principle of rational thinking about the connection between seeming and reality. We now turn to Rowe's criticism, recast as an objection to our principle BEE.

Rowe observes that:

Most existing objects are such that there are conditions which if satisfied, the experience will follow. This is an important point we often rely on in judging whether a particular perceptual experience is veridical or delusory. A book, for example, is such that if a normal perceiver is rightly placed, eyes open, attentive, etc., the perceiver can be expected to have an experience which he takes to be one of seeing a book. If we know that several subjects satisfy the conditions but do not have the experience this will be grounds for taking a particular subject's putative experience of the book as delusive rather than veridical.[7]

Rowe continues:

God, however, is not such an object. God may choose to reveal himself to A but not reveal himself to B under similar conditions. This means that the failure of a number of subjects to have the experience of God under conditions similar to those in which A had such an experience need not count against A's experience being veridical.[8]

But this, says Rowe, raises a serious problem:

Since we don't know what circumstances make for delusory religious experiences and we don't know what the conditions are [in] which, if satisfied, one would have the experience of God if there is a God to be experienced, we can't really go about the process of determining whether there are or are not positive reasons for thinking religious experiences to be probably delusive.[9]

Rowe's remarks suggest the following argument against the application of BEE to alleged experiences of God:

(1) BEE applies to an alleged experience of O (or an object of kind K) only if we know how to go about discovering whether or not an alleged experience of O (or an object of kind K) is delusory.

(2) We know how to go about discovering whether or not an alleged experience of O (or an object of kind K) is delusory only if we know either under what circumstances a person would be likely to have a delusory experience of O (or an object of kind K) or under what circumstances a person would be likely to have an experience of O (or an object of kind K) were O there to be experienced.

(3) In the case of alleged experiences of God, we know neither under what circumstances a person would be likely to have a delusory experience of God nor under what circumstances a person would

---

[7] William L. Rowe, "Religious Experience and the Principle of Credulity," *International Journal for Philosophy of Religion* 13 (1982): 90.
[8] Ibid.
[9] Ibid., pp. 90–91.

be likely to have an experience of God were God there to be experienced.

(4) Therefore, BEE does not apply to alleged experiences of God.

In this argument, to say that S's experience of O is delusory is to say that S has an experience which *seems* to be of O, whereas in actuality it is *not* an experience of O. That S's experience is delusory in no way entails that O is absent or does not exist. O might very well be present when S has a delusory experience. The experience will nevertheless be delusory because whether O is present or not, S has not experienced O. And in (1) to know "how to go about discovering whether or not an alleged experience of O (or an object of kind K) is delusory," means to know how to find positive reasons for thinking an alleged experience delusory or not delusory.

Rowe's requirement that we be able to know how to go about discovering whether or not an alleged experience of O (or an object of kind K) is delusory is less demanding than would be the requirement that we be able to have positive reasons for deciding whether O was absent.

The idea of (1) is, then, that if we did not know how to go about discovering whether or not an alleged experience of O (or an object of kind K) was delusory, then in every case in which a person, S, would just *seem* to have an experience of the appropriate sort we would just have to take S's word for it. We would have no check on what *seemed* to be the case, and would be doomed to an unacceptable gullibility.

(1) would require that BEE be amended in some such way as the following, call it "BEER":

> If a person, S, has an experience, E, which seems (phenomenally) to be of a particular object, O (or of an object of kind K), and we know how to go about discovering whether or not an alleged experience of O (or an object of kind K) is delusory then everything else being equal the best explanation of S's having E is that S has experienced O (or an object of kind K), rather than something else or nothing at all.

In (2), by knowing "circumstances" which make for delusory or genuine experiences, Rowe seems to mean empirically discoverable and specifiable *perceptual conditions*. This presumably would include both the perceptual state of S at the time of the experience and the relevant empirically discoverable environment in which S is having the experience. Let the relevant perceptual conditions be P. Rowe seems to envision the formulation of what we will call "perceptual generalizations" of the form:

> If a subject, S, has a putative experience of an object O (or of an object of kind K), and S is in P, then S's putative experience is likely/unlikely to be of O (or of an object of kind K).

So the idea of (2) is that if we knew in what circumstances, P, an alleged experience of a certain sort would be likely to be delusory, then one way of going about deciding whether S was having a delusory experience would be by checking whether S was in P. S's being in P would count in *favor* of the experience being delusory. And if we knew in what circumstances, P', an alleged experience of a certain sort would be likely to be genuine, then another way would be to check whether S was in P'. S's being in P' would count *against* the experience being delusory. According to (2) these are the only ways of going about finding whether or not an alleged experience was a delusory experience.

The idea of (3) is, as Rowe sees it, that God can choose to reveal Himself to one person and not to another. But in that case we could never give any perceptual conditions, P, in which it would be likely that S would be having a delusory experience of God, nor any perceptual conditions, P', in which S would be likely to be having a genuine experience of God. And that is because for any conditions which any person is in, God could choose either to be revealed or not to be revealed to that person in those conditions. It would always be up to God whether S would or would not experience God truly, and would not be a function of what perceptual conditions S was in. For instance, if S were to have an alleged experience of God and in exactly the same perceptual conditions nobody else did, the latter fact would not count at all against the genuineness of S's experience. Hence, whenever a person has what *seems* to be an experience of God we just have to take her word for it. In fact, S would have to take her own word for it. She would have no way of checking whether her putative experience was genuine. But then, Rowe concludes, we cannot apply BEER to cases of alleged experiences of God.

Were Rowe's argument sound we would have to conclude that we could not count any alleged experience of God as evidence for its own truth. But there are serious shortcomings to Rowe's argument.

To start with, BEER could not *replace* BEE as a sound principle for arguing from appearance to reality. And that is because BEER requires that we know how to go about finding positive reasons for whether or not an alleged experience of O was the "real thing." But, surely, in order to know such things we must be able to rely upon putative experiences of O. It is only by relying on putative experiences of O that we could even begin to come to know enough about the behavior and properties of the putative object in question to be enabled to have any idea about when an alleged experience might very well be delusory or when quite likely authentic.[10] But in order to do so we must rely on BEE before we could ever come to apply BEER. So Rowe could not very well argue for BEER replacing BEE.

Rowe's argument is best construed, therefore, as arguing not that BEE affords *no* evidential support whatsoever, but rather as arguing that the evidential support provided by BEE alone is weak, as contrasted with the evidential support provided by BEER. To be sure, when faced with putative experiences of an object O, BEE must get us started finding reasons which count in favor or against any given alleged experience of O being delusory. As time goes on, however, if we are unable to discover positive reasons for or against an alleged experience being delusory, then our evidential situation with respect to the truth of the alleged experiences is much weaker than it would have been had we discovered the appropriate positive reasons. BEER is the principle that applies when we succeed in finding such positive reasons. Only BEE applies when we fail. So Rowe could argue that we are limited to arguing from alleged experiences of God to God's existence from BEE alone, and therefore our conclusion is evidentially weak, and especially so relative to what might have been had we been able to argue from BEER to the same conclusion. In what follows we will therefore construe premise (1) of Rowe's argument as:

(1A) BEE affords good (i.e., not weak) evidential support, everything else being equal, when applied to an alleged experience of O (or an object of kind K) only if we know how to go about discovering whether or not an alleged experience of O (or an object of kind K) is delusory.

Given this as Rowe's first premise, we find it to be seriously faulty.

Our first reply to (1A) is paraphrased from an idea of William Alston's, raised in a somewhat related context:[11] Whether or not the application of BEE will yield ways of discovering whether an alleged experience of an

---

[10] This is not quite right, since we may have experience only of O-like objects, and make predictions about O on that basis from a well-confirmed theory. See footnote 4, this chapter.

[11] Substantially this line is taken by William P. Alston in *Perceiving God: The Epistemology of Religious Experience* (Ithaca: Cornell University Press, 1991), pp. 216–20.

object is delusory will depend upon what sort of object is revealed to us in alleged experiences to which we apply BEE. The employment of BEE *might* reveal to us an object about which we can discover reasons for or against alleged experiences of it being delusory. But then it might not. We might learn enough about the object in question to come to know that it is of such a nature that it does not lend itself to ways of discovering whether alleged experiences of it were delusory or not. BEER unjustifiably limits beforehand what results we might come up with when relying upon BEE. And it limits those results to what we typically could expect when applying BEE to physical objects, and rather stable, gross ones at that. But to limit the results beforehand is to stack the deck against alleged experiences of God, since what is revealed about God in alleged experiences of Him shows that He is precisely that kind of being about whom it is very difficult to know that a putative experience of Him was delusory. And this inference follows not only from the sporadic distribution of such putative experiences, but from the content of what is revealed in those experiences—from the way God is experienced to be. Hence, BEER represents what William Alston calls, "epistemic imperialism," an imperialism which insists on imposing on all subject matter what is appropriate to stable, gross physical objects in particular.

This reply, while fine as far as it goes, does not go far enough for our aim of showing the *strong* rationality of belief in God on the basis of experience. To be strongly rational on our argument it would have to be rational on the deliverances of BEE when applied to alleged experiences of God to believe that God was experienced, and not rational to believe that God was not experienced, everything else being equal. But the above reply in defense of BEE seems to show only that a belief based on BEE that God was experienced would be rational, but not that it would not be rational to believe otherwise because of a rejection of BEE on grounds of (1A). It does not seem to show that it would not be rational for a person to reject BEE on the grounds of (1A). A person might be entirely justified in refusing to take the chance on going with BEE when doing so might be acquiescing in one grand delusion supported by relatively weak evidence. She might ask herself how she could tell whether there really was a being like God is supposed to be or whether the evidence was just too sporadic to be anything but weak, and so not apply BEE to the case of God. So it seems that believing that BEE does not apply in the case of God could be a rational belief in this context. But in that case, we will not have shown that it was *strongly* rational to believe God was experienced on the basis of BEE.[12]

We therefore wish to supplement this reply to (1A) with the following observation. Rowe wishes to endorse (1A) because he believes, apparently, that unless we knew how to go about finding whether or not an alleged experience of O was delusory, then any alleged experience of O would have to be accepted as evidentially efficacious. We would have to take any alleged experience of O at face value. But if any alleged experience of O must be taken at face value, then the evidential power of such an experience would be greatly diminished or cancelled out entirely. Such an alleged experience has (significant) evidential power only if we could have reason for or against thinking an alleged experience of O delusory, and found in fact that it was not delusory. If alleged experiences of O, however, could not be *exposed* to the possibility of being shown delusory, then their evidential value would be seriously discredited.

Even if Rowe were right that the (significant) evidential value of an alleged experience of O depended upon the evidential value possibly being counterindicated and upon such a possibility not having materialized, surely it is wrong to suppose that this condition could be realized only were it possible to find reasons for thinking such an experience delusory. An apparent experience of O is delusory, recall, if it seems to be an experience of O, but is not. But the evidential value of an alleged experience of O could be challenged in other ways. For example, if we had reason to believe that *even if O were not present* S would have thought he was experiencing O, then the evidential value of S's experience would be compromised *even if S's experience were not in fact delusory*, that is, even if S were really and truly experiencing O (unbeknown to S and to us).[13] In such cases, the evidential value of S's alleged experience of O could be exposed

---

[12] In the context of Alston's presentation of this reply, it is intended to establish only what we have called "weak rationality," so our response is no criticism of Alston.

[13] Suppose you ask your friend to check whether the freezer is cold by putting his hand inside and seeing how it feels. He reports that the freezer is cold. One way you might find out that your friend's report was not trustworthy would be by learning that you had forgotten to plug in the freezer. But another way would be by learning that your friend suffered from a circulatory problem that made him feel cold in his hands regardless of circumstances. (Let's suppose it is possible for your friend to feel cold in his hands for two reasons at the same time: both because he feels the cold of the freezer and because of his circulatory problem.) If the latter happened, you would have learned that his feeling cold in his hands was not evidence for the freezer's being cold, even if the freezer had in fact been cold.

to defeat, even if we had no idea how to find out if the putative experience was *delusory*.

Hence we find (1A) to be ill-supported by the requirement that an alleged experience of O could have significant evidential value only if exposed in principle to the finding of reasons for thinking it delusory. So BEER seems too strong a principle, if what we are after is a way of securing challenges to the evidential value of alleged experiences.

Applying this rejoinder to the case of putative perceptions of God, in principle we could imagine having reason to think that even were God not appearing to S, S might very well have thought he was experiencing God. In fact many of what are called "reductionist explanations" of putative perceptions of God are best understood as making just that sort of claim. The reductionist explanations range over an array of pathological and non-pathological conditions of perceiving subjects. We might discover, for instance, a strongly confirmed theory about human psychology which together with what we know about S would have as a consequence that we could have expected S to have thought he was having an experience of God when he did, whether or not God was really appearing to him. In such a case the evidential value of S's experience would be greatly discredited without our yet having any reason whatsoever for thinking that S was having a *delusory* experience.

In Chapter 5 we consider the reductionist charge that putative experiences of God *in fact* lack evidential value. We will show that this charge is unfounded. But our reply there in no way blunts the point that apparent perceptions of God *could* have been discovered to lack evidential value for such reasons, reasons having nothing to do with showing apparent perceptions of God to be delusory. So experiences of God are exposed to evidential defeat. That they are not typically defeated in this way allows us to conclude, on what Rowe might plausibly maintain, that they typically do have evidential value. Hence, after all that Rowe has said and done, it remains strongly rational for us to believe that God is experienced.

We pass to a consideration of premise (2) of Rowe's argument.

According to (2) the only way we could go about discovering whether or not an alleged experience of O (or object of kind K) was delusory would be by discovering perceptual generalizations which made delusory experience likely or which made it likely that a person was having a genuine perception of an object, were it there to be experienced. Note that as before the employment of BEE must precede the discovery of such perceptual generalizations, for it will be only by relying on the results of BEE that we could gain any idea about the nature of the alleged object, and hence get any idea about what would make for delusory and nondelusory experiences. So (2) must be understood to imply that the employment of BEE can be only provisional until the time comes when we discover reliable perceptual generalizations that would afford positive reasons for thinking an experience delusory or not. As long as that time has not come, or especially as soon as it becomes clear to us that no such perceptual generalizations will be forthcoming, our justified dependence upon BEE is greatly limited or minimal at best.

But there is reason not to accept (2), because there are positive reasons, all based on experience, relevant to determining whether an alleged experience of a certain object was delusory or not, short of discovering relevant perceptual generalizations.

For one thing, on BEE of course an alleged experience counts in favor of its own genuineness. But Rowe's argument insists that BEE is insufficient reason for deciding that the alleged experience was the real thing. A natural reply would be to invoke STING to argue that the frequency and variability of conditions in which such experiences take place count more than does BEE alone in favor of the genuineness of such experiences. Hence, BEE and STING together give more of a reason to think that experiences of that sort are not delusory than does BEE alone, independently of our knowing any perceptual generalizations relative to that type of experience. Hence one way of going about discovering positive reasons as to whether an experience was delusory or not would be to look to see whether it occurred again, how often, and under what varied conditions. So (2) is false. And of course, BEE and STING can be applied to alleged experiences of God. Of course, not everybody experiences God, and those who do don't perceive Him all the time. Were that not so the case for concluding that God exists would be stronger than it is. But (2) provides no good reason for ruling against alleged experiences as providing a *good* case for God's existence, nonetheless.[14]

Having used BEE and STING for the experience of God, we could then find other reasons relevant to whether or not an alleged experience of God was delusory. For example, a subject might have an alleged experience of God, well supported by BEE and STING, in which God told her that an earlier alleged experience of hers was delusory. This would constitute a reason, whether or not decisive, for thinking the alleged experience in

[14] Later in this chapter we will return in some detail to the issue of the relative rationality of belief in God and in physical objects based on alleged experiences of each.

question to have been delusory. Or suppose a subject has had experiences which he thought were of God until he has an experience of God which convinces him, by its content and power, that the previous experiences were not of God at all. He now has positive reasons for deciding whether the previous experiences were delusory. So we do know how to go about discovering positive reasons for thinking an alleged experience of God delusory, without necessarily being able to come up with appropriate, true perceptual generalizations, a further reason for not accepting (2).

Second, a positive reason for thinking an alleged experience of O to be delusory which would not employ perceptual generalizations, would be if predictions made on its basis did not turn out. And if the predictions did turn out, that would be positive reason for thinking an alleged experience of O to be not delusory. Neither of these would *prove* the case, but would be what Rowe is looking for: positive reasons for thinking one way or the other. In order to check predictions we needn't know true perceptual generalizations governing alleged experiences of the type in question. At most we would have to know true perceptual generalizations governing the reliability of our experience of the fulfillment or lack of it of the predictions. Hence, (2) is false.

In the case of any experience, E, of God, by a subject, S, a general prediction warranted on the basis of E would be that, everything else being equal, we could expect to find that others also have alleged experiences of God. To the extent this prediction is borne out we will have a positive reason for thinking that E is a genuine experience of God.[15] And with regard to a particular experience in which it seems that a subject has been visited by God and has been told of a coming future event she otherwise would not likely have known about, whether the event occurs is surely relevant, if not decisive, to whether she had really experienced God.

Finally, there is another way to discover that alleged experiences of God were probably delusory without invoking perceptual generalizations. Suppose typical reports of alleged experience of God involved attributing to God fantastic goings-on massively disruptive of the natural order, reminiscent, say, of some mythological stories told about Greek gods. In that case we could have good reason to doubt their veracity, since we have good reason to believe that such things never happen. This would be especially true when the reports were not very large in number and were confined

---

[15] Similarly, were the experience true we could expect certain moral and spiritual development to follow or to be accelerated. See William P. Alston, "The Fulfillment of Promises as Evidence for Religious Belief," in *Faith in Theory and Practice: Essays on Justifying Religious Belief,* ed. Elizabeth S. Radcliffe and Carol J. White (Chicago: Open Court, 1993), pp. 1–34.

to a small locale or a specific type of person or circumstance, rather than widely varied. So we have here another way that could have been available to us to determine that alleged experiences of God were probably delusory, without having to bring in perceptual generalizations of the sort that concern Rowe. (It should be noted that the negative assessment of such reports should be distinguished from a possibly positive assessment of a claim to have experienced God's performance of a miracle in violation of a law of nature. The latter may deserve credence, for example, when we grant that God exists and is omnipotent. But of course our present discussion may make no such assumption.)

In fact, of course, alleged experiences of God are not normally reports of bizarre happenings in violation of the natural order. So they are free of suspicion on the present grounds.

We have ways, therefore, of going about the task of weighing whether a person's apparent experience of God was delusory without having to employ perceptual generalizations concerning experiences of God.

But even were (2) to be true, it is far from clear that

(3) In the case of alleged experiences of God, we know neither under what circumstances a person would be likely to have a delusory experience of God nor under what circumstances a person would be likely to have an experience of God were God there to be experienced.

is true, because it is far from clear that alleged experiences of God do not satisfy its conditions. And that is because (2), as already noted, must recognize the validity of BEE, at least provisionally. But what is known by applying BEE is that God is often experienced as a maximally valuable being, and that when one experiences God typically one experiences the decentering of one's self, to some degree or other, so that God can be one's value center. So what is suggested by experiences of God is that, generally speaking at least, if one is unable to decenter oneself to at least some degree this would prevent, block, or interfere with one's ability to perceive God. And the history of alleged experiences of God lends plausibility to the claim that often only people who are open to God in this way actually do perceive Him.

So we can specify what amounts to a perceptual state of S in the case of perception of God, such that S's being in that state is a positive reason for thinking that S is not experiencing God even if he seems to be. Specifically, if S is an egotistical and selfish person who abuses others and claims to have had an experience of God, that would be a reason, everything else being equal, for thinking his experience delusory. This would especially be the case if S continued in his self-centered abusive behavior after and between alleged experiences of God. Of course, it need not *necessarily* be delusory. After all, it might happen that God in His wisdom decides to reveal Himself to a scoundrel, although the history of alleged experiences of God shows that this is not generally the case. But then, Rowe is seeking only "positive reasons" for thinking a specific experiential episode delusory. And in the case of God, we have such. To be sure we have not set down perceptual generalizations which refer to the *sense* conditions under which S allegedly experiences God, but to insist here upon sense conditions only would be epistemic imperialism with a vengeance.

It may be true that in the case of God we do not have as many perceptual generalizations, and ones as detailed as we do in the case of tables and chairs, and so it might be argued that the case for God's existence presents a lower likelihood than does the case for tables and chairs. This may be so, but it does not yet follow that the case for God is not a good case, nonetheless.[16] In any event, we have been given no reason to think (3) is true.

We conclude that Rowe's argument fails to discredit the evidential value of alleged experiences of God when BEE, or BEER, and STING are applied to them.

III

We began this chapter with Michael Martin's objection that the use of BEEN in God's case neutralized the results obtained from applying BEE in God's case. We then went along with the reply that BEEN could not be applied in the case of God because we could not make out the distinction between *experiencing God's absence* and *failing to experience God's presence after a thorough search*. In doing so, we were going along with the implicit assumption that knowing by experience that God was absent would have to be a matter of inferring this from the failure to experience God's presence in appropriate circumstances. But suppose we were mistaken about this. Suppose it were possible to have a direct (putative) experience of God's nonexistence. And if so, perhaps we have to rethink our replies to Martin and Rowe.[17]

Suppose it were possible to seem to experience God's nonexistence.

---

[16] Later in this chapter we return in some detail to the issue of the relative rationality of belief in God and in physical objects based on alleged experiences of each.

[17] This section draws upon some ideas found in Jerome I. Gellman, "A New Look at the Problem of Evil," *Faith and Philosophy* 9 (1992): 210–16.

Suppose a person could gaze onto the starry heavens and have what seemed to him to be a vivid experience of God's nonexistence. Or, to give this suggestion more concrete plausibility, consider that sometimes people assert that they believe God does not exist on the basis of their experiences of particularly painful and horrifying evils. For example, while some survivors of the Nazi Holocaust were somehow strengthened in their religious faith by their deeply disturbing experiences of brutality and murder, other survivors came out of the Holocaust proclaiming that they no longer believed God existed. They became agnostics. And others proclaimed more strongly that they now believed—on the basis of their experiences in the ghettoes of Europe and in the Nazi death camps—that God did not exist.

Philosophers, used to presenting the problem of evil as an evidential argument, might be tempted to suppose that the latter were arguing in an implicitly deductive or inductive way from the evil they experienced to the nonexistence of God. The argument would be that God couldn't exist or most likely did not exist, given those evils. But there may be another way of understanding the conversion of these people to atheism. The philosophers' "argument" from the "problem of evil" might be a discursive variant upon what is really for these people an (alleged) experience of God's non-existence. Perhaps these people who witnessed horrific evils and declare that God does not exist were (allegedly) experiencing God's nonexistence in the evil which they knew. They experienced this nonexistence not in the sense of reaching the conclusion that God didn't exist on the basis of the evil they knew. Rather, they *perceived* the world as Godless, as without God. And they perceived this within the utter repugnance and revulsion of the evil they knew.

Look at it this way: Poets have written of *seeing* eternity in a grain of sand, and ordinary mortals sometimes experience God's presence through the beauty and symmetry of a snowflake. We need not assume that the poet is implicitly advancing a cosmological argument from the existence of sand, nor ordinary mortals urging an implicit version of an argument for the existence of God from the exquisite shapes of snowflakes. They are both having alleged experiences of God on the occasion of perceiving certain features of the world. But then neither need we assume that, for example, Holocaust survivors who experienced horrific evils and turned atheist must be inferring God's nonexistence rather than just seeming to experience it.

Perhaps worries will arise about the coherence of the idea of an experience of God's nonexistence, especially because for us "God" is a proper name, with the properties ascribed to proper names in Chapter 1. Given this point of view it may be less than perspicuous what could be *meant* by an alleged experience of God's nonexistence, for reasons we will now explain.

In Chapter 1, we endorsed the view that a proper name is a "rigid designator," which designates its object regardless of the definite descriptions true of it. On the view of Saul Kripke, ascribed to J. S. Mill, and sometimes called "Millianism," on which proper names are rigid designators, there is a problem with the semantic meaning of negative existentials in which proper names are in the subject-place. Consider, for example:

(SC) Santa Claus does not exist.

We cannot say that in (SC) "Santa Claus" refers, directly as it were and not via the benefit of descriptions, to Santa Claus, and that (SC) is saying about *him* that he does not exist. That is because there exists no such thing as "Santa Claus." And we can't "point to" a nonexistent "Santa Claus." On Kripke's theory of rigid designation, therefore, (SC) should express no proposition whatever, since its subject term is robbed of any semantic function, given that it fails to refer.

Now a similar problem would arise for the Millian for the alleged experience that God does not exist. Recalling that to experience God entails that God exists and is the object of the experience, a Millian has no problem with:

(EG) S experiences God's existence.

for "God" refers to a specific being, whom S is experiencing. But when we consider:

(NG) S experiences God's nonexistence.[18]

a problem arises. For how will the Millian understand the semantic content of (NG)? Surely it is not to be understood as stating that there exists a particular being, God, such that S experiences *His* nonexistence?

Our view of proper names, however, does not coincide with Kripke's, for, as explained in our first chapter, we have understood "rigid designation" as a pragmatic category only and not as a semantic one. With regard to the semantics of proper names we reject standard descriptivist theories

[18] On our use of the locution, "S experiences X's nonexistence," it entails that X does not exist.

but leave open the possibility that the Nominal Description Theory might be true. We argued that this openness to the Nominal Description Theory in no way clashes with a commitment to proper names having the pragmatic function of rigid designators.

Hence, on the semantic level we are not adverse to an analysis upon which (NG) becomes something roughly like:

(NGN) S experiences that "God" has no bearer.

But that surely is not the whole of it, since "God" in (NG) figures pragmatically as a rigid designator. Since we distinguished between successful and failed rigid designators, we would say that if (NGN) were true, then "God" would be a failed rigid designator.

Now recall that in our first chapter we endorsed the view that the use of a proper name ordinarily takes place within a "naming game," a game which sets the parameters, albeit roughly, beyond which a name fails to name. With regard to the name "God," we claimed the naming-game normally governing it requires that God be described at least by the minimum condition (N):

> God is:
> (1) the most perfect actual being,
> (2) who is very high on the scale of perfection,
> (3) whose perfection is vastly greater than that of the second most perfect actual being, and
> (4) upon whom other beings in some important way are dependent.

(N) tells us that the game is one of naming a being who is such that it falls within the limits set down by the conditions: being the most perfect being there is, possessed of high perfection, far above any other being in perfection, and having the universe dependent on it.

In our previous discussion we noted that if the being who lies at the inception of the pertinent referential chain for God, for example, the being who appeared to Adam, failed to fulfill these requirements in some way, then the natural conclusion would be that this being was not God, and that therefore "God" had failed to refer. And we can now add a further observation: it may be possible for a person to have an experience which discloses experientially that the universe is such that there exists no being who falls within the parameters set by (N). Such a person's experience then shows that "God" is a failed rigid designator.

For example, there are those who claim to be able to experience *dependence* as an attribute of the world or of things within the world. By the same measure, others might be able to experience *independence* as an attribute of the world or of things in it, in the sense of their not being dependent or importantly connected to anything outside it. But in that case, they will have experienced that (N)(4) was not fulfilled, and thus will know via experience that the name "God" did not refer. Finally, one may be able to *experience* that the world is such that it is not accompanied by any being who is very high on the scale of perfection, and experience that fact within the very experience of horrendous evils. In that case, (N)(2) will have been experienced as not fulfilled, and thus that "God" does not refer will have been known by experience.

So now we can say that to experience that God does not exist might take various forms, including: experiencing the very being who has been experienced in the past by, say, Adam and Moses, and who has been thought to be God, as delineated by (N), yet experiencing that it was not properly described within the parameters of (N), and was therefore not "God"; experiencing the world in such a way that one experiences that one of its attributes is that it is not God's world, i.e., is not accompanied by any being fulfilling the minimum requirements of (N); and experiencing the world as abandoned, as without connection to a supremely valuable being.

But if we are to countenance the possibility of a direct experience seemingly of God's nonexistence, then we must amend our previous responses, respectively, to Martin and Rowe. With regard to Martin, if we admit that a person could seem to perceive that God does not exist, then we come up against Martin's claim that we should accept his principle BEEN just as readily as we accept our principle BEE. Recall BEEN:

> If a person, S, has an experience, E, which seems (phenomenally) to be of the absence of a particular object, O (or of an object of kind, K), then *everything else being equal* the best explanation of S's having E is that S has experienced the absence of O (or of an object of kind, K).

Our earlier problem with BEEN hinged upon the difficulty of determining that a person had experienced God's absence or nonexistence, rather than only having failed to experience God's presence. We argued that we didn't know enough to *build up* the distinction between the two. For that reason we denied that BEEN could be employed for alleged experiences of God's nonexistence. But now we are considering that there could be an experience in which God's nonexistence is detected phenomenally within the experience itself. In that case, God's alleged nonexistence could be perceived without being grounded first in the building up of the distinction between "experiencing God's absence" and "failing to experience God." So we remain with no objection in principle to the application of BEEN to alleged experiences of God's nonexistence, and there seems to be no basis upon which we could accept BEE but reject BEEN.

On the assumption that direct (alleged) experiences of God's nonexistence are possible, we hereby accept BEEN's application to alleged experiences of God's nonexistence. And so we remain with no objection in principle to considering such alleged experiences as counterevidence to alleged experiences of God.

But the *practical* implications of this admission are in fact negligible. For all that follows from this admission is that with respect to any single putative experience of God's nonexistence that there might be, the best explanation of it would be, everything else being equal, that the person was experiencing God's nonexistence and that God really did not exist. But from that it hardly follows that the experiential evidence for God's nonexistence seriously challenges the experiential evidence for His existence. In order for this to follow, we would have to have reports that people actually have had alleged experiences of God's nonexistence, or have some other good grounds for believing that such alleged experiences have taken place. And the numbers of such episodes would have to be such as to give *significant* counterevidence, relative to the experiential strength of alleged experiences of God. Then we would have to argue from BEEN and the analogue of STING, call it "STINGEN," for the nonexistence of an object, that the negative perceptual evidence undermined the positive perceptual evidence. But we do not *have* such significant counterevidence. There may actually be enormous numbers of people across cultures and down though history who have had seeming experiences of God's nonexistence, but we lack *evidence* that this is the case. How many people do we *know* about, who actually have seemed to *experience* God's nonexistence?

Suppose, though, we asserted that large numbers of alleged experiences of God's nonexistence have actually occurred among sufferers of great evil—such as Holocaust survivors who came to deny God's existence—thinking of these sufferers as having direct experiences of their atheism rather than thinking of them as only arguing to that conclusion. Even so, this would not give us good evidence for God's nonexistence. The number of such people and the variability of the circumstances of their experiences could not be compared to the number and variability of circumstances attaching to alleged experiences of God.

But in fact the evidence from such experiences is far weaker than that. For to the extent to which alleged experiences of God's nonexistence take place under conditions of great horrendous suffering, to that same extent the alleged experiences of God's nonexistence take place in circumstances which severely discredit their evidential value. For conditions of great stress and danger create *pathological circumstances*, circumstances in which a subject might very well be expected to seem to experience God's nonexistence, everything else being equal, even if God really did exist. Hence, apparent experiences of God's nonexistence under conditions of experiencing horrendous evils are evidentially suspect. So an argument from apparent experiences of God's nonexistence under such conditions could not very well challenge our argument from BEE and STING.

Of course, the other side of this reply is that if situations of great danger and stress are indeed pathological then it would also be true that in them a subject might very well seem to experience God's presence even if God didn't exist, and that therefore in such situations the evidential value of such experiences is severely compromised. We accept both directions of this way of arguing. In Chapter 5 we discuss at length the implications of this for our argument from alleged experiences of God, and note that there is no grounds for thinking that alleged experiences of God typically or often do take place under pathological circumstances. But on the claim we are now considering, that we should locate alleged experiences of God's nonexistence in situations of great suffering, it would turn out that alleged experiences of God's nonexistence did *typically* take place under pathological conditions. And for this reason their evidential integrity is well damaged, since there is reason to think that such seeming experiences would very well have taken place in such circumstances, even if God existed.

Hence we can only conclude that an argument from BEEN and STINGEN to the nonexistence of God does not succeed, and Martin has given no good objection against our argument from BEE and STING.[19]

We now return to Rowe's objection to the evidential value of alleged experiences of God. Were we to suppose it at least *possible* for there to be

---

[19] As for an argument to the effect that if God were absolutely perfect He would not allow to take place any experiences in which it seemed that God did not exist, on the grounds that this would be a great evil, we refer the reader to our discussion of the problem of evil in Chapter 7 of this work.

direct experiences of God's nonexistence, we would have at our disposal a way of finding positive reason for thinking an individual alleged experience of God delusory. Suppose we were to investigate and find massive evidence of alleged experiences of God's nonexistence. That would be acceptable, positive reason for thinking an individual alleged experience of God delusory. (And we could have this positive reason, without necessarily knowing any perceptual generalizations either for or against an alleged experience being delusory.) In that case, then, Rowe's premise would be false that:

(2) We know how to go about discovering whether or not an alleged experience of O (or an object of kind K) is delusory only if we know either under what circumstances a person would be likely to have a delusory experience of O (or an object of kind K) or under what circumstances a person would be likely to have an experience of O (or an object of kind K) were O there to be experienced.

Since we would then know a way to go about investigating whether or not an alleged experience of God was delusory, Rowe's principle BEER would be satisfied. The only question remaining would be whether there was massive evidence of seeming experiences of God's nonexistence.

As we have already noted, however, the evidence we have in favor of evidentially respectable occurrences of apparent experiences of God's nonexistence is negligible. Hence, although we know how to go about looking for a positive reason for thinking that an individual claim to have experienced God is delusory, we have not found that reason in fact. We can now proclaim in good conscience, as far as anything Rowe has argued, that the very fact that alleged experiences of God's nonexistence *could* have been great in number and thus *could* have shown an individual presumed experience of God to be delusory, but aren't and haven't, strengthens the evidential power of a presumed experience of God.

The conclusion is that even were we to recognize the possibility of putative experiences of God's nonexistence, and thus have to retract our earlier rebuttal of Martin and Rowe, that would not require changing our negative assessment of their objections. Our argument from BEE and STING stands.

IV

In this chapter we have been defending our use of BEE as a fundamental principle of rationality governing our experience, and we have been de-

fending the success of BEE, with STING, in establishing overall the truth
of experiences of God, everything else being equal. In addition we have
argued that alleged experiences of God pass the test of BEER as well. In
this section we turn to one final objection, based on the failure of many
people to ever experience God and on the intermittent nature of the experience by those who do have it.

Before that objection we note that according to BEE and STING, the
likelihood that God is experienced is strengthened by the great number of
such alleged experiences and the great variations in conditions in which
they occur. This notwithstanding, putative experiences of God are far less
frequent, ubiquitous, and uninterrupted than are experiences of physical
objects. The latter are afforded to nearly every human being in one form
or other throughout their waking life. By comparison, experiences of God
are measured out only relatively meagerly, only sometimes, not to everyone, and not even to all cultures. So some would argue, should it not
follow by comparison that believing in God on the basis of alleged experiences of Him is less than rational?

Some would also claim that although we have argued that having ways
to find out whether an alleged experience of O was delusory was not a
necessary condition of testing the evidential value of the experience, it
must be admitted that having such ways strengthens the evidential value
of an experience. And although we suggested ways relevant to checking
whether alleged experiences of God were delusory, it must be conceded
that they are far less impressive than they normally are in the case of physical objects. The perceptual generalizations are fewer and less commanding.
This poses another question. Should it not follow that by comparison believing in God on the basis of alleged experiences of Him is less than
rational?

But of course this line of thinking is not at all compelling. It might be
the case that believing that God exists on the basis of alleged experiences
of Him is less rational than believing in physical objects on the basis of
experiences of them without it following that believing in God on that
basis is less than rational. The belief in physical objects might have rational
support far beyond what is needed to render it rational. Hence, belief in
God could be less rational than belief in physical objects, yet still be adequately rational.

This raises, another question. Is believing in God based on alleged experiences of Him at least *less* rational than believing in physical objects based
on alleged experiences of them? This is the interesting question, and our
answer is that it need not be, even conceding the facts about the relative

number of experiences of God in comparison to experiences of physical objects, and conceding the differential in the power and nature of the potential evidence that an experience is delusory.

The impression that in the given circumstances believing in God based on experience must be less rational than believing in physical objects based on experience seems to be based implicitly on some such principle as the following:

> For any belief-candidates, A and B: if on S1's evidence, E, A is likely to degree N, and on S2's evidence, E', B is likely to degree M, and N is greater than M, then relative to E and E', S1's belief that A is more rational than S2's belief that B.[20]

Let us call this the principle of "Commensurate Rationality," or "CR". CR applies to any belief candidates including ones that are not mutually exclusive of one another. Thus CR is not a principle for choosing between competing belief-candidates, but only for calibrating relative rationalities of various belief-candidates. Also, A and B can be the very same belief candidate, variously supported by different evidences for different subjects.

Now, let A be the belief that physical objects exist and let E be what we know of experiences of physical objects. And let B be the belief that God exists and let E' be what we know of experiences of God. On E alone that physical objects exist is more likely than it is that God exists on E', because of the differential in the number of cases each is based on, and because of the differential in the number and power of the ways of determining whether an alleged experience was delusory. CR implies that for that reason, relative to E and E', believing in physical objects is more *rational* than is believing in God.

But CR should not be accepted as it stands, for believing in either of two belief candidates could be equally rational relative to two given bodies of evidence, respectively, even though one was more *likely* than the other relative to those respective bodies of evidence. And that is possible because for any given belief-candidate there could be a ceiling beyond which *rationality* would no longer increase despite increments in likelihood. Beyond that ceiling more evidence would no longer make any difference to the

---

[20] A stronger principle would be that of "proportional rationality": "For any belief-candidates, A and B: if on S1's evidence, E, A is likely to degree N, and on S2's evidence, E', B is likely to degree M, and N is greater than M, then relative to E and E', S1's belief that A is more rational than S2's belief that B to the same degree that M is greater than N." This principle is stronger, however, than what is needed for the argument we are now considering.

degree of rationality involved in holding that belief, because the likelihood would be so high *already* that the rationality would be secured already in a maximal way.

An example will illustrate the point. Suppose S has seen 130,000 elephants in Bengal, and believes on that basis that elephants are flourishing in Bengal. And suppose that S's friend has seen 130,001 elephants, and believes on that basis that elephants are flourishing in Bengal. (And suppose they both have the same standard for judging what makes for the flourishing of elephants in Bengal.) S's friend's belief is more *likely* relative to her evidence than is S's belief relative to *her* evidence, based as it is on a larger sample class. But S's friend's belief that elephants are flourishing in Bengal is not any more *rational* than S's belief that elephants are flourishing in Bengal. And that is because S's belief is already as rational as can be. Increased likelihood does not make it any more rational.

Examples need not be limited to cases where the differences in likelihood are minuscule, as in the above example. Our conclusion would not be changed were S's friend's belief to be supported by the sighting of 1,300,000 or even 13,000,000 elephants, while poor S had experienced only his 130,000. The point would stay the same: S's evidential base is enough to confer maximal rationality on S's belief. His belief is as rational as can be. The fact is that S's friend's belief would benefit from vast over-evidence relative to the needs of establishing the maximal rationality of the belief that elephants are flourishing in Bengal.

Suppose then we replace CR with CR.1:

> For any belief-candidates, A and B: if on S1's evidence, E, A is likely to degree N, and on S2's evidence, E', B is likely to degree M, and N is greater than M, then relative to E and E', S1's belief that A is more rational than S2's belief that B, provided that S2's belief that B (on E') is not as rational as can be.

CR.1 says nothing about when a given belief-candidate would or would not be as rational as can be. But this is as it should be, since these matters will surely depend on the belief-candidate in question, perhaps on the believing subject, and on the circumstances. In addition, we should expect that it is often a matter of judgment as to whether the point of maximal rationality has been reached, and less a matter of applying a calculus of rationality in order to decide.

Let us now consider the application of CR.1 to the relative rationalities of believing in God and physical objects relative to experience. From the fact that the existence of physical objects is more likely relative to alleged experiences of them than is the existence of God relative to alleged experiences of Him, which we concede, it does not yet follow from CR.1 that belief in God is less rational than belief in physical objects, relative to the respective experiences. It would follow only if the likelihood of God's existence were not such as to make that belief as rational as can be relative to such experiences.

Putative experiences of God have been widespread in the history of the world, in many different circumstances. These include radically different historical circumstances, various religious and cultural settings and different economic and sociological conditions. Persons of varying cultures, world-outlooks and mind-sets have claimed to have perceived God, in great numbers. On BEE and STING this makes it very likely, everything else being equal, that God really is experienced and does exist. Couldn't this likelihood make it as *rational* as it can be relative to that evidence that God exists? This suggestion will no doubt not meet with much enthusiasm on the part of many readers. But perhaps we can say a few things that would tend to blunt their resistance.

We suspect that at least some of the resistance to the idea that belief in God is as rational as can be relative to the facts about experiences of God would come from illicitly importing into the issue reasons the reader might have for thinking that the evidential value of these experiences is defeated by other considerations. But the claim we are now considering is not that belief in God is rational as can be *overall*, but that it is so *relative to the facts about the experience of God* as inferred from the application of BEE and STING. After all, at this stage of our argument we have not been so bold as to claim that BEE and STING establish the strong rationality of believing in God, overall. So far at least, we have been making this claim only *everything else being equal*.

The question is, then, whether when considering only the evidence of experiences of God, with no other evidence, belief in God is as rational as can be. Answering this question in the affirmative is entirely consistent with affirming that overall belief in God is not as rational as can be. Once this is acknowledged some of the resistance to the idea that the belief in God is as rational as can be relative to the facts about experiences of God might be dissipated. And resistance might thereby be weakened to the thought of a belief in the existence of God relative to facts about experiences of God being as *rational*, though not as *likely*, as belief in the existence of physical objects relative to experiences of them.

A further source of resistance to the idea that belief in God may be as rational as can be, based on what is known about experiences of God, may come from a lingering impression that the fact that so many people may be presumed to never experience God somehow must count against the evidential value of alleged experiences of God. This entire chapter has been devoted to rebutting this charge as it has been articulated in different ways by philosophers. But perhaps we can add a few observations to what has been written here in order to attempt to dispel worries about this and thus weaken further resistance to the idea that belief in God may be as rational as can be relative to experiences of God.

If we accept the deliverance of BEE and STING concerning the genuineness of experiences of God, we can be in a position to explain *on that basis* why it is that more people do not experience God.

Typically, experiences of God reveal a type of being who apparently cannot be coerced to appear. We cannot experience God merely by our choosing. Thus a comparison of the experience of God to the experience of (most ordinary) physical objects is less apt than would be a comparison between the former and the hearing of a secret. Because what is heard in a secret is heard *as* a secret there is a built-in explanation of why so many others don't know what the hearer knows. Hence, that others don't know what the hearer knows counts not at all against one who seems to have heard a secret. In a similar way, the fact that many people seem never to be aware of God at all counts less against the truth of experiences of God than it would otherwise. Not that God is a secret, but God is experienced as not being readily invoked.

Furthermore, for all any of us knows, God may be appearing to people who for one reason or another are incapable of conscious awareness of God. For all we know, God is appearing to all people all the time, including those of us who insist we have never had an experience of God. But the fact that nevertheless God is not consciously experienced by all of us can be explained, at least partially, in various ways. Many people do not have a sufficient psychological set to know they were experiencing God even were God to be appearing to them. Still others are adamant atheists who would resist becoming aware of God even if He were readily accessible to them.

We have also noted how being incapable of decentering oneself and being closed to having God as one's value center can plausibly prevent one's becoming aware of God's presence. Often, to recognize God as God requires a readiness to perceive one's value center as outside of oneself in the first place. Unless the subject were psychologically and spiritually ready for this, she might never be aware of God as God.

Experiences of God might for this reason remain well beyond the awareness of the subject or be misunderstood as experiences of something else. For example, a subject may think he was experiencing a "creative force" within, which description need not have momentous consequences for the decentering of his self, when in actuality he was experiencing God. Perhaps many of us are not capable of experiencing something other than ourselves, or what we ourselves are part of, as the center of our value. So perhaps for that reason we never seem to be experiencing God.

So we could rely on BEE and STING for support for the belief in the genuineness of alleged perceptions of God and also for some explanations provided by what is disclosed in such perceptions, for why more people are not aware of God. So the fact that more people aren't aware of God counts for less than it might otherwise have done.

We conclude that it cannot be shown by CR.1 that belief in the existence of God relative to the evidence of experiences of God is less rational than belief in physical objects relative to perceptions of them.

This having been said, however, nothing in the overall argument of this book depends upon both beliefs being equally rational. The task we have set ourselves is more modest: to show that belief in God is overall strongly rational based on experiences of God. That conclusion is not damaged by the admission that relative to their respective evidences belief in God may be less likely and less rational than belief in physical objects. Being less likely and less rational is perfectly consistent with being very likely and very rational.

In conclusion, the attacks we have considered against BEE and against our employment of it stemming from alleged failures to experience God or alleged experiences of God's nonexistence are not convincing. They do not succeed in displacing our confidence in the power of principles BEE and STING to establish a strong presumption in favor of there being genuine experiences of God and thus of God's existing. So far forth, our argument stands.

[4]

God and
Religious Diversity

In this chapter we take up the issue of religious diversity as a challenge to our argument from alleged experiences of God to the strong rationality of believing that God is experienced and thus exists.

Various philosophers have challenged the justification of relying on the truth of alleged experiences of God, in light of the diversity of religious experiences found in the world's religions. Antony Flew has protested that:

> Religious experiences are enormously varied, ostensibly authenticating innumerable beliefs many of which are in contradiction with one another . . . The varieties of religious experience include, not only those which their subjects are inclined to interpret as versions of the Blessed Virgin or senses of the guiding presence of Jesus Christ, but also others more outlandish presenting themselves as manifestations of Quetzalcoatl or Osiris, of Dionysus or Shiva.[1]

Flew seems to be arguing in this passage that there are both contradictions and diversities between religious experiences that render unjustified any reliance on purported experiences of God.

John Hick has also recorded several distinct problems deriving from the diversity of religions:

> The history of religions sets before us innumerable gods, differently named and often with different characteristics . . . What are we to say . . . about all these gods? . . . Many of them could co-exist without contradiction. On the other hand, the gods of the monotheistic faiths are thought of in each case as the one and only God, so that it is impossible for there to be more than one

[1] Antony Flew, *God and Philosophy* (London: Hutchinson, 1966), p. 126.

instantiation of this concept. It is thus not feasible to say that all the named gods, and particularly not all the most important ones, exist- at any rate not in any simple and straightforward sense.

Further, in addition to the witness of theistic religion to this multiplicity of personal deities there are as yet other major forms of thought and experience which point to non-personal ultimates . . . Surely these reported ultimates, personal and non-personal, are mutually exclusive.[2]

In this quotation Hick is raising three distinct epistemological problems with religious diversity. And these three problems are the topic of this chapter.

One problem arises from the fact that in different religions in which it is claimed that God is experienced, God is claimed to be experienced in different ways, ways incompatible with one another or at least widely varied. From this there ensues what we will call the "Argument from Multiple Theisms." A second issue arises from the purported experience in the world's religions of hordes of lesser deities. This will pose the "Argument from Multiple Deities." And a third problem arises from the purported experience in different religions of beings each claimed to be experienced as absolutely perfect (or supreme), where the properties of at least some of them are allegedly incompatible with properties attributed to God on purported experiences of Him. This we will call the "Argument from Multiple Perfect Beings."

We will be looking at each problem area in turn to see how each may be thought to create a problem for relying on apparent experiences of God, and contend that the facts of religious diversity present no obstacle to our argument.

I

We begin with the Argument from Multiple Theisms. We take up first a strong version of it which we will call the "Argument from Incompatibility." According to the Argument from Incompatibility, in different religions in which God is supposed to be experienced, He is putatively perceptually known in ways which ascribe to Him *logically incompatible* properties from one religion to another. These putative experiences cannot all possibly be true. At least some must be false. On the basis of the experiences alone, however, we have no reason to prefer one over another, con-

[2] John Hick, *An Interpretation of Religion: Human Responses to the Transcendent* (London: Macmillan, 1989), pp. 233–34.

tradictory, one. So we cannot justify accepting one experience as true rather than another. But even more, since the deliverances of putative experiences of God are so widely incompatible, we have good reason to deem *unreliable* the entire enterprise of forming judgments on the basis of alleged experiences of God. Thus, we are rationally obliged to suspend judgment concerning the truth of incompatible experiences.[3]

There are two directions in which we might look for incompatible experiences of God. The first would be in the direction of incompatible revelations from God. It might be argued that God is allegedly experienced in different religions as revealing, respectively, incompatible propositions or incompatible commands or as revealing His will in incompatible ways. One religion reports a putative revelatory experience of God in which God issues a command or reveals a truth *incompatible* with a putative revelatory experience of another religion. Hence, the argument would go, God is ascribed logically incompatible properties in different religions.

A second direction to look might be to the fact that God seems to be experienced in one religion as having a character or nature *incompatible* with the way He is experienced in other religions. For instance, it is sometimes thought, in the popular mind at least, that Christians typically experience God as "loving," Moslems, as "just," and Jews perhaps as somewhere in between. But each of these ways of experiencing God, it may be claimed, is *incompatible* with each of the others. So, different religions, respectively, ascribe incompatible properties to God in this way as well.

Given these supposed widely incompatible ascriptions to God from different religious traditions, respectively, putative experience of God should be judged an unreliable way of trying to get at the truth of things.

If this argument is correct, this line of reasoning continues, then our argument from BEE and STING fails. This is the Argument from Incompatibility.

In order for the Argument from Incompatibility to be successful it must meet two conditions. The first is that alleged incompatibilities of ascribed properties to God must be widespread enough to render reliance on alleged experiences of God an unwarranted or unreliable procedure. If the incompatible ascriptions were only few and far between, relative to the total number of sightings of God, we could just discount the former and be left with a large enough number of apparent experiences of God which

---

[3] An argument along these lines is presented and defended by Stephen Grover in "Religious Experiences: Skepticism, Gullibility, or Credulity?" in *Faith in Theory and Practice: Essays on Justifying Religious Belief*, ed. Elizabeth S. Radcliffe and Carol J. White (Chicago: Open Court, 1993), pp. 103–15.

displayed no incompatible ascriptions between them. In that case, it would be highly unreasonable to bar reliance in general on alleged experiences of God, on the grounds provided by the Argument from Incompatibility. If there were massive perceptions of a volcano at a certain location, say, and then one day we got some reports of an eruption and other reports denying that an eruption took place, it would be highly irrational on those grounds to suspend judgment about the existence of the volcano. At most we would have some reason for thinking that at that time maybe one side had not observed the same volcano as the other, or the like.

Secondly, the Argument from Incompatibility is successful only if it convinces us that two alleged experiences of God being incompatible is a good reason for thinking that they are not reliable experiences of *God*, that their incompatibility robs them of evidential value on behalf of their being experiences of *God*, everything else being equal. Not every pair of experiences allegedly of a given object and which have elements incompatible with one another need be rejected as being truly of that object. In some cases the incompatibility may be overcome by other perceptual evidence, including evidence provided by the very experiences in question, that strongly suggests that both perceptions are of a single object and that the elements that are inconsistent must then be explained by various differences in the contexts of experience. For example, from the fact that two people give contradictory perceptual reports about another person whom each of them takes to be the president of the United States it does not follow so far forth that they are not both perceiving the president of the United States or that they do not know that they are or that their perceptions are not good evidence that they are each perceiving the president of the United States. After all, they may each have perfectly sound perceptual grounds for thinking that they are perceiving the president, and the incompatibility may be due merely to "local" differences in the way they perceive the president. The discrepancy might be due to "local" differences of vantage points or perspective, different lighting, expectations of the observers, or the like. All of these differences are perfectly compatible with each observer having excellent grounds for thinking that he really is observing the very same person, the president. And even if we are inclined to think that the local discrepancies at least *count* against its being the same person who is being perceived, we can readily imagine that there is overwhelming counterevidence, including perceptual evidence, that it is the same person being perceived in both instances. So, the Argument from Incompatibility has to be able to show not only that two alleged experiences of God are incompatible, but that the incompatibilities are of such a nature that they show the experiences in question to be unreliable indicators overall on the "global" level of the presence of God.

Accordingly, our first reply to the Argument from Incompatibility is that incompatibilities arising out of alleged inconsistent revelations are not widespread enough to render reliance on alleged experiences of God an unwarranted or unreliable procedure. In the vast majority of cases of alleged experiences of God across religions the subject experiences only God's very presence, or only God's acting in some way toward her, such as consoling her, or perceives God as revealing His will as it pertains solely to the subject herself. In the first two instances, no revelation of a truth or of God's will is involved at all. And the third instance as well does not concern the revealing of some true proposition, but only of some directive personal and private to the subject. It is highly unlikely, though theoretically possible, therefore, that two such "revelations" will involve incompatibilities. The place to look for incompatible revelations is in revelations of true propositions or in directives meant to apply to all of humankind or to large groups of people. But these sorts of revelations are miniscule in number when compared to the total number of alleged experiences of God known to have occurred. So in the total number of alleged experiences of God, pairs of incompatible revelations which entail incompatible properties in God on the basis of experience alone can be expected to be very small indeed, and thus their power to render unreliable or to appreciably contribute to the unreliability of the entire "enterprise" of experiences of God is negligible. Even were we to subtract them from the total experiential evidence for God's existence, our evidential base will be more than enough to make belief in God strongly rational.[4]

Second, we wish to argue with regard to those alleged experiences of God which do seem to be incompatible revelations and which seem to disclose incompatible Divine characters, that it is much harder than the Argument from Incompatibility would have us believe to establish on that basis alone that an alleged experience of God was delusory with regard to its being an experience of *God*. It is easier than the Argument from Incompatibility would admit to ascribe the incompatibilities to local differences within a common perception of God.

We begin this second reply by attending to allegedly incompatible revelations, where throughout we reserve the term "revelation" to refer to the revealing of true propositions or of God's will for all of humankind or for

---

[4] This reply does not apply to incompatibilities in God's character as revealed in alleged experiences of Him.

large groups of people. We believe that allegedly incompatible revelations do not show the experiences in question to be unreliable indicators of the presence of God. First, let us characterize two alleged revelations, R_1 and R_2, as *incompatible* when either of the following is true (where in these definitions each proposition in itself is logically consistent and each command in itself is logically obeyable):[5]

(1) Proposition P_1 is revealed in R_1, and P_2 in R_2, and the conjunction of P_1 and P_2 entails a contradiction.

(2) Command (or God's will) C_1 is revealed in R_1 to a subject (or subjects) S_1, and C_2 in R_2 to S_2, and it is not logically possible both that S_1 obeys C_1 and that S_2 obeys C_2.[6]

or (3) Proposition P_1 is revealed in R_1 and command (or God's will) C_2 in R_2 to S_2, and S_2's obeying C_2 will imply the falsity of P_1.[7]

On the face of it, the mere fact that two alleged revelations, R_1 and R_2, are incompatible in the above sense is not yet a reason for thinking that they cannot both be experiences of God. Why can't there be in each case a correct identification of God by the subject, an identification made independently of the content of the revelation? And why should the remaining incompatibility not be ascribed to "local" differences in the conflicting perceptions? Why should the very question of whether it was God who was being experienced be raised at all? Even if we are inclined to believe that incompatible revelations at least *count* against its being God who is perceived in both instances, why should we suppose that the content of the revelations was all the evidence that the subjects who had the experiences had to interpret the experiences? There may very well be independent, overwhelming perceptual evidence in the experiences that each is, after all, of God. So the very fact that alleged revelations clash may indeed count

[5] Of course revelational incompatibility need not be a function of just two revelational episodes. An incompatibility can result from combining several revelations on one side with several on another side. We have limited ourselves to revelational pairs only for convenience.

[6] The typical case of alleged incompatibility will be when S_1 is S_2, or is included in the subjects S_2.

[7] As we have noted earlier in this work, there could be other senses of "revelation" besides one involving propositional content or commands. For example, on what George Lindbeck calls the "experiential-expressive" model of understanding the relationship between religion and experience it could turn out that most apparent experiences of God are "revelations," in the sense of being the type of experience which grounds religious doctrines and behavior as "expressive" of that experience. See George Lindbeck, *The Nature of Doctrine: Religion and Theology in a Postliberal Age* (Philadelphia: Westminster Press, 1984), chapters 1 and 2.

against their both being from God, but this would be quickly overcome by the additional perceptual evidence.

We are supposing that alleged revelations are only a small minority of apparent experiences of God. And incompatible alleged revelations are a smaller minority than that. So we have good independent reason for thinking that God is experienced, and have no reason so far forth to think that a subject involved cannot independently identify the experience as being of God. Thus we have good reason to believe that if there is an incompatibility between alleged revelations, the incompatibility should be best explained as a "local" difference between the experiences.

Plausible explanations of incompatibility can be sought from the subject end of such experiences as well as from the object end. The incompatibility may be ascribed to a misunderstanding on the part of one or another of the subjects involved, or both. The subject just may not quite have understood what God wanted. Or it can be ascribed to one or another of the two subjects, or both, when experiencing God *imagining* that God was imparting a revelation. Neither of these possibilities would give sufficient reason for thinking that either or neither of the subjects had actually perceived God. It happens frequently that one person misunderstands another, and happens sometimes that one person thinks someone is communicating with him when she is not.

But perhaps it will be protested that in the case of *God* we should not expect that a person would misunderstand what has been communicated or that he would imagine in the midst of an experience of God that God was communicating to him when He wasn't. Even so, there are plausible explanations from the object end of the alleged revelations. There are several possible explanations of how or why God could or would issue incompatible revelations. For example, considering type (1) incompatibilities, God might simply wish one addressee to believe what is incompatible with what He wants another addressee to believe. And considering type (2) incompatible revelations, God might wish to *test* an addressee by issuing a command He does not wish carried out, and which is at odds with a previous command. Or God might desire only a temporary suspension of a previous command. Maybe, even, God very much wants us to be in the dark and perplexed by the whole question of why He would give incompatible commands in the first place. Or, finally, there is nothing logically untoward in simply supposing that God gives incompatible commands for His own inscrutable reasons although we have no idea what these reasons might be.

There is doubt that we should be prepared to entertain any of these ideas in an actual case of alleged incompatible revelations unless we had good reason to do so. But as far as we can see, we do have good reason for doing so, given the independent justification we have for believing that God is experienced and given the fact that the subject of an alleged revelational experience should presumably be able to identify that it is God being experienced, independent of the revelational content. So we have every reason to ascribe the incompatibility between alleged revelations to "local" differences rather than to global delusion about God's being experienced.

Now it might be protested that at least some of our explanations of why God might give incompatible commands are not *possible* explanations, because they imply that God could issue a command He did not mean to have fulfilled. And it might be protested that there could not be any *possible* explanation of why God would reveal incompatible propositions, because that would imply that God could reveal a falsehood. But these, it might be protested, contradict a traditional belief about God's nature, a belief implied by God's absolute perfection. God is considered in the major religious traditions of the West to be absolutely trustworthy. But it cannot be the case that God is absolutely trustworthy yet reveals a falsehood, or reveals a command He does not mean to have carried out. When an absolutely trustworthy being reveals a proposition it must be true. And when an absolutely trustworthy being issues a command He must really wish it to be fulfilled. Hence, it is not possible that *God* issue a command He does not mean to have obeyed or that *God* reveal a falsehood.

Leaving aside the doctrinal position here being enunciated, it is not clear that apparent experiences of God support the conclusion that God cannot reveal a proposition that is not true and cannot issue a command He does not wish to have fulfilled. For while the experience of God's absolute perfection may be assumed to support God's absolute trustworthiness, the doctrinal position may be construing the trustworthiness too narrowly. It supposes that the trustworthiness of God must reside in trusting His *word*. But this is not necessarily so. The absolute trustworthiness of God need imply no more than that God *Himself* is to be perfectly trusted. That means that whatever God does is done for God's own, perfectly good reasons. *God* is to be trusted no matter what. But from that it does not follow that God cannot reveal a falsehood or issue a command that He does not mean to have performed. What follows is only that if God does reveal a falsehood or does issue a command that He does not mean to have fulfilled He can be perfectly trusted to be doing so for the best of reasons. So even if

God reveals incompatible revelations and we are unable to fathom why this should be so, we can perfectly trust that God has done so for His own inscrutable reasons, reasons flowing from His perfection.

God, after all, can allow innocent children to suffer horrible tortures and painful deaths for His own good, inscrutable reasons, without that compromising His perfection. And that is because He has sufficient reasons for allowing these things, reasons we can perfectly trust.[8] Similarly, God could reveal a falsehood or give a command He does not mean to have carried out, for His own good reasons, reasons we can perfectly trust.

We suggest, therefore, that God's being perfectly trustworthy need not imply that God cannot tell a falsehood or cannot issue a command He does not mean to have carried out.[9]

In fact, there are clear examples from within religious tradition of God giving a command He does not mean to have fulfilled and of God revealing a false proposition. In the Genesis story of the binding of Isaac, God commands Abraham to sacrifice his son. Subsequently God's angel stays Abraham's hand. In giving the command, God creates in Abraham the false impression that He wishes Isaac to be sacrificed. But God was only testing Abraham. God never wished for the command to be carried out.

And in Genesis 18:12, we read that Sarah laughs at the thought of her having a baby, since she is beyond child bearing age, and because, so she says, *Abraham* is old. In the next verse, God tells Abraham that Sarah had said that *she* herself was old, and mentions nothing about Abraham. A Jewish teaching claims that God changed Sarah's words and told Abraham a falsehood, telling him that Sarah had used the term "old" of herself, whereas she had actually used the term of Abraham. God does this, on this teaching, for the sake of preserving "peace in the home" between husband and wife, hiding from Abraham Sarah's having blamed him, in part, for her present inability to have a child.[10] Whether or not one accepts the exegesis,

---

[8] This position is defended in detail in Chapter 7.

[9] We may assume, though, that if God wishes to be in communicative relation with creatures, something allegedly attested to by experiences of God, He can be expected to want to generally tell the truth and generally give commands which He wishes the recipient to carry out. Otherwise, subjects will learn not to take God's communications at face value.

[10] See Genesis Rabbah, 48:18. The Hebrew term used for "falsehood" can also be translated as "fabrication." The actual wording of the Midrash refrains from explicitly ascribing the falsehood to God, instead ascribing it to the "verse." But since the verse is supposed to be a quotation of God's words to Abraham, the clear implication is that God has told a falsehood. The ascription of the falsehood to the verse rather than to God may be attributed to the reluctance to say openly that God had spoken falsely, which no doubt reflects in turn the conviction that this is not a common sort of event and that we should ordinarily trust not only God but also His word.

we have here a clear case of a religious teaching which ascribes to God the telling of a falsehood for a good reason.

That God has revealed incompatible revelations entails incompatible properties in God only when auxiliary premises are added, drawn from religious doctrines. Such auxiliary premises might include the previously mentioned doctrine that God will not reveal a falsehood, or that God intended one revelation to be eternal and unchanging, and that it was not meant solely to educate up until a time when it could be safely abrogated, or until a new revelation would be granted. Or it might include the claim that God intended one revelation to be binding without any temporary suspension at any time by any person for some higher purpose. It seems that in general the derivation of incompatible properties in God on the grounds of incompatible revelations would depend upon such doctrinal auxiliary premises. But what can be derived from doctrinal beliefs is beside the point of our concerns, since we have been addressing the evidential value of alleged experiences of God with particularistic religious doctrines set aside.

Hence we conclude that God's issuing incompatible revelations should not be expected to entail the ascription of incompatible properties to God.[11]

We do not wish to be so dogmatic, however, as to insist that no auxiliary premises that would facilitate the entailment could possibly be known to be true by experience of God. And that is because we do not wish to be dogmatic about what can and cannot be known about God from experience. We in fact hold rather liberal views on that. However, we are confident that there will be few cases of alleged incompatible revelatory experiences of theistic religions. And when these few cases are judged in light of the generality of alleged experiences of God in which no incompatibilities arise, they become evidentially inconsequential.

We conclude, therefore, that both from the subject end and from the object end of incompatible alleged revelations there are ways available for explaining the difference between the alleged revelations as local differences only, and we have not been given a good reason by the Argument from Incompatibility for thinking that the difference points to a global delusion about God being experienced.

[11] Lurking in the vicinity is an argument that because of alleged experiences of incompatible commands or incompatible revelations of the Divine will no one really knows which religion, if any, is the true one. This is an issue for the epistemology of religious belief. However, it is not related to the subject of this book since we are not engaged in an assessment of the truth claims of any religion aside from the claim that God is experienced, and thus exists.

II

We turn to the second alleged incompatibility within experiences of God: between God's nature or character as experienced in one religion as opposed to another religion.

It must be pointed out, as a first step, that differences in God's character do not at all divide along the lines of distinct religions. These differences, on the contrary, reside within religious traditions themselves. God is experienced in a variety of ways within each of Christianity, Islam, and Judaism. One need only be reminded of the priest's sermon in *Portrait of the Artist as a Young Man* to realize how the God of anger and vengeance has loomed large in the Christian experience of God. Or one could think of Rudolf Otto's characterization of religious experience as evoking dread and terror[12] or of Jonathan Edwards's sermon "Sinners in the Hands of an Angry God."[13] In the mystical tradition of Islam, Sufism, God is regularly experienced as no less loving than in the most rapturous mystical perceptions of the Catholic mystic Bernard of Clairvaux.[14] And the typical experiences of a Jewish Hasid are of a God overflowing with love for the subject of the experience.[15]

According to traditional Jewish thinking, Abraham experienced God as a God of love, while Isaac experienced God as a God of justice, while Jacob knew God as a combination of the two.[16] These variable ways of experiencing God are central to the traditional Jewish way of thinking about God and are accentuated in the daily prayers where God is addressed as "The God of Abraham, the God of Isaac, and the God of Jacob," rather than simply as "The God of Abraham, Isaac, and Jacob."

According to a valuable study by John B. Carman, religious traditions in general are characterized by the ascription of what Carman calls "polar

[12] See Rudolf Otto, *The Idea of the Holy*, trans. John W. Harvey (London: Oxford University Press, 1957).

[13] See Jonathan Edwards, *Selected Writings of Jonathan Edwards*, ed. Harold P. Simonson (New York: Ungar, 1970).

[14] See Annemarie Schimmel, *Mystical Dimensions of Islam* (Chapel Hill: University of North Carolina Press, 1975). For Bernard, see Etienne Gilson, *The Mystical Theology of St. Bernard*, trans. A. H. C. Downes (London: Sheed and Ward, 1955).

[15] See Joseph Weiss, *Studies in East European Jewish Mysticism*, ed. David Goldstein (Oxford: Oxford University Press, 1985); and Rivka Schatz Uffenheimer, *Hasidism as Mysticism* (Jerusalem: Magnes Press, 1993).

[16] An obvious exception to Abraham's experience of God as loving is when Abraham is commanded by God to sacrifice his son, Isaac. That this experience is so untypical for Abraham is central to various Jewish understandings of the testing of Abraham. In this connection see Jerome I. Gellman, *The Fear, The Trembling, and the Fire: Kierkegaard and Hasidic Masters on the Binding of Isaac* (Lanham, Md.: University Press of America, 1994).

attributes" to God.[17] And as Carman shows, the "coincidence of oppo-
sites" is not an uncommon theme in Christian theology.[18]

It is therefore a gross distortion of actual, living religions to think that
the differences in how God is experienced fall along lines dividing recognized religious traditions one from another. The truth is that perceptions of
God differ within religious traditions themselves. Even if we were to grant
that the intra-religious differences may be less extensive than the inter-
religious ones, were the present form of the Argument from Incompatibility correct, that same form of argument would tend to show there to be
a radical incoherence in how God is perceived to be within particular
religious traditions themselves. This should give us reason to doubt the
efficacy of this argument. And we shall now argue as we did with regard to
incompatible revelations, that it is far harder to verify this sort of incompatibility than the Argument from Incompatibility would lead us to think.

The idea we are presently examining is that God's being experienced to
have a loving character, for example, is at logical odds with an experience
in which God is perceived to have a just character. However, this does not
present a problem of incompatible ascriptions to God. God's having a loving character would be incompatible with God's having a just character
only if it were logically impossible for God to have both. But surely it is
logically possible for it to be the case that every act God does is a full
expression of His love and also a full expression of His justice. He so
arranges the world, let us suppose, that when he subsequently acts His love
is perfectly congruent with His justice. Characters are logically incompatible only if they require incompatible results. But God could so arrange
things that His love and His justice coincided perfectly.[19] So if one person
or group of people experienced God's character or nature as loving and
another person or group experienced God's character or nature as just,
they may both be experiencing the true nature of God, a nature both
loving and just.

Actually, less than that will do. It would be enough were God's love and

---

[17] See John B. Carman, *Majesty and Meekness: A Comparative Study of Contrast and Harmony
in the Concept of God* (Grand Rapids, Mich.: Eerdmans, 1994).

[18] See especially chapter 18 of Carman, *Majesty and Meekness*.

[19] This is not entirely correct, however, if we take into account the existence of free will.
Given that what free creatures do is up to them, it might be the case, for all we know, that
God cannot create a world in which His love was perfectly congruent with His justice. This
would happen were God obliged to create at least some free creatures who would act in ways
that God would not want to respond to with both love and justice. This problem may be
overcome by our suggestion in the next paragraph that God's having two characters of a
certain sort does not require perfect congruence between them.

justice congruent *for the most part*. That would be enough to establish God's character as both loving and just, since, after all, God can sometimes act out of character, or at least *seem* to be acting out of character when He is not.

In order to generate incompatible properties in God on the basis of different characters of God what we need is at least some alleged experiences showing that God's character is *exclusively* of one sort, with other alleged experiences showing that God's character is exclusively of another, *logically incompatible* sort. Or we need alleged experiences showing that God's character is exclusively of one sort, and that God never can seem to act out of character, with alleged experiences showing God acting out of *that* character.

Now there may actually exist such incompatible pairs of experiences of God's character, but we hope enough has been said here to have convinced the reader that they must be fewer in number compared to what might commonly be thought. And such pairs are surely a very small part of the totality of alleged experiences of God by various religions. Hence, the Argument from Incompatibility based on allegedly incompatible characters of God has no power to upset our use of BEE and STING to establish the experience of God.

We conclude that the Argument from Incompatibility, based either on alleged incompatible revelations or on alleged incompatible characters of God, fails to weaken our argument from BEE and STING that God is actually experienced, and thus exists.

III

We said at the outset that the Argument from Incompatibility was a *strong* version of an argument derived from the facts of religious diversity that might be brought against our argument. It is a "strong" argument in the sense that it argues that because of the incompatibilities, we have very good reason *not* to assign all of the various alleged experiences of God to one being. We have found this argument wanting. At this point the defender of the Argument from Incompatibility may be tempted to retreat to what we can call the "Argument from Diversity." This argument would not claim that there are incompatibilities in the way God is experienced in different religions, but that the very *diversity* in the ways that God is allegedly experienced is sufficient to undermine our argument from BEE and STING.

Each case of an alleged incompatibility which we have argued against was a case in which God was experienced differently, and at times radically so, in various alleged experiences of Him. But then, one may wish to argue, while we may have no sufficient reason to think that all of these experiences *could not* be of one being, still we do not yet have sufficient reason to assign the diverse experiences to one being. When we think of the different alleged revelations from God and of the strikingly different characters God allegedly possesses, wouldn't the better part of wisdom be to at least withhold judgment as to whether or not all of these reflect the doings or the character of just one being? In the face of the facts of religious diversity, we should refrain from asserting that it is one being, God, who is experienced across religions. Instead judgment should be suspended.

This Argument from Diversity would begin to sound credible only if it were true that God could not be identified as God across religions without recourse to the content of an alleged revelation or to the seeming character of God as allegedly revealed in an experience. But why should we think this to be true? It isn't true that the only way to identify a *person* is to rely on what she says or how her character seems to be. There are plenty of other ways to make the identification. And there is no reason to think that God could not be identified in an experience of Him in ways other than by reference to what He reveals or how His character seems to be.

As presented in Chapter 1, the ways of identifying God include recognition-identification of God by way of reference to conditions under which God might be expected to appear and not appear, by way of locations or range of locations at which God might be expected to appear and not appear, by phenomenal features similar to those reported in the past, by an overall perceptual gestalt, and by how God can be expected to nonperceptually or quasiperceptually affect one. In addition, God can identify Himself to a perceiver in what we have called "auto-identification." So there are plenty of ways for God to be identified independently of what He reveals or what character He displays.

Experiences of God within a particular religious tradition constitute a *network* in which a fund of experiential knowledge about God is built up and shared. As time goes on and God is more widely perceived, the fund of knowledge about Him and about the conditions in which He may be experienced and not experienced is enriched in various ways.

The network may be presumed to have developed to be so complex that some later identifications may be made in ways entirely different from earlier ones. The network may have overlapping identifying features or may involve mere "family resemblances" between identifying marks sufficient to warrant identification. In this way, variegated means of identifying God are established entirely upon perceptual grounds together with independently warranted background knowledge. The network can always be augmented by God's auto-identification or by a personal experience in which God appears in a way hitherto unfamiliar, the identification based upon the retroactive reflection that God could have been expected to appear in this way.

In at least some of the experiences of God in the network, God is perceived as an absolutely perfect being and in others as (but) a supremely valuable being. These types of experiences intertwine with others in which God is not so experienced but which share with the former common features, or features bearing a family resemblance to the former, or features associated with the former by God's auto-identification.

Within a single religious tradition no problem need arise over the diversity in God's character as divulged in experiences of Him. The network can provide other ways for making the identification, and God can auto-identify Himself as well across character differences.

In addition, for each of the world's religions in which God is said to be experienced, the network includes, prominently the experience of an intimation of God's plenitude or inexhaustible fullness, a fullness the presence of which is revealed without being displayed. In Christian mysticism this sometimes has been referred to as the "Divine Abyss."[20] In this type of experience, God is identified as God and is also experienced to be far more than is disclosed in the present experience, or in any experience. In fact, this inexhaustible fullness seems to be one of the ways in which recognition-identification of God is made. Given the prominence of this type of experience within each of the world's theistic religions, a person who experiences God's character as being of one sort can well appreciate how another person in her same tradition, or she herself at another time, might very well experience God in another way, out of the fullness of God's being. But all along it will be *God* who is identified as who it is who is being perceived.

All this has been said with regard to a network of experiences within a single religious tradition. But similar considerations apply to reidentifying God across experiences which span different religious traditions. Let the "network set" be the set of networks of experiences of God in different religions in which God is experienced. Each such religious network is a

---

[20] See Evelyn Underhill, *Mysticism: A Study in the Nature and Development of Man's Spiritual Consciousness* (London: Methuen, 1945), p. 339.

member of the network set. Judging from the literature, the great majority of alleged experiences of God across the network set are quite congenial to one another. (Any resistance to this idea would have to come from focusing much too narrowly upon alleged revelations from God, and from not giving sufficient weight to the more common types of experience of God.)

The experiences in one member of the network set bear resemblance to those in another member of the network set, similar to those between experiences within any given member, although not to the same extent. In the different theistic religions, God is equally experienced as either an absolutely perfect being or a supreme being. Also, the fund of identifying features of God built up in one member of the network set and linked up with such experiences overlaps with and bear various similarities to the corresponding funds of other members of the network set. And, finally, the experience of God's hidden, inexhaustible fullness is an experience common across religions.

Of course there are differences in the perception of God from one member of the network set to another. But the differences are embedded within an extensive, rich context of overlapping and similar experiences of God, as far as one can judge from what is said about such experiences in different theistic religions. The situation here no more bars the identification of God from one member of a network set to another than it does with respect to varied richly endowed ways of identifying a single human person.

In fact, in light of the experience, common to members of the network set, of God's inexhaustible fullness, there is even less reason here than elsewhere for barring identification across the varied networks. The nature of God as revealed in experiences of Him suggests and invites the possibility that God, independently identified, is known differently, in part at least, by different people.[21]

We therefore see no good reason not to, and good reason to, conclude that each member of the network set reflects a rich collection of experience of the same object as every other member of the network set. And that object is God.

All of this is said independently of particularistic doctrinal beliefs pertaining to God's true revelation or having to do with to whom God reveals Himself or to whom He would never reveal Himself, etc. When doctrinal factors are added in, the situation may be expected to change. However, as

[21] If we wished, we could elevate the claim that cohering network sets are of or about the same being into a principle of the "Ontological Unity of Cohering Happenings," or "OUCH." In our list of principles, then, OUCH would follow BEE and STING.

we have been emphasizing throughout, our inquiry is directed at the evidence from alleged experience of God across the world's religions, *sans* considerations flowing from particularistic religious doctrines.

We conclude, finally, that the Argument from Multiple Theisms, in the form of either the Argument from Incompatibility or the Argument from Diversity, poses no challenge to our argument from BEE and STING that God is truly experienced and thus exists.

IV

This brings us to the second alleged problem posed by religious diversity, the Argument from Multiple Deities. This argument begins with the recognition that the world's religions are populated with a myriad of gods. As John Hick has put it:

> A collection of names of Mesopotamian gods made by A. Deinel in 1914 contains 3,300 entries . . . In Hesiod's times there were said to be 30,000 deities . . . And if one could list all the past and present gods of India . . . and of the Near East . . . and of southern Europe . . . and of northern Europe . . . and of Africa . . . and also of the Americas, Australasia, northern Asia and the rest of the world they would probably form a list as bulky as the telephone directory of a large city.[22]

Hick asks about these gods, "What are we to say, from a religious point of view, about all these gods? Do we say that they exist?"[23]

If we focus in this section exclusively on the *lesser* gods—those not claimed to be either absolutely perfect or supreme beings in our sense— from the perspective of our inquiry mere *belief* in these gods does not pose a problem. From the perspective of our inquiry these gods pose a problem only when they are said to be the objects of human experience. On our principles BEE and STING, to the extent that a god, say Frigg, is claimed to be experienced, to that same extent it is rational to believe that Frigg exists and not rational to believe that Frigg does not exist. But if it were not claimed that Frigg was actually experienced, no problem would arise. Hence, the Argument from Multiple Deities must insist upon the alleged *experience* of the multitude of lesser deities, arguing that were all the gods (or many of them) allegedly experienced, BEE and STING would imply the strong rationality of believing in all of them no less than BEE and

[22] Hick, *An Interpretation of Religion*, pp. 233–34.
[23] Ibid., p. 234.

STING imply the strong rationality of believing in God on the basis of alleged experiences of Him.

So we can state the argument as follows:

(1) If it is strongly rational to believe in God on the basis of alleged experiences of God, then it is equally strongly rational to believe in a telephone-book size list of lesser gods on the basis of alleged experiences of them.

(2) It is obviously not strongly rational to believe in a telephone-book size list of lesser gods on the basis of alleged experiences of them.

Hence,

(3) It is not strongly rational to believe in God on the basis of alleged experiences of God.

This may plausibly be taken to be a reconstruction, in our terms, of Flew's argument cited at the start of this chapter, and to be a summary of Hick's intention in the above quotation. This is the Argument from Multiple Deities.

It is not clear how many gods in the telephone-book size list are believed to have actually have been experienced, or are believed in for other reasons. Given that one of the "functions" of the gods is to serve as aids in explanation and control of natural events, it stands to reason that many gods are believed in for explanatory reasons alone without ever having supposedly been known in experience. And if Robin Horton is to be believed, the *predominant* role of the gods in African religions, and we may assume elsewhere as well, is precisely in explanation rather than in "communion."[24] So BEE and STING can be expected to obligate us, at most, to the existence of only *some* of the gods in the list, undoubtedly, though, still many in number.

Considering now just those gods who have been claimed to have been known by experience, premise (1) is ill-formulated if intended to be justified in light of BEE and STING. For what follows from the respective applications of BEE and STING is not (1), but at most:

(1a) If it is strongly rational to believe in God, *everything else being equal*, on the basis of alleged experiences of God, then it is equally

[24] See Robin Horton, *Patterns of Thought in Africa and the West* (Cambridge: Cambridge University Press, 1993), chapter 1.

strongly rational to believe in a telephone book-size list of lesser gods, *everything else being equal*, on the basis of alleged experiences of them.

But even (1a) does not result from the respective applications of BEE and STING. For while it is true that any single alleged experience of a god is as well supported by BEE as is any single alleged experience of God, it is false that the experiences of a given god are as well supported by STING as are the experiences of God. This is because the sheer number of reports of experiences of a god such as Frigg and the extent of the varied historical and cultural conditions of these alleged experiences would never begin to compare to the comparable facts for God. Hence, it is simply false that on BEE and STING the rationality of believing in one of the gods is *equal* to the rationality of believing in God. The rationality of believing in God on BEE and STING is surely more impressive than it is for belief in any god. So (1a) is false.

The Argument from Multiple Deities might proceed to argue, though, that even if BEE and STING do not confer the *same* rationality on belief in the gods as they confer on belief in God, they nevertheless supposedly do convey *some* positive degree of rationality on the former belief, and if so there must be something seriously wrong with these principles.

But this more modest argument founders on the fact that what is concluded from either BEE and STING is concluded only "everything else being equal." If the present, more modest, argument is right in rejecting the conclusion that it is rational to believe in the gods, this is only because not everything else *is* equal. We feel ourselves to be in possession of reasons, good reasons, for doubting the existence of the gods. These considerations *overcome* the evidential value provided by BEE and STING in favor of the gods' existence. They do not challenge the validity of these principles in the first place. So there is no fault to be found here with BEE and STING at all.

Among the reasons we have for thinking that in the case of the gods not everything else is equal are the essentially fantastic nature of the gods and the bizarre character of the reports and conditions under which they are allegedly experienced. These factors clash with general confidence in the regularity of nature or the, at best, very rare suspension of that regularity. The fact is that the more bizarre and fantastic reports are and the more that the bizarre penetrates the very details of the report the more reason we have to believe that the report has no evidential basis at all or only a very slim one. And generally reports of experiences of the gods have this character. No such allegations of the bizarre need be attached to alleged experiences of God. These alleged experiences are rarely reported to have implications of a fantastic or otherwise bizarre nature, and only rarely involve claims of suspension of the regularity of nature.

As a matter of fact, neither Flew nor Hick ever explicitly states why (2) is false. Perhaps they are bothered by the sheer number of gods to be believed in. But Flew does write, as in the quotation at the start of this chapter, of some of the gods being "outlandish." So maybe Flew, and perhaps Hick as well, think it is not rational to believe in these lesser gods at least in part because of their alleged fantastic and bizarre natures. But to the extent to which this is their reason for rejecting alleged experiences of such gods, to that same extent, we are now suggesting, there is a basis for distinguishing between the experiential evidence for the existence of the gods and that for God.

Reasons for rejecting the existence of the lesser gods are defeaters of the application of BEE and STING to alleged experiences of the lesser gods, and are not reasons for rejecting BEE and STING in the first place. And the defeaters are relevant to our argument from BEE and STING only if they apply also to the case of alleged experiences of God. But then this would have to be argued directly for alleged experiences of God. Actual reasons would have to be given for thinking that in the case of God everything else was not equal. These, of course, are matters worth considering, and we are in the midst of considering them. But the Argument from Multiple Deities in itself is a nonstarter.

V

We turn now to the final argument from religious diversity against our argument from BEE and STING, the Argument from Multiple Perfect Beings.[25] There are religious traditions in which deities not identified as "God" are allegedly experienced, and allegedly experienced or known from experience to be perfect beings. Judging from how these deities are described, we may be able to say of some of them that the network of alleged experiences of them, stripped of their mythological elements, is similar enough to the network set of God-as-experienced for it to be pos-

[25] The present argument applies as well to alleged multiple experiences of supreme beings who are not necessarily perfect. For simplicity's sake we omit this complication in the argument. In addition, a somewhat similar argument could be devised in terms of "ultimates" that are not beings at all, such as *sunyata*, or emptiness, in some Buddhist teachings. And treatment of it would be accordingly somewhat similar to our treatment of the Argument from Multiple Perfect Beings. We leave the working out of the details to the reader.

sible to say that they are God under a different name.[26] But other deities are experienced to be very different from God. Specifically, some deities are experienced to be impersonal beings. An example is Brahman in some Hindu traditions. In those traditions, though not in other Hindu traditions, "Brahman" is allegedly experienced to be a being possessed of maximal possible value but who is *impersonal*, unlike God who is typically experienced to be a personal being.[27] Following Hick, we will say that a being is personal if it interacts with other beings, having what Hick calls "ethical qualities."[28] A "nonpersonal" being does not interact with other beings and lacks ethical qualities. On the Argument from Multiple Perfect Beings, the problem is not just that Brahman is allegedly experienced to be *different* from God.[29] In Hick's words, Brahman and God are "mutually exclusive." The claim is, then, that the existence of God is logically incompatible with the existence of Brahman. God is allegedly experienced to be a being who is *both* maximally valuable and personal. And Brahman is allegedly experienced to be a being who is *both* a maximally valuable being and impersonal. But there can be only one maximally valuable being, and it cannot be both a personal and an impersonal being.[30] Hence, it cannot be the case that both God and Brahman exist.

However, as far as the facts of experience are concerned, we have no good reason to say they both do not exist. But we also have no good reason for concluding that one *rather than* the other does not exist. So, we have a problem with accepting our argument from BEE and STING on behalf of God's really being perceived and hence existing. And of course the same should be said for an argument for the existence of Brahman, or for any other allegedly experienced being, if any, who is allegedly possessed of both maximal value and the attribute of being impersonal.

This is the gist of the Argument from Multiple Perfect Beings.

As a first response, it should be pointed out that if we had to compare,

[26] In this connection see R. C. Zaehner, *Hinduism*, 2d ed. (London: Oxford University Press, 1966), chapter 6.

[27] In still other strands of Hindu culture "Brahman" is thought of as a person or as not a "being" at all. For a historical presentation of the various ways in which Brahman has been understood in Hindu culture, see Troy Wilson Organ, *Hinduism: Its Historical Development* (Woodbury, N.Y.: Barron's, 1974). For an excellent conceptual clarification of "Brahman" in Hindu thinking, see the introduction to *The Brahma Sutra: The Philosophy of Spiritual Life*, ed. and trans. S. Radhakrishnan (London: Allen and Unwin, 1971).

[28] See Hick, *An Interpretation of Religion*, pp. 264 and 338.

[29] Unless otherwise noted, references to "Brahman" will be to Brahman as impersonal.

[30] We argue at the start of Chapter 1 that there could not be more than one maximally valuable being.

on BEE and STING, the phenomenon of experiencing God as personal with that of experiencing Brahman as impersonal, the former would be more supportive of God than the latter would be of impersonal Brahman. That is on account of the greater variety in conditions under which alleged experiences of God as personal take place relative to those of Brahman as impersonal. The fact is that the latter are far more localized and culture-bound than the former. In fact, within Hindu culture itself the conception of a personal ultimate being strongly dominates, and alleged experiences of an impersonal ultimate being are in the decided minority. So on STING, alleged experiences of God as personal support God's being actually experienced and personal more than do alleged experiences of impersonal Brahman support the existence of such a being. Nonetheless, we are not confident that this differential is sufficient to make it rational to believe, in light of the Argument from Multiple Perfect Beings, that God is experienced and not rational to believe that impersonal Brahman is experienced. And so we pass to a second response to the Argument from Multiple Perfect Beings.

We said that alleged experiences of Brahman create a problem for our argument from BEE and STING. But how exactly are we to conceive of the problem involved here? One way of conceiving of it would be to think that because of the "mutual exclusion" of God and Brahman, alleged experiences of God (and of Brahman) are simply too unreliable to employ alleged experiences of God as a way of establishing God's existence. We should therefore turn our backs on alleged experiences of God as a source of truth.

But this way of conceiving the problem would not be warranted by the facts. When faced with conflicting experiences we should first see whether we can explain away recalcitrant elements by reference to the conditions under which one or another of the experiences took place. If this fails or seems too hard to do, we should seek to adjudicate between the conflicting experiences as best as possible. If what were involved were only one single experience, or just a few, conflicting with another single one or with just a few, or if the matter were not momentous, the rational recourse might very well be to suspend judgment and not bother with the whole matter. But the matter here at hand is momentous. The experiencing of God is a massive phenomenon in terms of the sheer numbers of such alleged experiences across religions down through history. It is a phenomenon that occurs under widely varying social, cultural, psychological, and economic conditions. And the same can be said for the phenomenon of the alleged experiencing of Brahman (with some reservations, as expressed earlier).

When faced with two experiential phenomena of this sort, the rational way to proceed is to attempt to explain away the differences between them by reference to the conditions of perception, and if this fails, to resolve to harmonize between the recalcitrant phenomenal features of the recurring perceptions. It is not rational to abandon the field. The attempt at harmonization should be guided by the desire to accommodate as much of the appearances as is possible as indicative of reality. Any adjudication which in this regard saves more phenomenal content than another is to be preferred, everything else being equal. This approach may be a corollary of BEE and STING themselves, since these principles would require maintaining whatever content is given to experience which is *not* contradicted by other experiences.

Now there does not seem to be much chance of accounting for the differences in alleged experiences of God and of Brahman by the respective perceptual conditions, including, say, cultural factors leaning to the personal here and to the impersonal there. This is not promising, given the variety of conditions involved in each case, as well as in light of the fact that in Hindu culture experiences allegedly occur of a personal "Brahman" and of a "Brahman" who does not seem to be a "being" at all, in addition to those of an impersonal Brahman. So the burden seems to fall on harmonization between the respective experiences.

So if there is a real problem here, it must have to do with the attempt to adjudicate between the recalcitrant appearances. And indeed, the Argument from Multiple Perfect Beings, or its like, is typically dealt with by philosophers by way of offering what are regarded to be plausible adjudications. Such is the way of Swinburne and Hick, for example. We shall soon be considering what each of them has to offer. But there is an epistemological point that must be made before turning to these attempts at harmonization. It has to do with what happens if no plausible way of harmonizing the conflicting appearances suggests itself. Would the rational course be to *then* refuse to rely on alleged experiences of God? It is most important to note that this would not be the rational course. Given the massiveness of the phenomenon of alleged experiences of God, and given the rich variations of conditions under which they occur, the rational approach to having failed to come up with a plausible harmonizing of the "God appearances" with the "Brahman appearances" would be to continue to rely on the alleged experiences of God, but to do so together with a resolve to seek adjudication together with the understanding that some elements of what is given in those experiences might have to be abandoned in a successful harmonization.

Of course, we would also be bound to acknowledge the alleged experiences of Brahman and to seek adjudication of them with the alleged experiences of God. But there need be no epistemological problem involved in doing so. Since, as we have argued, "God" is a name, and supposing "Brahman" is as well, there need be no epistemological problem in supposing that the very being, God, who is perceived as personal, and the very being, Brahman, who is perceived as impersonal, are one and the same being (on the grounds that each is a maximal being), as long as one is committed to seeking an adjudication of the discrepancies. And, once again, the reason for seeking an adjudication rather than giving up the game is that there is massive perceptual evidence in favor of the existence of both God and of Brahman.

We propose, then, that supposing that alleged experiences of Brahman logically conflict with alleged experiences of God, the rational course is to believe that God is really and truly experienced, and thus exists, and to resolve to bring about and hope for the emergence of a plausible explanation or harmonization. This stance should be tempered by an awareness that some of what is included in how God appears might then have to be abandoned, though we know not what or how much. The Argument from Multiple Perfect Beings should be seen, therefore, as presenting the sort of problem which faces scientists from time to time: conflict between massive groups of observations, where each group has good, solid credentials in itself. It is best under such circumstances to try to credit as true as many observations as possible and to hope for the best.

So we conclude that the Argument from Multiple Perfect Beings can be successful at most in showing that some harmonization is required and that some of the elements of what is revealed about God might have to be given up. It does not show that relying on alleged experiences of God to infer God's existence must be grossly inappropriate.

But are there no plausible ways available to harmonize alleged experiences of God as personal with those of Brahman as impersonal? Richard Swinburne has proposed what we may call "ascent to generality" as a harmonizing mechanism when religious experiences conflict. Swinburne writes:

> The fact that sometimes . . . descriptions of the object of a religious experience are in conflict with descriptions of the object of another religious experience, only means that we have a source of challenge to a particular detailed claim, not a source of skepticism about all the claims of religious experience. Babylonian astronomers reported the movements of holes in the firmament:

Greek astronomers reported the movements of physical bodies in the heavens. The conflict between them did not mean that there were no specks in the sky of which both groups were giving further descriptions.[31]

Swinburne suggests that a claim based on a religious experience can avoid other conflicting claims by paring down the existence claim, by what we are calling "ascent to generality,"—putting it in a nondetailed way as an experience of "some supernatural being." To follow this suggestion, however, would be a drastic retreat from the richness of the content of those experiences, and should be avoided if at all possible in the name of the desire to save appearances as much as possible.

John Hick has been expounding for some time now an extensive, well thought out response to the problem of conflicting experiences of God and other deities or "ultimate" beings. He proposes what he calls the "pluralistic hypothesis."[32]

The "pluralistic hypothesis" states that:

The great world faiths embody different perceptions and conceptions of, and correspondingly different responses to, the Real from within the major variant ways of being human; . . . within each of them the transformation of human existence from self-centeredness to Reality-centeredness is taking place.[33]

The "Real," for Hick, like Kant's "thing-in-itself," is not experienced directly or in and of itself. In itself the Real is beyond all human cognition. Rather, says Hick, the Real has "masks" or "faces" which are experienced by human beings. These faces appear within the act of cognition of the Real, and differ depending upon what a particular culture or religion brings to and thus imposes upon its experience of the Real in itself. This view of Hick's is akin to Kant's theory of human cognition according to which humans impose conceptual categories upon the thing-in-itself, which latter possesses none of the properties determined by those categories. The difference between Hick and Kant is that for Kant the categories of cognition are universal for all human experience, whereas for Hick, culture-relative categories are employed in application to the Real.

The Real in itself, says Hick, is therefore neither personal nor impersonal, these categories being imposed upon the Real in the act of perception and cognition, issuing out of different cultural contexts. What the Real really is, according to Hick, is forever beyond our knowledge, save for

[31] Swinburne, *The Existence of God*, p. 266.
[32] See Hick, *An Interpretation of Religion*, especially chapter 14.
[33] Ibid., p. 240.

some purely formal and abstract characterizations. The latter includes the Real's being the most valuable possible being, but does not include any specific attributes upon which the perfection of the Real may be alleged to depend.

Religions, for Hick, are human responses to the Real, grounded in the respective cultural "masks" imposed on the Real in experience, with the task of directing human hearts toward the Real and away from selfish interests. Experiences of the "masks" or "faces" of the Real are adequate to the religious life, says Hick, since they serve adequately the purpose of educating believers to strive to be directed toward the Real rather than directed toward their own needs and desires.

We believe there is something valid and important about Hick's approach, but also believe that it has some unattractive features. The first is that on Hick's Pluralistic Hypothesis there is a degrading of the perception of God as compared to the experience of a physical world. People are normally not Kantians about their ordinary, daily commerce with the world. They do not suppose that they are not really seeing the tree and that the tree is only a "face" or "mask" of something else, of a tree-in-itself, or of a more inclusive "thing-in-itself." They take themselves to be seeing the very tree before them. This is so even though people's perceptions of the world around them are sometimes at odds with one another and require reconciliation. When inconsistencies arise they do not seek refuge in a noumenon-phenomenon distinction. Rather, they adjudicate the differences the best they can, while staying within the conviction that they are experiencing the very world around them *itself*. They seek for explanations for why inconsistent perceptions obtain. And when people in general fail to come up with a good explanation they still never seek to solve the problem by going over to the Kantian distinction. This practice reflects the common sense robust sense of reality people generally have about the world of physical objects around us.

But to propose the Pluralistic Hypothesis, as Hick does, is to separate off the perception of God into a category employed nowhere else, a category which diminishes the robust sense of the reality of God in alleged experiences of Him. We should not be so ready to assert that God Himself is only a "face" or "mask" of something else, of the unexperienced Real when we don't do the same for dissonant sense perceptions. Doing so, we submit, undervalues the force and sense of reality of experiences of God. We would do better, therefore, to seek other ways of responding to the Argument from Multiple Perfect Beings, before resorting to the drastic, singular step of making God a phenomenon of an unexperienced noumenon.

Also, Hick advances his solution as an *hypothesis*, albeit one claimed to be supported by statements theists have made about God. Offering a hypothesis or theory is a fine way of harmonizing between conflicting perceptions, but if the harmonization can be accomplished just as well by attending solely to features of the respective perceptions, that is to be preferred. We now present such an harmonization.

As we noted earlier in this chapter, in the network set of alleged experiences of God, we find that alleged experiences of God often include the perception of God's inexhaustible fullness. Let us elaborate a bit more on that subject. God's fullness is only intimated, not open for view: God revealed is God hidden. God is revealed, but also appears as a plenitude, beyond—infinitely beyond—what is disclosed in any experience of Him. God is revealed as (largely) hidden, because He is so very full. This does not mean that God can be identified *in spite* of His being hidden, but that the experience of His being hidden positively aids in the identification of God as God. Whatever God reveals of Himself, furthermore, is experienced as coming out of the very plenitude which is beyond being encompassed by the subject.

William James affirms that one of the "marks" of mystical experiences is their "ineffability," wherein, "the subject of it immediately says it defies expression, that no adequate report of its contents can be given in words."[34] And William Alston, after offering many examples of alleged experiences of God says, "One cannot but be struck, in our examples as well as elsewhere, by the constantly reiterated insistence that the experience is *indescribable*."[35] Alston then cites these two reports:

(1) "For the eyes of the soul behold a plenitude of which I cannot speak; a plenitude which is not bodily but spiritual, of which I can say nothing."

(2) "although God seems at that moment very far from the soul, He sometimes reveals His grandeur to it in the strangest way imaginable. This way is indescribable; and I do not think that anyone could believe or understand it who has not already experienced it."

Alston concludes, "Citations could be multiplied ad libitum."[36] He then goes on to argue against James as follows:

> Nevertheless, I feel that this is blown out of all proportion . . . Our subjects manage to say quite a lot about their experiences and about what they take

[34] William James, *The Varieties of Religious Experience* (New York: Mentor, 1958), pp. 292–93.
[35] William P. Alston, *Perceiving God: The Epistemology of Religious Experience* (Ithaca: Cornell University Press, 1991), p. 31.
[36] Ibid., pp. 31–32.

themselves to be experiencing . . . One can hardly take literally the claim that the experiences are *ineffable*."[37]

Alston suggests that the ineffability claim is meant to convey no more than that use must be made of metaphors and symbols to give an adequate description of an experience of God.

Alston is surely right that we cannot take the ineffability claim literally, if the latter be understood as denying that anything at all can be said about God. This interpretation of the claim would roundly contradict both formal and material descriptions of God given by persons who have had such experiences. And Alston is also correct in seeing the role of metaphor and symbolism in descriptions of mystical experiences. But we suggest a different, more direct explanation to account for the many instances of the ineffability claim in face of material descriptions of God offered by those very subjects who make the claim. We propose that in making material claims about God, subjects are responding to that aspect of their experience in which something about God is openly revealed to them, such as God's intense love, and that when they at the same time make the ineffability claim, they are responding to that aspect of their perception of God in which God is known to be an inexhaustible plenitude, a plenitude only intimated but not open to view. The overwhelming sense of God's hidden, infinite plenitude is the ground of the claim of the ineffability of the experience. That aspect of God which is openly present is the ground of the material description, despite God's ineffability in other respects. It would be most correct to say, then, that the experiences are ineffable in some respects but not in others.[38]

We are not claiming that God is always perceived as an inexhaustible plenitude. But experiences in which God's hidden, inexhaustible plenitude is revealed are a significant element in the network set of religions in which God is allegedly experienced. And if we are right about how to understand the ineffability claim, these experiences may be even more common to the network set than we may have otherwise supposed, since the ineffability of an experience may not always be reported along with the aspect of it which is effable.

Now given this feature of God as revealed in experiences of Him, it

[37] Ibid., p. 32.
[38] For more on ineffability, see William P. Alston, "Ineffability," *Philosophical Review* 65 (1956); Keith E. Yandell, "Some Varieties of Ineffability," *International Journal for Philosophy of Religion* 6 (1975): 167–79; and Alvin Plantinga, *Does God Have a Nature?* (Milwaukee: Marquette University Press, 1980).

follows that the perceptual claim that God is personal can be combined with the perceptual claim that God is not *only* personal. God is personal, but also possessed of an inexhaustible plenitude beyond whatever may be revealed in experiences in which God is seen as personal.

A particularly striking instance of the claim that God is not *only* personal, and that His personhood is but part of a larger plenitude can be found in the writings of Martin Buber. The instance is striking because Buber's fame rests largely on his influential advancement of the idea that God can only be known as a "Thou," as an eternal Thou who exists in mutual I-Thou relationships with humans.[39] Late in his celebrated work *I and Thou*, Buber writes that God:

> Whatever else he may be in addition, enters into a direct relationship to us human beings through creative, revelatory, and redemptive acts, and thus makes it possible for us to enter into a direct relationship to him . . . The concept of personhood is, of course, utterly incapable of describing the nature of God; but it is permitted and necessary to say that God is *also* a person . . . Of God's infinitely many attributes we human beings know not two, as Spinoza thought, but three: in addition to spiritlikeness—the source of what we call spirit—and naturelikeness—exemplified by what we know as nature, also thirdly the attribute of personlikeness. And only this third attribute, personlikeness, could then be said to be known directly in its quality as an attribute.[40]

God, then, is not *only* a personal being. He is also an inexhaustible being, possessed of an inexhaustible, hidden plenitude, save for that part of the plenitude with whose open, revealed presence the subject is graced. Indeed, God's personhood itself is best thought of as experienced as coming out of the hidden plenitude itself.

Given all of this, *judging from what is revealed of God in experience*, we can readily see how it could be possible for God to be experienced in ways other than and contradictory to His being a personal being. For instead, other features of God could emerge into the open out of the plentitude, just as God's personhood does. God could be experienced wholly as an impersonal being. And we can readily understand how it could be possible that the experience of God as a wholly impersonal being would be pure "bliss and joy," as are experiences of impersonal Brahman.

So, we can readily understand how God could be Brahman.

[39] Although we cite Buber for support, we do not mean to endorse his doctrine that God can be known *only* as personal. This denial of ours is our way out of the bottle.

[40] Martin Buber, *I and Thou*, ed. and trans. Walter Kaufmann (New York: Charles Scribner's, 1970), p. 181.

The idea is not that God actually possesses contradictory properties. Rather, the idea is that out of God's inexhaustible plenitude He has the innate power to appear as either personal or as impersonal. Or to put it differently, God has an "aspect" which is personal and an "aspect" which is impersonal. Out of the plenitude can emerge either of these aspects in the absence of the other.

So here we harmonize experiences of God with those of Brahman, saving appearances quite well. This retains the appearances of God as maximally valuable, personal, and a largely hidden plenitude, and retains the appearances of Brahman as maximally valuable, impersonal, and a "bliss and joy."

This manner of adjudicating the problem does not require Swinburne's ascent into generality, nor Hick's Kantian-like distinction between God-as-experienced and God-in-Himself. We might have been driven to make Hick's distinction, had God *Himself* been experienced as *only* personal and not also as possessed of an inexhaustible, hidden plentitude. For in that case we might have been driven to pass from the way God is *experienced* to the way God is "in Himself." But once we acknowledge that experiences of God includes the features we have described, we needn't be dislodged from thinking how God is *experienced* to say that when Brahman is experienced it can very well be God who is being experienced.

Unlike Hick, therefore, we are prepared to entertain the thought that God *Himself* is experienced both as a personal being and as an impersonal being.

Unlike Hick, in light of our earlier remarks about the epistemologial situation in the absence of any satisfactory adjudication, we do not feel obliged to offer our proposed harmonization as *the* correct, true one. It is sufficient for our purposes that it be a plausible possibility, thus showing that there are plausible ways of solving the problem at hand, short of abandoning the argument from BEE and STING to God. Perhaps, we will live to find other harmonizations, equally or more plausible.[41]

In the meantime, we conclude that the fact that some allegedly perfect beings such as Brahman are experienced as impersonal does not give a

---

[41] Another possible harmonization would be to claim that God is personal only by *analogy* to the way a human is personal, and that this way of God's being personal does not really contradict God's being impersonal (the latter presumably in a non-analogical way). Yet another possible harmonization would be to argue that the impression that God is personal/impersonal was false or illusory, fitting for a "lower" apprehension of God, to be discarded upon entering into the true perception of God as an impersonal/personal being. Each of these possibilities is more radical than the one we have proposed and seems to us initially less plausible than what we have offered.

reason for thinking that alleged experiences of God cannot be relied on to give the truth about God's existing. It remains strongly rational to believe that God is experienced and so exists, because given the large number and wide distribution of alleged experiences of God, and given their distinctive content, it has not been shown that we must discount the evidential value of alleged experiences of God in the face of alleged experiences of "ultimate" impersonal beings.[42]

---

[42] Steven Katz claims that an unbiased examination of reports of mystical experiences from different traditions shows how very different these experiences are, respectively, from each other. (See Steven Katz, "Language, Epistemology, and Mysticism," in Steven Katz, ed., *Mysticism and Philosophical Analysis* [New York: Oxford University Press, 1978], pp. 22–74; and Katz, "The 'Conservative' Character of Mysticism," in *Mysticism and Religious Traditions*, ed. Steven Katz [New York: Oxford University Press, 1983], pp. 3–60.) Katz documents well the disparity in theological thinking and in descriptions of experiences in different mystical traditions, and concludes that these are a good reason to suppose that it is false that one and only one being is disclosed in all of these traditions.

Katz himself relies heavily upon a "conceptualist" theory of perception, which says, roughly, that S perceives O only if S forms a concept of O, and that different concepts make for different perceptions. We reject this theory in the name of the appearance theory of perception presented in Chapter 1. (On this point see Alston, *Perceiving God*, pp. 186–87.)

The conceptualist theory of perception aside, documenting descriptive discrepancies unfortunately does not guarantee phenomenal discrepancies of any significance to us. And that is because we must distinguish grades of *abstraction* of descriptions. Some descriptions are closer to the phenomenal level than others. Suppose there is a particular man that Jones and Smith both see. Smith says she has seen "the president of the United States," while Jones says he has seen "the former senator from Massachusetts." These are widely divergent descriptions, but also highly abstract ones, and thus we can make little case for a phenomenal discrepancy on the basis of *their* discrepancy, even if Smith and Jones reject each other's descriptions as incorrect. Descriptional difference adds up to phenomenal difference only to the extent to which the descriptions are close to the phenomenal level.

But of course the same may be said for conflicting descriptions of mystical experiences. In any given case, it is an open question as to what level of abstraction is involved in the description, and hence an open question whether we have an instance of divergent phenomenal content or only of abstract description unrelated or only tenuously related to divergent phenomenal content. In fact, when the descriptions are taken from highly metaphysical, ramified systematic theologies, as are most of Katz's examples, we have good reason to think that divergences in description might *not* reflect important differences at the phenomenal level.

It is a difficult matter to decide in any given case the level of abstraction of a description employed to report a mystical experience. But there are some possible ways of finding out, at least roughly, what is what. A mystic can be queried as to whether his use of a particular description is more like saying that something is red or like saying it is beautiful or like saying it is the president of the United States or like saying it is composed of subatomic particles. In this way, by analogy, we can hope to come to some idea of the level of abstractions used in descriptions of mystical perceptions, and its closeness to description of phenomena. Of course such an enterprise cannot be undertaken for mystics long gone. But since the descrip-

And so we conclude that our argument for the strong rationality of believing that God is experienced and thus exists survives all of the objections brought against it from the facts of religious diversity.

---

tions are, as we have noted, within highly ramified, metaphysical, systematic theologies we have reason anyway to think that mystics' descriptions often do not reflect phenomenal differences to any exciting extent.

In any case, we have argued that there need be no insuperable problem with saying that an object experienced in one tradition in a way different from the way God is experienced in another is the same as God, given the way God is experienced as an inexhaustible plenitude.

For an important discussion of Katz's argument, see Donald Evans, "Can Philosophers Limit What Mystics Can Do? A Critique of Steven Katz," *Religious Studies* 25 (1989): 53–60.

Reductionism

I

The "reductionist" objection to our argument that it is strongly rational to believe that God exists consists of the claim that subjects who allegedly experience God are generally in conditions such that their being in those conditions annuls whatever value their experiences might be thought to have in favor of God's really being perceived. If this objection were correct, then even though it may be true that, everything else being equal, we are to believe that apparent experiences of God really are of God, nonetheless, everything else would *not* be equal, and there would be little or no reason to think God was ever actually experienced.

The "reductionist" claim can come in two versions, the "Truth Reductionist" or "T-Reductionist" claim, and the "Evidence Reductionist" or "E-Reductionist" claim. Both make the same "Circumstantial Claim":

> There are specific circumstances (which the reductionist has in mind), C_1, C_2, . . . C_n, such that generally, when a subject, S, allegedly experiences God, S is in one or another of C_1, C_2, . . . C_n.

They differ over the significance of this fact. *T-Reductionism* is the view that:

> S's being in one or another of C_1, C_2, . . . C_n, is a good reason for thinking that S is not experiencing God.

And *E-Reductionism* is the view that:

> S's being in one or another of C_1, C_2, . . . C_n, is a good reason for
> thinking that S's alleged experience of God is not adequate evidence
> that S is experiencing God.

Reductionism, then, consists of two parts, the Circumstantial Claim and
the "reductionist" assertion, the former focusing on truth, and the latter,
evidence.

The specific circumstances which the reductionists have in mind in the
Circumstantial Claim can be divided between pathological and nonpathological circumstances or conditions of the experiencing subject. We will
divide the Circumstantial Claim, and thus the respective reductionist arguments, into two, one being the claim that alleged experiencers of God are
generally in some pathological condition or other (the "Pathological
Claim"), and the other that they are generally in some relevant nonpathological condition or other ("the NonPathological Claim"). There is, of
course, a third possibility, and that is the claim that alleged experiencers of
God are either in some pathological condition *or* in a relevant nonpathological condition. In light of our discussion of the first two, however, it
will not be necessary to deal with this third claim.

We will begin with the reductionist arguments from the Pathological
Claim.

An instance of what we may call the "T-reductionist argument from the
Pathological Claim" has been recorded by C. D. Broad. "It is said that such
experience always originates from and remains mixed with other factors,
e.g., sexual emotions which are such that experiences rising from them are
very likely to be delusive . . . They seem much more likely to produce false
beliefs and misplaced emotions."[1] According to this point of view, which
Broad himself does not accept, alleged experiences of God "always" have
some pathological explanation or other, making it likely that they are not
really experiences of God after all. Caroline Franks Davis has portrayed
what we may call the "E-reductionist argument from the Pathological
Claim" as arguing that an appreciable number of alleged experiences of
God take place with subjects in pathological conditions, and that:

> The operation of [pathological] factors has been shown in non-religious cases
> to increase the likelihood of unveridical perceptual experiences; and in con-

[1] C. D. Broad, *Religion, Philosophy, and Psychical Research* (London: Routledge and Kegan
Paul, 1953).

junction with certain sets, these factors can make it highly probable that the subject will have certain perceptual experiences, whether or not the apparent percept is actually present . . . Experiences produced by such factors cannot provide good evidence on their own for the alleged percept.[2]

The E-reductionist argument from the Pathological Claim was once advanced by Bertrand Russell who wished to reject the evidential value of alleged experiences of God in general on the grounds that: "From a scientific point of view, we can make no distinction between the man who eats little and sees heaven and the man who drinks much and sees snakes. Each is in an abnormal physical condition, and therefore has abnormal perceptions."[3]

Davis lists the following pathological circumstances that have been most suggested as being included in the purview of the Pathological Claim:[4]

1. Hypersuggestibility—akin to hypnotic suggestion, either self-induced or induced by external factors such as brainwashing or an emotional environment
2. Severe deprivation—physical, economic or social
3. Severe sexual frustration
4. Intense fear of death—creating defence mechanisms
5. Infantile regression—as a solution to unconscious conflicts
6. Pronounced maladjustment—insecurity, stress, and anxiety
7. Mental illness—or related states.

This list will serve as the basis for our discussion of the Circumstantial Claim with regard to pathological states of the experiencing subject.

While no one would deny that some persons who have putative perceptions of God are in one or another pathological state, the "Pathological Claim" is not interested in claiming only that. It claims that *typically* or *generally* persons who seem to be experiencing God are in some pathological state or other. This is a very broad claim, meant to apply not only to contemporary supposed experiences of God but to the generality of such putative experiences across cultures and religions down through history.

Now the Pathological Claim could be endorsed from one of two possible approaches. It could be maintained that it is an empirical generalization

[2] Caroline Franks Davis, *The Evidential Force of Religious Experience* (Oxford: Clarendon Press, 1989), p. 193.

[3] Bertrand Russell, *Religion and Science* (London: Oxford University Press, 1935), p. 188.

[4] Davis, *Religious Experience*, chapter 8. This work came to our attention during the writing of this book and proved very helpful in the writing of this chapter.

from observations of subjects of alleged perceptions of God. Or it could be maintained as part of an a priori position, a world-outlook, on which it is believed that subjects having alleged experiences of God simply *must* be in pathological circumstances. And they must be in pathological circumstances because that would be the only way to explain the experiential data, since the idea that God is really experienced is ruled out from the start.

When the Pathological Claim is presented as an empirical generalization it is beset with grave difficulties. We will not go into detail on the subject here, since Caroline Franks Davis has done so with impressive thoroughness. We will make do with a summary of three general findings which, according to Davis upset the Pathological Claim when made as an empirical generalization:

(1) There are problems with the scientific reliability of several studies that have been conducted on the pathological circumstances that could possibly explain experiences of God.

(2) Many studies that might be thought at first glance to be relevant to the Pathological Claim are not necessarily so. They are studies of populations identified and graded as to their *religiosity*. Such studies cannot be assumed to have valid implications for the population of subjects who have had putative experiences of God. Religious subjects who have apparent experiences of God are only a proper subpopulation of those marked as religious by such studies, and may display different characteristics from the religious population at large. And subjects who are not religious by the criteria of these studies are also known to have had apparent experiences of God.

(3) In any case, scientific studies do not confirm the Pathological Claim. At most they show that being in some pathological circumstance or other is a factor for *some* persons having putative experiences of God. The impression that matters are otherwise is influenced, no doubt, by studies concentrating on conversion experiences and on other dramatic cases in very specific kinds of public settings. In these cases we may be right to suspect pathological conditions more than in other situations. But the phenomenon of apparent experiences of God is vastly more widespread than are instances of dramatic conversions at public meetings. Taken together the investigations that have been conducted don't even begin to show that *typically* or *generally* persons who have had putative experiences of God throughout history and across religions have been in pathological circumstances of one kind or another. That inference, if it is an inference, is a sheer jump to an unfounded conclusion.

The fact is that nobody really knows or even has a good reason, based

on observational evidence, for thinking that typically subjects having putative experiences of God are in some pathological circumstance. Hence no
form of reductionism, neither T-reductionism nor E-reductionism, is supported if the Pathological Claim is intended to be an empirical generalization.

Most often, we believe, the Pathological Claim is part of what we may
call a "skeptical claim." That is, one hears it said that "maybe" or "for all
we know" subjects having apparent experiences of God are in some pathological state. And it is then asserted that *for that reason* the apparent experiences should not count in favor of God's really being experienced. We call
this a "skeptical claim" for it would have it that what *might be the case for all
we know* should count against what *is* the case. What might be the case for
all we know is that most or many subjects who have apparent experiences
of God are in one or another pathological circumstance. What *is* the case,
on the other hand, is that across religions and through the course of history
subjects *have* apparent experiences of God. These latter count for authentic
experiences of God, on principles BEE and STING. We should not allow
what *might* be the case for all we know (e.g., for all you know you are
dreaming, you are being fooled by an evil demon, etc.) to count against
what *is* the case (e.g., it seems to you that a table is in front of you, and
therefore everything else being equal you should believe there is a table in
front of you). To invoke "what might be the case for all we know" is a
turn to skepticism.

In addition, the claim that for all we know subjects having putative
experiences of God are in some pathological state or other has some initial
implausibility. After all, judging by the literature, through hundreds of years
of history and across various theistic religions there is an impressive variety
in the persons who have had apparent experiences of God. They do not on
the surface line up as a group bearing similarities to pathological subjects.

So what we have is really nothing more than a *suspicion* that typically
subjects who have alleged experiences of God are in one or another pathological condition. But on what is this suspicion grounded?

The suspicion that the Pathological Claim is true might be based, first of
all, on reasons for thinking that God does not exist. The question of how
the argument from alleged experiences of God fares against alleged counterevidence to God's existence is one taken up in the last two chapters of
this work. In the meantime in this chapter we wish to determine whether
alleged experiences of God establish God's existence, *everything else being
equal*, save for reductionist considerations. So we put aside the issue of
counterevidence to God's existence for the present.

Perhaps the suspicion that the Pathological Claim is true might grow out of the fact that an experience of God is typically not a shared experience, but one an individual has when others, even in his close proximity, do not have it. This might suggest to some that a person who reports such an experience must be hallucinating or be given to hypersuggestibility or to some other pathological condition which would explain why he seems to perceive what others do not. We dealt with this sort of suspicion in Chapter 3 and concluded that this sort of consideration does not have the power to detract from the strong rationality of believing that God really is experienced.

The suspicion might also stem from a tendency to believe in an a priori manner, as it were, that God just couldn't really be experienced, and so that something *has* to be wrong with the suggestion that He is.

The a priori suspicion of putative perceptions of God brings us to the second way in which the Pathological Claim might come to be endorsed. As opposed to being an empirical generalization, the Pathological Claim may be held as part of a world-outlook which denies as a matter of principle that God could be experienced. If the Pathological Claim is so held, pathological circumstances will be invoked as what *must* be the plausible explanation of why some people think they are experiencing God when they aren't. The idea that God is really and truly experienced is ruled out in this world-view from the start. This position, then, is not jumping to conclusions, but seeking for plausible explanations, given the initial outlook.

The a priori position does not wish to take account of the *evidence* in favor of God's being experienced, but instead makes its belief that God is not experienced the measure of what might be true or not. We are prepared to acknowledge that there are persons for whom the impossibility of there being an experience of God is such a basic belief that nothing we say could influence their thinking. We are also prepared to acknowledge that this position could be a (weakly) rational one.[5] From the start our argu-

---

[5] We have argued in Jerome I. Gellman, "Religious Diversity and the Epistemic Justification of Religious Belief," *Faith and Philosophy* 10 (1993): 345–64, that belief in God may properly be what we called there a "rock-bottom" belief which, among other characteristics, is held without evidence. Similarly, belief in God's nonexistence may be such a belief. A "rock-bottom" belief is not held *because* it is rational, but rather, it helps determine what other beliefs shall be deemed acceptable. It might be that the logic of rock-bottom beliefs justifies their endurance against counterevidence. For that reason we do not rule out the rationality of a dogmatic rejection of experience of God.

We remind the reader that an admission that rejecting the evidence in favor of experience of God need not be irrational does not entail that belief in God based on that evidence is not

ment does not pretend to show that a person can be rational only if she accepts our conclusion. In our Introduction we acknowledged that a person might be rationally justified in rejecting our argument in the name either of severely particularistic religious doctrines or nonreligious doctrines which exclude the possibility of God's being known by experience. Both types of doctrines are "bracketed" or set aside in our deliberations. At the same time we invite persons of the a priori persuasion to consider the evidence and maybe change their minds.

The known facts about subjects having putative experiences of God are that sometimes such persons are in one or another pathological state. Even were we to discount all of these cases, however, this would presumably make but a small dent in the total evidence we have for there being genuine experiences of God, and thus for God's existence. Hence, as an objection to our argument from BEE and STING, reductionism is not successful.

II

In this section and the next we want to take a close look at T-Reductionism and E-Reductionism, respectively, as applied solely to those alleged experiences of God acknowledged to take place in pathological conditions, that is to reductionism without the Pathological Claim that *typically* putative perceivers of God are in pathological circumstances. We will argue that T-reductionism is wholly unsuccessful with regard to actual pathological cases, but that E-reductionist considerations do weaken somewhat the evidential value of actual pathological cases. The conclusion we will argue for is that: (1) There is no reason to believe that in the pathological cases the subject is not experiencing God, and (2) There is reason to think that the evidential value of the pathological cases is *weak*, but that they have some evidential value, nonetheless.

The T-Reductionist claim regarding actual pathological cases of apparent experiences of God is that in these cases we have good reason to believe the subjects are *not* experiencing God. This is stronger than the charge that their putative experiences are not evidence that they are experiencing God. What grounds might a T-reductionist have for this stronger claim?[6]

---

strongly rational. For a belief *that p* to be strongly rational it is sufficient that there be *an* application of the principles of rationality on which it is rational to believe *that p* and not rational to believe that *not-p*. We continue to claim strong rationality for the belief that God exists.

[6] Throughout our remaining discussion we focus solely on the evidential brands of reductionism.

Focusing on the example of hypersuggestibility for an illustration of pathological circumstances, the T-Reductionist might wish to argue as follows:

(1) More often than not, when it is suggested to a hypersuggestible subject that he will perceive a (real) state of affairs, A, and the subject then seems to perceive A, A does not in fact obtain.

So,

(2) When it is suggested to a hypersuggestible person that he will be experiencing God, and then he apparently does experience God, then too it is likely that he is not really experiencing God.

This argument suffers from a fatal flaw: its premise is false. Surely, often in the course of their daily lives hypersuggestible people are told they will be perceiving certain objects or states of affairs and then they really do. The receptionist says, "Wait here and the doctor will be with you shortly," and she is. Or the wife says, "The phone is ringing," and the husband then hears the ring for the first time, and picks up the receiver to receive a call. The child is told she will find her lunch on the kitchen counter, and she does. And so on. The number of events in the daily lives of hypersuggestible persons when people suggest to them what they will experience must be very large indeed. And just as surely the vast majority of cases are such that what was suggested really does take place. Ordinarily the doctor comes, the phone is ringing, and the lunch is on the kitchen counter. So (1) is false, and we have been given no grounds for thinking that God is *not* experienced by persons in pathological circumstances.

Furthermore, in the case of hypersuggestibility, we should be very cautious about making an analogy between what hypersuggestibles can generally be brought to falsely think they experience and alleged experiences of God. The sorts of false judgments a person known to be generally hypersuggestible is prone to make might differ from the kind of false judgment that would be ascribed to hypersuggestibility on the part of a person who thought he had experienced God. General hypersuggestibility may not carry over to alleged experiences of God. To bring out the problem with this let us examine a study by Basil Douglas-Smith, in which subjects were tested for their general hypersuggestibility to see to what extent they may be hypersuggestible in connection with alleged experiences of God. In this study subjects were deemed to be hypersuggestible if they passed the "glow-card" test.[7] Subjects were given a card with a spot of ink on it, and told to report how long it took them before they began to see the spot glow in the dark. Subjects were apparently under the impression they were being tested for their ability to see in the dark. Subjects who thought they saw the spot glow were classified as hypersuggestible, for the simple reason that the spot could not glow in the dark at all. The hypersuggestible subjects, as opposed to others, thought they saw a glow because it had been suggested to them that the spot would glow. But it didn't, and couldn't. Subjects picked out in this way as hypersuggestible were then studied for whether they had seeming experiences of God to a degree significantly higher than others (which, by the way, they did not, in this particular study).

This sort of methodology implicitly suggests that we might very well have expected a correlation between being the sort of person who could think they see a spot glow when it doesn't and being the sort of person who might think they are perceiving God, when they aren't. But the analogy is implausible, as is in general the analogy between the sort of false experiences we can attribute to hypersuggestibles and alleged experiences of God. This is because in general the range of experiences a hypersuggestible person can be induced to think he has is rather narrow. It is implausible, for example, to think that *in general* a hypersuggestible person could be induced by suggestion into thinking he was viewing a skyscraper or an elephant when he wasn't. Studies dealing with hypersuggestibility, being aware of the general limits of hypersuggestive hallucination, select testing procedures precisely from states of affairs there is reason beforehand to think a hypersuggestible person could be induced to falsely perceive. The glow of a spot in the dark is the kind of percept we can imagine a hypersuggestible person thinking he has when he doesn't. On the other hand, studies asking hypersuggestible persons to report the instant they saw the table in front of them burst into flames could be expected to fall flat in determining an appreciable sample of hypersuggestibles.

In order to make an analogy to apparent perceptions of God, perceptions of God would have to be more like seeing a glow in the dark than like having a view of a skyscraper or an elephant or seeing a table burst into flames. But judging by what nonpathological subjects say about what we take to be genuine cases of experiences of God, experiences of God are more akin to seeing an elephant or a skyscraper than to seeing the glow of a spot in the dark. For one, from what can be distilled from reports, perceiving God is more akin to the perception of a gross physical object than to seeing a glow in the dark. To see a spot glow in the dark is not to perceive an entire object that might or might not be there, but a property of an object known to exist, a spot. And to perceive a glow is to detect a quite unstable and subtle property of the spot at that. To hallucinate a glowing spot, therefore, is one thing. To hallucinate God, in the vivid and convincing way often reported, another.

We have reason to think that *in general* a person susceptible to suggestions like the one that a spot would glow need not be susceptible as well to suggestions, direct or subtle, about having a perception of God. And in general in order for there to be a plausible basis for thinking a person could be brought to have an alleged experience of God via suggestion the person would have to be particularly highly vulnerable to suggestion, and to hallucinatory experiences of a rather narrow kind.

True enough, hypersuggestible people may be prone to mistaking one thing for another. Under the influence of a suggestive environment such a person may falsely take a dangling rope to be the tail of an elephant, for example, and in *that* way think he is seeing an elephant when he really isn't. So seeing an elephant when there isn't one need not be an entirely hallucinatory experience. But in order to create an analogy between such cases of misidentification and putative experiences of God we would have to be able to identify something that is not God which is appearing to a hypersuggestible subject, which we wish to say the person is misidentifying as God. Generally speaking, it is hard to see what that might be. In any case, we would also have to have independent reason for believing that the subject was not also experiencing God in order to know that he had mistaken something else for God.

Our excursion into the study by Douglas-Smith is meant to illustrate the point that we have reason to question whether a person infected by general hypersuggestibility would be pathologically prone to mistake what is not really an experience of God for an experience of God. And so we have reason to question whether hypersuggestibility is a reason for thinking that no real experience of God has taken place.

What has been said so far applies to the pathological category of hypersuggestibility, and we have found reasons to reject or question the T-Reductionist claim against alleged experiences of God when applied solely to subjects in this category. But perhaps a defense of T-reductionism could be formulated for the other pathological categories—severe physical, economic or social deprivation, severe sexual frustration, intense fear of death, infantile regression, severe insecurity, stress, or anxiety, and mental illness—which would apply to them and not to hypersuggestibility. The T-reductionist might point out that in all of these cases (although not in the case of hypersuggestibility) we have good reason to believe that a pathological person knows, at some level or other, that her suffering would be relieved if she could believe that God had appeared to her. And this "knowledge" is because of the comfort and support she could be expected to receive from such a belief. And we know also that pathological persons generally suffer severe mental anguish. Perhaps from these considerations the T-reductionist would want to argue that therefore a pathological person is especially prone to believe that God is appearing to her. Now suppose this is so. How would it follow from this that a pathological person who had claimed to perceive God had actually not perceived God but had only *seemed* to? The argument would presumably go along the following lines:

(1) When the belief of a person, S, that O was present serves a strong psychological need for S, then when it seems to S that O is present, more often than not O is not appearing to S.

(2) The belief of a pathological person (with the exception of the hypersuggestible) that God was appearing to them serves a strong psychological need for them.

So,

(2) When it seems to a pathological person (with the exception of the hypersuggestible) that God is appearing to them, more often than not God is not appearing to them.

Once again, the premise of the T-reductionist argument is wholly unsubstantiated, or just plain false. Surely very often when a person having a strong psychological need to believe in the presence of something forms the perceptual belief that it is present, it really is present. There are many persons possessing strong psychological needs for friends, a favorite chair, food, care takers, familiar surroundings, and the like. But surely in many such cases, often when it seems to the person in question that these things are present to him they really are present to him. And this may be true of most such cases. The T-reductionist has no grounds for thinking premise (1) to be true. So this T-reductionist way of arguing relies on a premise that is without support.

The T-reductionist might want to claim that in pathological conditions subjects don't have false *perceptions* of God but are only pretending, to themselves, to be having an experience of God whereas in reality they are not. They are not experiencing any phenomenal "God-content" at all. They are thus not hallucinating, but fabricating. That pathologicals are fabricating is an interesting claim, and might even be true. But even if it were true it would not follow that they were *not* perceiving God. At most it would follow that they were not aware that they were really perceiving God. In any case there would have to be evidence for the claim that pathologicals are fabricating before we could accept this argument.

We therefore conclude that in the various forms of it that we have considered, we have been given no reason to think that a person who is in a pathological condition and who seems to perceive God is not really perceiving God.

<h2 style="text-align:center">III</h2>

The E-Reductionist claim regarding actual pathological cases of apparent experiences of God is that in these cases we have reason to believe that the subject's seeming to experience God is not adequate evidence that God is being experienced. This is weaker than the T-reductionist charge that there is good reason to believe that God is not being experienced. We now turn to this claim.[8]

The E-reductionist argues that in pathological cases a subject's alleged experience of God is not adequate evidence that she is experiencing God because we have reason to believe that *even if she weren't experiencing God, it would have seemed to her that she was experiencing God.* But if we have reason to believe this, then its seeming to her that she is experiencing God does not count as adequate evidence that God was indeed experienced by her. The principle appealed to in this argument is apparently something like the following:

> If we have reason to think that even if S were not experiencing O it would have *seemed* to her that she was experiencing O, then, everything else being equal, that it seems to S she is experiencing O is not adequate evidence that she is experiencing O.

[8] The E-reductionist approach is relevant to the objection of William Rowe to principle BEE, discussed in Chapter 4. Rowe, recall, believes that unless we knew how to go about finding whether an alleged experience of God was delusory we would simply have to take the subject's word that God was really appearing to him, whenever it just seemed to him that was so. However, as pointed out in the earlier chapter, since E-reductionist considerations are relevant to the subject's alleged experience of God, we do not have to take the subject's word for it even were we to have no idea how to check if the alleged experience were delusory. And that is because we could discount the evidential value of the alleged experience of God whether or not God were in fact appearing to the subject.

Call this the "E-reductionist principle," or "ERP." An example of the application of ERP would be our being able to predict in advance that it will seem to a person that he sees a tree in the yard, because we know that a hologram of a tree was being projected there, and the person was going out to the yard. In that case, even if we supposed that he wouldn't be seeing an actual tree in the yard, we could predict he would be going to *seem* to see a tree. On ERP, therefore, the fact that it then seemed to the person that he saw a tree in the yard would not by itself, *everything else being equal*, be adequate evidence that he had seen a tree.[9]

ERP cannot help the E-reductionist negate the evidential value of pathological cases, however. It is simply false that *generally* we can predict in advance that a person who is in a pathological condition will be going to seem to experience God. After all, many pathological persons do not ever think they are experiencing God. Plenty of people under extreme stress, most mentally ill persons, and so on, never have such experiences. The distribution of such experiences among them seems no higher than in the general population.

We have already noted that in general the range of experiences a hyper-suggestible person can be induced to think he is having is very narrow. And this range does not plausibly suggest that we could predict in advance that he will have apparent experiences of God. What we said about hyper-suggestibility applies in general to other pathological cases as well. So ERP is applicable, if at all, to only a relatively small sector of the pathological cases. It leaves the evidential value of other pathological cases unaffected.

But suppose the world were different. Suppose we could predict in general that pathological people *will* be having experiences in which it seemed to them that God was appearing. Would that be reason to believe that its seeming to them that they were experiencing God was not adequate evidence that they were experiencing God? In order for ERP to apply, it would not be enough that we able to predict this. We would have to possess a reason for thinking that we could predict this even when we supposed that they will not actually be perceiving God. What would such a reason be like? To have such a reason it would not be enough to have reason to believe that being pathological was simply a sign or indication that a person will be seeming to experience God. That something is a sign or indication that an experience seemingly of O will take place is hardly a reason for thinking that O will not be experienced. We would have to

[9] Everything need not be equal, of course. If we added to the story that there were a hundred actual trees in the yard, then that a person seemed to see a tree would be good evidence that he had.

possess a reason for thinking that a person's being pathological will *cause* him to seem to experience God. But even that is not enough, for our reason would have to lead us to believe that a person's being pathological will cause him to *seem* to experience God, without that also being a reason for believing that a person's being pathological will cause him to *actually* experience God. We have this sort of reason in the tree-hologram case. That a tree-hologram is being projected in the yard is a reason for believing a person in the yard will seem to see a tree, without also being a reason for believing they will actually be seeing a tree.

Hence, even if all pathologicals could be predicted to be going to *seem* to experience God, ERP would apply only if we had reason to believe that a person's being pathological will cause him to *seem* to experience God, without that also being a reason for believing that a person's being pathological will cause him to *actually* experience God.

And so our question becomes, what reason have we to think that ERP applies? Any reason for thinking that it does will have to contend with the fact that there are reasons for believing, everything else being equal, that a person's being pathological may very well cause them to *actually* experience God, and not only to seem to do so. In a related context C. D. Broad once wrote, "The fact that those persons who claim to have this peculiar kind of cognition generally exhibit certain mental and physical abnormalities is rather what might be anticipated if their claims were true. One *might need to be* slightly 'cracked' in order to have some peep-holes into the supersensible world."[10] As it stands, Broad's statement is factually false. Persons who claim to experience God cannot generally be presumed to be pathological. And given the variety and number of nonpathological instances of presumed experiences of God, it cannot be said that in order to experience God one "might need to be" pathological. Nonetheless, there may be something correct in Broad's observation, and that is that pathological people might very well have a heightened sensitivity to God's presence compared to the general population, precisely because of their being pathological. A mentally ill person might very well be more open to or more accepting of God's presence than others, because of his need and because of his disengagement from mundane life. And a severely sexually frustrated person might very well be more receptive to the intimate nature of God's disclosure of Himself than are others who find intimacy in other ways more easily than she does. And so on. The needs of the pathological might

[10] C. D. Broad, "Arguments for the Existence of God: II," *Journal of Theological Studies* 40 (1939): 164.

very well make him more likely to find God and to acknowledge Him when He really appears, just as a hungry person is more likely to seek out and take note of food about than is a person who recently ate a gourmet meal.

Furthermore, if we were able to predict that in general a pathological person would be seeming to experience God, this might be because God was having mercy on such people in their suffering and therefore was revealing Himself to them. In actual fact we cannot predict in general that pathological people will be seeming to perceive God. But what we are now considering is what we would have reason to say were we to be able to predict this. And it seems to us that in such circumstances we would have some reason to think that God might very well be appearing in His mercy to such persons.

So we have two reasons to believe that if being pathological will *cause* someone to *seem* to perceive God, it might very well also cause them to *actually* perceive God. We might be reluctant to take these suggestions seriously were all alleged experiences of God had by pathological persons, and had by no one else. But since we have reason to believe, on the "non-pathological evidence" alone, that God is actually experienced, we have reason to believe that being pathological might very well cause someone to also perceive God.

From all of this we conclude that even were we able to predict that it would seem to all pathologicals that they were experiencing God, *from this alone* the argument from ERP would not be as strong as the E-reductionist would like, since the E-reductionist would have to deal with the fact that if being pathological causes one to *seem* to perceive God it might very well also cause one to perceive God.

In any case, since it cannot generally be predicted that it will seem to a pathological person that God is appearing to them, in fact, ERP does not apply.

IV

Let us now consider a second principle that an E-reductionist might wish to invoke against alleged experiences of God. Suppose we have reason to believe that S is especially liable to take an experience to be an experience of O even when the experience is not really adequate evidence for that belief. Hence, whether or not we could predict in advance that it will be seeming to S that she is experiencing O, were it in fact to *seem* to S that she was experiencing O, we would have reason to suspect that there was not adequate evidence for believing that S was experiencing O. The principle involved here may be stated as follows:

> If we have reason to believe that S is especially prone to taking what does not perceptually justify the belief that she is experiencing O as an experience of O, then *everything else being equal*, were it to *seem* to S that she was experiencing O that would not be adequate evidence that she was experiencing O.

Let's call this the "justification E-reductionist principle," or "JERP." An example would be where we had reason to think that a child was strongly prone to identify various objects as her teddy bear even when there was no adequate perceptual justification for doing so. On JERP, that it then *seems* to her that she sees her teddy bear, everything else being equal, is not adequate evidence that she does see it.[11] This is true even if we could not predict in advance that it was going to seem to the child that she was seeing her teddy bear, because, say, we could not predict in advance that there would be present any objects that the child would possibly misidentify as her teddy bear.

On JERP it could be argued that in those pathological cases where a person does have an experience which seems to him to be an experience of God we have reason to be suspicious, because we have reason to believe that he is especially susceptible to taking what does not perceptually justify believing he is experiencing God as an experience of God. This could be true even when we could not predict in advance that it was going to seem to him that he was experiencing God. And that could be because we may know in principle that people like this are especially liable to take that which does not justify their thinking that they experience God as an experience of God, without our knowing exactly what sorts of perceptual content would cause them to think unjustifiably that they were experiencing God. In that case we might not be able to predict in advance that it would be seeming to them that they were experiencing God, because we could not predict when they would be experiencing the sorts of things that would cause them unjustified impressions that they were experiencing God. Nonetheless, when it does seem to them that they are experiencing God we have good reason to suspect that there is not adequate evidence that they are actually perceiving God.

The E-reductionist argument is, then, that in pathological cases people

[11] There could be additional evidence to convince us she had, for example, if we too saw the teddy bear where she seemed to see it.

are especially likely or liable to take all sorts of experiences as perceptions of God in a perceptually unwarranted way. And that is because of either their severe psychological needs, which can be expected to be alleviated by these peoples' belief that God has appeared to them, *or* because of their hypersuggestibility. For example, if a person under great stress announces that she has had an experience of God, we should be suspicious, since her being under great stress could very well lead her to take some phenomenal content which did not warrant that belief as indicating the appearance of God. We should no more consider her report as adequate evidence, everything else being equal, that she did experience God than we should accept the report of the child given to identifying all sorts of objects as her teddy bear without adequate perceptual evidence. And JERP says that in both instances the report is not adequate evidence of its truth. To be sure there is a difference between the two cases, since we know actual instances where the child has taken something for her teddy bear which others can verify is not a teddy bear, whereas we do not know of actual analogous cases with pathological persons. Nonetheless, for different reasons, we have grounds for suspecting pathological persons.

In most cases, the bare fact that a person could mistake an experience which did not warrant believing she was experiencing God for an actual experience of God would not yet be a reason for discounting her apparent perception of God. The point here is, though, that in the pathological cases a person is especially susceptible to making such misidentifications of her experiences.

It does seems true in general that when pathological people do form the belief on perceptual grounds that God was present to them they are especially liable to have done so on inadequate perceptual grounds. Hence, although we cannot predict in advance that a person suffering from hypersuggestibility, physical, economic or social deprivation, severe maladjustment, mental illness, or the like, would or probably would have been going to have an experience which seemed to him to be of God, nonetheless when a person of that sort does report having experienced God we would do well to suspect his being susceptible to the unfounded taking of perceptual content to be indicative of God. If so, we have reason to conclude that everything else being equal the fact that he seems to experience God is not adequate evidence that he does.

The question that remains is to what extent everything else *is* equal. In our previous discussion of ERP we noted two reasons for thinking that a pathological person would experience God. Those reasons were that she might very well be more sensitive and receptive to God's presence than others and that God might very well appear to her in an act of kindness. However, the plausibility of each reason depended there on our temporarily pretending that pathological persons did regularly seem to experience God. In our present discussion, however, we are acknowledging that this is not so, and both reasons accordingly lose much of their plausibility. There still might be *some* reason to believe that a person who has reported that it seems to her that she is experiencing God might have detected God more readily than others do, or have been given a glimpse of God as a gift from God. But there is less of a reason for thinking this than there was in our previous discussion, and not enough of a reason for thinking that not everything else *is* equal and that there are equal counterconsiderations to the argument from JERP.

A different consideration, though, does somewhat blunt the argument from JERP, and that is that we have independent reason for believing that God really does appear to (some) people, namely to those, at least, who are not in pathological circumstances and seem to experience God. Had instances of apparent experiences of God been the lot solely or mainly of subjects in pathological circumstances, then the present E-reductionist reasoning would have been stronger than it now in fact is. And that is because we would then have had little *independent* reason for thinking that God ever was experienced. In that case, that a particular subject in pathological circumstances was seeming to perceive God would count for less than it now does. But in fact, as already noted, it is not plausible to think that subjects who seem to experience God are in special, pathological circumstances. So now, while we have reason to think that the evidence in such special circumstances is not adequate to prove that God has been experienced, we also have reason to believe that God does appear to people and that when they seem to have such experiences they really do. Hence there is at least *some* reason to think that God is indeed appearing to persons in pathological circumstances, as He appears to others.[12]

Finally, there is one other consideration that shows the application of JERP to the case of experiencing God to be somewhat weaker than in other applications of that principle. To appreciate it return to the example of the teddy bear. Its power as an illustration of JERP's plausibility comes

[12] The argument of this paragraph actually depends upon our argument in the following section of this chapter against thinking that generally those who seem to experience God are in some nonpathological condition which compromises the evidential value of their experience. Fully stated, the paragraph would depend on the claim that in general there are neither pathological nor nonpathological conditions which compromise the evidential value of apparent perceptions of God.

in part from the fact that the child's perceptual opportunities for being justified in believing she sees a teddy bear are highly restricted relative to the perceptual opportunities for not being so justified. Teddy bears tend to project a very narrow band of perceptual possibilities, whereas other things project innumerable possibilities of "looks" that do not provide adequate evidence that one sees a teddy bear, which "looks" the child in question, we are supposing, might take as a teddy bear. So the teddy bear example convinces us of the plausibility of JERP because we think of the many opportunities for the child being unjustified compared to the opportunities for being justified, and conclude that everything else being equal we should be very suspicious of the child's claim to have seen a teddy bear.

However, we do not know analogous facts in the case of God. For all we know God is appearing to all of us all the time, and we do not realize it. And for all we know, the ways in which God can appear are extremely various and rich. Furthermore, for all we know these ways are *augmented* in the case of pathological persons, augmented by reason of their unusual condition, and also because God chooses to appear to them in ways fitted to their limited or damaged ability to perceive and comprehend what transpires. Hence, for all we know the actual opportunities for justified perceptual beliefs that God is appearing to a pathological person may be very great, and may even be as great as the actual opportunities for unjustified perceptual beliefs. For all we know, the opportunities for justified belief that God is appearing to one are to be compared to when a teddy bear is always in the perceptual field of a child, and her opportunities to justifiably believe she sees a teddy bear are no less than her opportunities to unjustifiably think so.

From all of this we cannot argue, obviously, that JERP does not apply. After all, we are supposing that we *know* on general independent grounds that a pathological person is especially liable to take what does not perceptually justify the belief that she is experiencing God as an experience of God, but we do not *know* that the opportunities for justified belief that God is appearing to one approach the unjustified opportunities. To use the latter against the former would be to lapse into a skeptical claim. But what can be said is that the present argument from JERP has less force than what might be suggested by the examples used to illustrate JERP. And that is because, in the case of pathological subjects, there is more reason to think that they will be experiencing God than there is in the case of the child for thinking that she is perceiving her teddy bear. So we believe that the present considerations give us grounds for thinking that the E-reductionist argument from JERP is not as strong as in other cases that come to mind.

We conclude that the argument from JERP is a successful E-reductionist argument as applied to the pathological cases of seeming experiences of God, though we believe that the argument does not do away entirely with the evidential value of such cases.

With this we can summarize our discussion of reductionism as an argument from the Pathological Claim, as follows:

(1) T-reductionism and E-reductionism both fail as arguments from the Pathological Claim against the evidence in favor of God's being experienced across religions down through history.

(2) As applied to pathological cases alone of alleged experiences of God, T-reductionism fails to show that they are not experiences of God.

(3) As applied to pathological cases alone of alleged experiences of God, E-reductionism based on ERP fails to show that they are not adequate evidence of experiences of God.

and

(4) As applied to pathological cases alone of alleged experiences of God, E-reductionism based on JERP, succeeds in showing that they are not adequate evidence of experiences of God, without succeeding in showing that they have no evidential value at all.

V

The Circumstantial Claim, when asserting that alleged experiencers of God are typically in some *pathological* condition, does very little to weaken our argument from BEE and STING to the conclusion that God is experienced by human subjects. Perhaps, though, it will be claimed that typically experiencers of God are in some *non*pathological condition which robs their alleged experiences of their evidential value. The nonpathological conditions most frequently referred to in the "Nonpathological Claim" (that subjects having alleged experiences of God are in nonpathological conditions), as catalogued by Davis, are:[13]

---

[13] See Davis, *Religious Experience*, pp. 223–35.

(1) the internalizing of society's authority (due to Durkheim),[14]

(2) believing on the basis of wish fulfillment (due to Freud),[15] and

(3) being possessed of a religious "set" which makes one think or interpret an experience as being of God.

Here, as previously, we will have to distinguish between the Nonpathological Claim as an assertion of an empirical fact, and the reductionist spins put on the factual assertion.

The Nonpathological Claim itself is beset with several difficulties. Durkheim's claim that belief in God involves an objectification of the authority of a person's society has slender evidence in its favor if considered independently of the theoretical context in which it was enunciated. If Durkheim's entire theory is proposed for our consideration, it can hardly be considered an *established* scientific theory. We recognize that there are people who believe it with great sincerity and commitment. But while not doubting their right to do so, that fact hardly counts as *evidence* in its favor.

Freud's claim that the idea of God comes from a projection of a father figure coming from infantile regression and wish fulfillment has more intuitive plausibility than Durkheim's view. And some scientific studies appear to support it.[16] However, other scientific studies have raised doubts about the claim that religious belief *typically* can be characterized in this way.[17] In addition, the emphatic demands of the most developed spiritual souls in history for disinterested worship of God and for the decentering of self as a condition of true piety strongly suggest that there is a common religious orientation which disowns any utilitarian benefits to be gotten from religiosity.[18] This would presumably include disavowal of the benefits to be had from a benevolent Father in Heaven. Some philosophers of religion

[14] See, for example, Emile Durkheim, *The Elementary Forms of the Religious Life*, trans. J. W. Swain (New York: Free Press, 1965).

[15] See Sigmund Freud, *The Future of an Illusion*, trans. W. D. Robinson-Scott (London: Hogarth Press, 1962).

[16] See André Godin and Monique Hallez, "Parental Images and Divine Paternity," in *From Religious Experience to a Religious Attitude*, ed. André Godin (Brussels: Lumen Vitae Press, 1964), pp. 79–110. See discussion in Davis, *Religious Experience*, pp. 229–30.

[17] See Godin and Hallez, "Parental Images," and A. Siegman, "An Empirical Investigation of the Psychoanalytic Theory of Religious Behavior," in *Psychology and Religion: Selected Readings*, ed. L. B. Brown (Harmondsworth: Penguin Education, 1973), pp. 225–31. This work is cited by Davis.

[18] For a sustained study of the religious demand for a decentering of the self, see Merold Westphal, *God, Guilt, and Death* (Bloomington: Indiana University Press, 1984). For an anthropological theory that posits both instrumental and noninstrumental "communion" aspects of religion see Robin Horton, *Patterns of Thought in Africa and the West* (Cambridge: Cambridge University Press, 1993).

see this direction as the very essence of religious belief and practice.[19] But all of this counts against Freud's understanding of religion. Freud might wish to give this orientation itself a deep psychoanalytic interpretation which would make it cohere with his theory. But this would detract from the theory's initial plausibility which depends, after all, on the commonplace observation that God does seem, for many people, like a father. The evidence independent of psychoanalytic theory shows that for some, God is far less of a father than Freud makes out. We suspect that in propounding his theory Freud was looking at only a narrow slice of the religious phenomenon, and at an unsophisticated slice at that.

Freud's Nonpathological Claim is embedded in the context of a comprehensive psychoanalytic theory in which such terms as "infantile regression," "wish fulfillment," "father figure," and the like have massive theoretical connections with other terms in the theory. The Freudian claim would receive its greatest support were that theory an *established* one. But it is hard to agree that it is. It is highly controversial among students of human psychology. Hence it cannot serve as *evidence* in favor of a Nonpathological Claim.

A further grave difficulty with a Freudian (as well as Durkheimian) Nonpathological Claim for our present context is that Freud enunciated his theory about *belief* in God, and not specifically about having alleged *experiences* of God. Even were Freud right about the genesis of *belief* in God in general, still he might be wrong about whether putative *experiences* of God came about in a similar way. Some studies have shown that ego strength is correlated with very intense religious experiences.[20] Freud's theory of wish fulfillment and infantile regression applied to religious experience would predict ego weakness instead. Hence it might very well be that a Freudian theory, even if right about the formation of belief in God, is mistaken about the circumstances leading to apparent experiences of God.

We conclude that neither the Durkheimian nor the Freudian Nonpathological claims are sufficiently grounded in evidence to serve as a factual ground for a general reductionist attack upon experience of God.

In addition, even were Freud's factual claim to be accepted as true, Freud's reductionist use of it is faulty. In *The Future of An Illusion*, in addi-

---

[19] We are referring to John Hick, especially in *An Interpretation of Religion: Human Responses to the Transcendent* (London: Macmillan, 1989).

[20] See Ralph W. Hood, Jr., "Psychological Strength and the Report of Intense Religious Experience," *Journal for the Scientific Study of Religion* 13 (1974): 65–71. Once again I am indebted to my reading of Davis, who noted this study.

tion to arguing against the rationality of belief in God, Freud also has a
T-reductionist argument to the effect that:

(1) In most cases in which a belief, B, is an illusion, B is false.

(2) Belief in God is an illusion.

So,

(3) Probably, belief in God is false.[21]

where a belief is an "illusion" when it is held (solely or primarily) for
reasons of wish fulfillment. The first premise, however, is wholly unsupported. It is hard to know how Freud could claim to know or have good
reason for endorsing its truth. There are so many, varied beliefs based primarily on wish fulfillment that would have to be observed in order to
assess premise (1). Consider, for example, how many people there must
have been who were in the path of a hurricane who *believed* (not just
hoped) that the hurricane would not hurt them, out of a belief grounded
purely in wish fulfillment and without any evidential basis whatsoever. In
how many cases has the hurricane then veered and never touched them? If
we had to guess, it would be more rational to suppose that in more cases
than not such beliefs turned out to be true, for the simple reason that the
number of people actually hurt by a given hurricane is much smaller than
the number of people who were originally in its path. Or consider all of
the mothers and wives who have *believed* (not just hoped) with all their
hearts that their soldier boys would return home healthy and whole from
the war. The great majority of such sons, we may suppose, did return
healthy and whole, given that most soldiers do return home in that condition. And so forth. How would Freud even set about forming a convincing
sample-class for his projected probabilities? Freud is simply not entitled to
his first premise.

    As for those particular cases where we do become convinced that a
person is in either a Durkheimian or a Freudian nonpathological condition, the question of whether a T-reductionist or a E-reductionist argument will work against him and the validity of his experience is to be
answered by considerations parallel to those already discussed at length for
the Pathological Claim. We will not repeat that discussion, but only invite
the reader to make the comparisons and judge their adequacies. We repeat,
thus, our conclusion stated earlier for the Pathological Claim, in response

----

[21] See   ., *The Future of An Illusion*, sec. 6, pp. 26–29.

to the Nonpathological Durkheimian and Freudian Claim. Even for those cases where we know that a person is in these nonpathological conditions, reductionist arguments are either entirely unsuccessful or are somewhat weaker than the reductionist would like.

Consider now the empirical Nonpathological Claim, the claim that usually the subject of an alleged experience of God is in a religious "set." This idea is actually composed of two parts:

(A) Typically persons who have an experience of God are enmeshed in a religious "set" inculcated in them by religious teaching and training.
and

(B) This set is profoundly influential in their having alleged experiences of God.

We warn against taking this claim to imply that subjects who have alleged experiences of God typically are hypersuggestible. The latter condition is a pathological one and we have already noted that there is no evidence indicating that subjects of apparent experiences of God are pathological. The present *Non*pathological Claim is that set *alone* is typical of subjects having seeming experiences of God and that this influences them in a nonpathological way.

This form of the Nonpathological Claim has obvious plausibility, but we must caution against making more of it than is warranted. First to consider is that the specific nature or content of experiences of God are not always at all anticipated by those who have them, even when the subject is deeply religious and seeking a perception of God. The theme of unanticipated contents in experiences of God runs through various traditions. Consider this confession by Saint Teresa. "As I had no director, I used to read these books, and gradually began to think that I was learning something. I found out later that if the Lord had not taught me, I could have learned little from books, for until His Majesty taught it me by experience what I learned was nothing at all; I did not even know what I was doing."[22]

Likewise, the Hindu saint Ramakrishna testified that all the learning in the books had not prepared him for what he knew by acquaintance with God ("realization" of God). "What will you learn of God from books? . . . One cannot get true feeling about God from the study of books. This feeling is something very different from book-learning. Books, scriptures,

[22] Teresa of Avila, *The Life of Teresa of Jesus*, ed. and trans. E. Allison Peers (Garden City, N.Y.: Doubleday, 1960), p. 385, as quoted in Anthony N. Perovich, Jr., "Mysticism and the Philosophy of Science," *The Journal of Religion* 65 (1985): 72–73.

and science appear as mere dirt and straw after the realization of God . . . The one thing needful is to be introduced to the master of the house."[23]

And the Hassidic master and mystic Rabbi Israel of Koznitz said that before coming to his mystical master, the Maggid Dov Ber of Meseritz, he had read eight hundred Kabbalistic books. But after meeting the Maggid he realized he had learned nothing from them.[24]

Finally, it is a recurring theme in Buddhism, and especially in Zen Buddhism, that the initiate has an experience which he takes on the basis of the teaching to be the enlightenment toward which he was training, only to be told by the master that it was not. The master sends the initiate back for further training.

In all of these cases, the subject of an experience is deeply enmeshed in a religious set that is not influential in having the particular experience in the way or to the extent envisioned by the present Nonpathological Claim.

In addition, reports do exist of subjects, some religious, others not, who had "special" experiences that they felt they were not able to properly identify when they had them. Only later did they discover that a religious interpretation that saw them as experiences of God illuminated for them the true nature of what had transpired.[25] In such cases either the subject had no religious set to start with, or the religious set was not related to the experience in the desired way for the reductionist.

Nonetheless, it is obvious that most often, at least, a person who has an alleged experience of God is deeply embedded within a religious psychological set which is profoundly influential in that person having that particular experience. And the question now is just what a reductionist might justifiably be able to make of these cases against our argument from BEE and STING for the strong rationality of belief in God.

The T-reductionist would have to argue that the religious set is what entirely by itself causes a person to label a religious arousal as an "experience of God," when she is not experiencing God at all.[26] The T-reductionist infers from the subject's having a religious set the fact that she has *not* experienced God. We dismiss the T-reductionist claim for reasons similar to those brought against it for the Pathological Claim, which reasons, if

---

[23] *The Gospel of Sri Ramakrishna*, trans. Swami Nikhilananda (Sri Ramakrishna Math: Mylapore, 1964), p. 614.

[24] See Gershom Scholem, *Major Trends in Jewish Mysticism* (Jerusalem: Schocken, 1941), p. 333.

[25] See a discussion of this phenomenon in Davis, *Religious Experience*, pp. 161–65.

[26] More accurately, the T-reductionist could argue that the set plus pathological conditions do it together. We ignore this form of the argument, however, since we have already rejected the idea that alleged experiencers of God are mostly pathological.

anything, apply more strongly here. There is absolutely no reason to believe that *in general* a person's merely having a certain cognitive or psychological set would cause her to have a delusory experience in accordance with that set. And there is no reason to believe this for the case of experience of God in particular.

The E-reductionist argument, if analogous to what we have seen above, would have to argue either that given a person's religious set we could predict in advance that he would be going to seem to experience God, or that he would be especially prone to form an unjustified perceptual belief that God was appearing to him.

But here too there is absolutely no reason to think that *in general* a person's merely having a certain psychological *set* would cause her to seem to have experiences of some object, O, even were O not really appearing to her. And there is absolutely no reason to believe that *in general* a person's merely having a *set* would cause her to be incapable of discriminating between the perceptually justified and unjustified. Admittedly any of these misapprehensions or disabilities can appear and do appear from time to time. But just as surely they do not take place in a regular or systematic way *just because* a person has a certain cognitive or psychological *set*. Why should it be different in the religious case?

True enough, it is generally only religious people who have apparent experiences of God. But we do not suspect the justification of alleged observations by scientists who have been rigorously trained to make skilled observations that others find difficult, just because their training has created in them a particular cognitive and psychological *set*. So why should we suspect the justification of alleged observations of religious persons just because they have been "trained" in religious thought and living, merely because this has created in them a certain cognitive and psychological set?

Admittedly, in the case of the trained scientist who makes alleged observations others have not been trained for and so cannot make, we have independent reason for thinking she is making justified judgments on the basis of her observations, reasons having to do with what follows from well-confirmed theories about the subject matter in question. It is true that there does not seem to be such independent evidence in the case of alleged experiences of God. But in any case, we are arguing for the strong rationality of believing that God is experienced, based solely on the evidence of alleged experiences of God.

All of this only shows that the evidence in favor of God's being experienced may not be as strong as the evidence in favor of the truth of alleged, regularly occurring scientific observations backed up by a well-confirmed theoretical structure. It does not show that the evidence in favor of God's being experienced is not good evidence, nonetheless. And we do claim that it is good evidence. After all, that God has been and is putatively experienced within various religions is a good reason, everything else being equal, for believing that He is experienced. Now it *might* be true that having a religious set in fact systematically causes people to think they are experiencing God on inadequate evidence. So it *might* be true that not everything else *is* equal. But we do not know that. This is not true *for all we know*. What is true for all we know is that we have evidence that God is experienced in fact. To argue otherwise we have to have a reason for believing that not everything else is equal.

We suspect that one of the attractions this E-reductionist argument may have comes from confusing the mere having of a religious set with being religious and *hypersuggestible*. Those attracted to E-reductionism may be picturing those who have a religious set as impatiently looking for anything that might be taken as God's appearing to them, anxious to pronounce the same as God's appearance. This hypersuggestibility hypothesis creates suspicion of any alleged experience of God subsequently had by persons possessing religious sets. But of course this hypersuggestibility is not what is meant by the "having of a religious set," and we reject the confusing of the two as unfounded. But precisely this picture, we suspect, might be what gives some measure of plausibility to an E-reductionist argument from the having of a religious set.

A person's cognitive and psychological set influences, obviously, the way in which he experiences reality. But as long as that influence is within normal, reasonable bounds we do not deem the set to have had an insidious influence upon perception, and certainly not to the extent of calling the perception into question on a "global" level. Experiences of God within a religious tradition constitute what we called in Chapter 4 a "network" of experiences through which a fund of alleged knowledge about God is built up and shared. There are differences within a given religious tradition plausibly influenced by the subject's individual set. Nonetheless, there is plenty of overlap in the reidentification of God from one experience to another. Thus within a religious tradition the influence of set need not be insidious. And in our earlier discussion we called "the network set" the set of networks of experiences of God of different religions in which God is experienced. Differences in the perception of God occur from one network of the network set to another. And these may be attributed, at least in part, to the respective sets of different religions.[27] But at least some of these differences are reconcilable in light of the experiences of God's hidden fullness, discussed at length in Chapter 4, common to different traditions, making it eminently understandable that differences appear. And in any case, all of the differences are embedded within a much more extensive, rich context of overlapping and similarity of experiences of God. Hence, since the variations in experiences of God across different traditions which may be the result of variations in the respective religious sets do not bar our reidentifying God across traditions, we conclude that the influence of the respective sets upon the experience had is not insidious.[28]

We therefore conclude that the fact that persons who have apparent experiences of God are typically possessed of a religious set does nothing to discredit the evidential value of their experiences.

And so we conclude that, all told, E-reductionism, as T-reductionism before it, fails to damage in any appreciable way the evidential value of the fund of alleged experiences of God across religions down through history.

[27] They may equally reflect the fact that God appears differently to different traditions for His own inscrutable reasons.

[28] Steven Katz has argued that experiences of those trained in mystical traditions are so infected by their respective theology and expectations that we have good reason to think they are not all experiencing one reality. Katz's argument is strengthened by the inclusion of Buddhist and other Eastern mystical traditions in which no claim is made to have experienced God. Leaving out those traditions, we see no reason to accept Katz's claim for traditions in which God is allegedly experienced. See footnote 40 in Chapter 4. See also, Katz, "Language, Epistemology, and Mysticism," in *Mysticism and Philosophical Analysis*, ed. Katz (New York: Oxford University Press, 1978), pp. 22–74; and Katz, "The 'Conservative' Character of Mysticism," in *Mysticism and Religious Traditions*, ed. Katz (New York: Oxford University Press, 1983), pp. 3–60. See also Perovich, "Mysticism and the Philosophy of Science"; Huston Smith, "Is There a Perennial Philosophy?" *Journal of the American Academy of Religion* 55 (1987): 553–66; and Sallie B. King, "Two Epistemological Models for the Interpretation of Mysticism," *Journal of the American Academy of Religion* 56 (1988): 257–79.

[6]

Evidence against
God's Existence I

I

We argue in Chapter 2 that the best explanation, everything else being equal, of apparent experiences of God is that God is really experienced, and so exists, basing our argument on the two principles BEE and STING.

Following our argument, we devoted the ensuing chapters partly to a defense of BEE, but mainly to replying to charges that everything else is *not* equal, and that accordingly we could not rest with the conclusion that God is experienced, and thus exists. It is now time to summarize our replies to these charges and form an interim judgment on our argument from BEE and STING.

In Chapter 3 we considered a number of objections which, in one way or another, grow out of the observation that many people do not seem ever to perceive God, and that those who allegedly do perceive God almost always do so in a private experience not shared by others at the same place and time. In considering such objections we conceded that the likelihood of God's being experienced would be higher than it is were we able to specify more *perceptual generalizations* about under what perceptual conditions we could expect and not expect an experience of God to occur, as we can for the analogous case of perception of physical objects. And we also found that our argument would create a greater probability on its behalf than it does were humans graced with experiences of God as numerous as their perceptions of physical reality. However, as noted, these truths fail to show that it is not strongly rational to believe that God is experienced on the basis of apparent perceptions of God.[1] And our reasons for saying that were, in the main, that we do have at least *some* perceptual generalizations to aid us in the case of experience of God, that in any case there were other ways of testing the evidential value of alleged experiences of God, and that the evidence in favor of the existence of physical objects on the basis of experience is in any case vastly more evidence than is needed for rational belief. Hence, neither of the above considerations shows that the belief that God is experienced cannot be strongly rational.

In light of the frequency of alleged experiences of God over history and across religious traditions, and noting the variable conditions under which such putative experiences take place, we concluded that while considerations raised in that chapter showed that the belief that God was experienced was less *probable* than the belief that physical objects were, we have good reason to think the belief strongly rational nonetheless.

In Chapter 4 we rejected the charge that our argument from BEE and STING was defeated by alleged problems growing out of the facts of religious diversity, including problems of multiple theisms, of multiple, lesser, deities, and of multiple perfect beings.

In Chapter 5 we closely examined various reductionist arguments against our argument. We acknowledged that undoubtedly *some* alleged experiences of God are suspect because the subject seems to be or might be in some pathological condition. But as far as can be judged from the literature, it is not plausible to think that most or even a significant portion of subjects who seem to experience God are pathological. And while it is true that persons having putative experiences of God are typically in a nonpathological religious set, that too, we argued, is no reason for doubting the genuineness of their experiences.

In summary, we note that our argument would be stronger:

(1) Were God to appear to mere mortals with the frequency of their experiences of physical objects.

(2) Had we a richer store of perceptual generalizations by means of which we could find reasons for thinking God was not really appearing to a person.

(3) Were God experienced in exactly the same way by everybody in every religious tradition in which He is experienced.

---

[1] The reader is reminded that a belief is *strongly* rational when in light of the total relevant evidence there exists *some* reasonable application of the canons of rationality on which it is rational to believe that p and not rational to believe that not-p.

(4) Had all religions experienced God's revelation as being one and the same.

and,

(5) If no person who experienced God was ever found to be in a pathological condition.

But from all of these together it does not follow that our argument is not a *good* argument so far considered. And we hereby submit that it remains a good argument because:

(1) The frequency and variability in the conditions in which God is allegedly experienced create a strong presumption, on BEE and STING, that God is experienced and hence exists.

(2) We do have a small number of what amount to perceptual generalizations for investigating alleged experiences of God which can give us a reason for thinking that God was experienced or that He wasn't. And there are other ways to check the evidential value of alleged experiences of God. We do not have to take a person's word for it. In addition, we learn from BEE and STING that God is not an object about which more perceptual generalizations could reasonably be expected.

(3) Although it would be easier to identify God across experiences of Him were everybody to experience Him in the same way, there is sufficient overlap in how God is experienced to identify Him nonetheless.

(4) The number of alleged pairs of revelations that there is reason to believe are really contradictory is apparently negligible within the total number of alleged experiences of God.

and

(5) There is no evidence that across religions and down through history most or an appreciable number of persons allegedly having experiences of God were pathological. There is every reason to deny this.

We conclude that so far forth our conclusion stands that God is experienced, and thus exists, everything else being equal.

II

The objections so far examined all had to do with alleged defects or shortcomings at the perceptual end of purported experiences of God. What remains for us to consider in this chapter and the next is evidence against God's being experienced which stems from the alleged object end of such experiences. We have in mind arguments *against* God's existence. To the extent to which there are indications that God does not exist, to that same extent there is evidence that God is never really experienced. But of course there just being evidence against God's existence is not enough to neutralize or defeat our argument that God is experienced, and so exists. The evidence would have to be such as to make the proposition that God does not exist more likely than the proposition that God is experienced. But even that would not yet show that God did not exist or that God was not actually experienced. For we would have to consider as well arguments in *favor* of God's existing, which proceeded independently of the positive evidence from experience. If the combined strength of all of the arguments in favor of God's existence, including ours from BEE and STING, were greater than the arguments against God's existence, then we could continue to maintain that God exists and is experienced, even if the strength of the arguments against God's existence were greater than that of the argument from BEE and STING alone.

So in order to reach a final verdict on the enterprise in which we are engaged, we would really have to address ourselves to the various arguments that have been proposed for and against God's existence.

Alas, it is beyond the limits of this work to attempt to reach a final verdict. Doing so would require another book at least as long as this one. Neither can we hope to do justice in the confines of this work just to the arguments against God's existence that have been proposed at one time or another, leaving aside the arguments in favor of God's existence. We can, however, hope to accomplish two more modest tasks to which we dedicate the remainder of this chapter and the following chapter. The first, briefer, task will be to put the evidential threat into proper perspective by blunting the impression that seems to be quite common in some circles, that there is "out there" an impressive assortment of rational arguments directed against God's existence, arguments commonly known and accepted by many. And we will do this mainly by driving a wedge between contemporary intellectual reasons for not adhering to theistic *religions*, and arguments actually directed against believing in *God*. We will point out that typically (with the possible exception of the problem of evil) the intellectual causes of the falling away from theistic religion are not correctly thought of as even being *directed* against God's existence. Hence, even if the former were all sound they wouldn't be relevant to showing that God did not exist. We will also expose an "existentialist argument" against God's existence to be devoid of evidential value.

Our second task will be to examine closely the two arguments which are, prima facie, the strongest arguments around against the existence of

God. We have in mind the argument, actually a cluster of arguments, to the effect that the concept of God is beset by internal contradiction, and the argument from evil, especially the so-called "probability argument from evil." We will show that neither of these is successful as an argument against God's existence.

Having accomplished these two tasks, we will not have established thereby that there *are* no good arguments against the existence of God. We will not have considered other arguments that have been raised against God's existence. Nevertheless, we will have gone an appreciable part of the way toward arguing that there is no good argument against the existence of God that would upset our conclusion from the experience of God. We will thus have done all we can in this work to show not only that, everything else being equal, it is strongly rational to believe God exists in the light of purported experiences of God, but that everything else *is* equal, and so that it *is* strongly rational to believe that God exists.

III

Without doubt, a major cause of disbelief in God in today's world is disillusionment with and alienation from theistic religions. God is abandoned along with the theistic religion that one is brought up in, or else God is never seriously considered because religion is never seriously considered. But the more common intellectual reasons for leaving theistic religion or for never considering religion seriously in the first place are not really relevant to the question of whether God exists. Even if sound, these causes would not be even prima facie rational reasons for not believing in God. The belief in God, then, is guilty by association, relative to the more common intellectual reasons for not adhering to a theistic religion. And while it may be understandable that a person who had no interest in religion might also not be interested in the question of God, that does not mean that she has *evidence* against belief in God, even if she were to have evidence or good cause against her religion, or any extant religion, being true.

One of the primary causes of people turning their backs on theistic religion has to do, no doubt, with evidence that has been thought to show that various doctrines or styles of thinking or scriptural passages of these religions are false or seriously suspect. The nineteenth-century confrontation between the theory of evolution and religious belief provides an obvious example, as does the earlier clash between new theories of astronomy and cosmology and ones cherished by the Catholic Church. Also, new fields of inquiry such as Bible criticism have convinced many that what is claimed for the biblical text in traditional religions cannot possibly be true. And in general, the scientific view of the world is defended as being at odds with the world-outlook implicitly found in the scriptural writings of Western religions.

Evidence against any religious doctrine or style of thinking or scriptural passage of one religion or another is not relevant, however, to the question of whether God exists.[2] The question of God's existence can be settled in the affirmative, even if no known religion is true or acceptable as is.[3] Our argument, specifically, that God exists because allegedly experienced, does not depend for its cogency on any religion at all being true or largely true as is. In particular, the fact that purported experiences of God historically occur most often to people who adhere to a religious life is in itself not a reason for thinking that the alleged experiences can be taken as true only if the surrounding religions can be so taken. All that need be acknowledged is that adherence to a religion prepares one or trains one for the possibility of experiencing God. And this can be so even though the religion might not be true as is. It need only have the spiritual power to direct one toward God.

Neither is there any good reason to think that if God existed contemporary theories of cosmology and astronomy would be false. And there is no good reason to believe that if God existed then a theory of evolution would be false.[4] And there is no good reason to believe that if God existed the theory that Scriptures were put together from disparate documents would have to be false. At most there is reason to think that if these theories are correct then certain scriptural passages and other traditional texts or cherished beliefs are false, at least when taken literally. But from this it hardly follows that there is evidence that God does not exist.

The above observations pertain to specific scientific or historical theo-

[2] An obvious exception are doctrines entailed by God's existence. If they are false, God does not exist. Our point is, though, that commonly these aren't the kinds of doctrines rejection of which leads to abandonment of religion. Not excepted are doctrines which entail God's existence. They may be false without disproving God's existence. For example, a religious doctrine that God revealed a certain truth entails that God exists. But that doctrine's being false does not count against God's existing.

[3] We should add here the reminder that as argued earlier even were we to discount all claims made for the revelation of religious doctrines from God, that would make a very small difference to our argument from BEE and STING.

[4] An exception would be the argument that the suffering of animals and humans entailed by evolutionary theory was incompatible with God's existence. This would be a version of the problem of evil, to be discussed at length in the following chapter.

ries. In addition, one often hears that the most impressive advancement in our scientific understanding of the world has rendered intelligible entire areas of our experience which were hitherto opaque to natural explanation and which thus used to call forth an explanation in terms of God's activity in the world and history. So the "hypothesis" of God is no longer needed to adequately explain what previously was otherwise without explanation.

This line of thinking, however, does not supply us with any evidence against God's existence. Even if correct, at most it shows that what might have been taken once as evidence for God's existence is no longer to be taken as such. But that fact is hardly evidence *against* God's existence.

In response to our reply, it might be argued that if we have no need for an hypothesis, then we should at least refrain from believing it. So since we have no need for the hypothesis of God's existence we should refrain from believing that God exists. Now, without questioning the epistemic principle here invoked and without bothering to investigate whether God is not still a good explanatory hypothesis in other matters, we wish to point out that this response to our reply carries no weight when set within the context of our argument on behalf of genuine experiences of God. For our argument shows that everything else being equal, it is strongly rational to believe that God is experienced. And the reason for that is that on BEE and STING that God is experienced is the best *explanation*, everything else being equal, of the fact that people *seem* to perceive God. So the existence of God recommends itself to us as the best "hypothesis" for explaining the facts of alleged experiences of God. So it is just false that due to scientific advances we no longer have any need of the "hypothesis" that God exists.

We conclude that without further argument it is difficult to see how our scientific understanding of the world could yield evidence that God does not exist, as opposed to affording evidence against other religious dogmas. True enough, some have adopted atheistic outlooks as a result of the impact of science upon their understanding of the world. But they may merely be guilty of making God guilty by association. And even where their belief is impeccably (weakly) rational, that does not yet show that there is anything in scientific theories which counts as *evidence* against God's existence. It only shows that a person could fail to believe in God and be (weakly) rational.

There are other common reflective causes of the contemporary alienation from religion which are similarly not relevant to the question of God's existence. In the second half of the twentieth century a moral sensibility has arisen which judges various aspects of traditional theistic religions to be morally unacceptable or repugnant. We include in this category a feminist consciousness which condemns as immoral the way in which women have been neglected or subjugated within traditional religious behavior and theologies. And we include as well a universalist thinking which finds particularistic moral codes or teachings, allegedly displayed by some traditional religions, to be morally reprehensible.

But even were we to embrace these moral assessments, we would have no reason whatever to conclude that God did not exist. The most that could be argued would be that if God is really wholly good then the offensive scriptural passages, religious doctrines, attitudes, and practices could not have really come from *God*. It would not follow in the least that God did not exist. If one did draw such a conclusion it would likely be another case of finding God guilty by association.

Finally, in addition to these intellectual causes of alienation from religion, there is a kind of argument, or maybe more of a mood, which no doubt is a contributing factor to contemporary disbelief in God. We have in mind what is expressed, for example, by Sartre, which can be stated baldly in argument form as follows:

(1) If God exists, then I, Sartre, am not free to choose myself.

(2) But, I, Sartre, am free to choose himself.

(3) Hence, God does not exist.[5]

In this argument, God's existence is portrayed as antithetical to a person's freedom, not in the sense in which a person is free to choose between alternative actions, such as moving her finger or refraining from doing so, but free from having an "essence," free from having a plan for her imposed from without her own being, and thus free to choose herself.

What is Sartre's *evidence* that (2) is true? If he has no evidence for thinking that he, Sartre, is free to choose himself, but states this as a basic belief or outlook of his on life, then maybe, granting (1) in the meantime, Sartre has a reason for thinking that God does not exist. But that reason does not count as evidence against God's existence, in the sense that concerns us in this study.

But let us not be dogmatic about this. Perhaps Sartre has evidence for the truth of (2). Perhaps, for example, Sartre *seems* to experience his freedom, seems to experience himself as one who is free to choose himself, and so on BEE it is rational to conclude that everything else being equal

[5] See Jean-Paul Sartre, *Existentialism and Humanism*, trans. Philip Mairet (London: Methuen, 1948), pp. 27–29.

Sartre *is* free to choose himself. And so perhaps Sartre has evidence that God does not exist.

But, even were we to concede that Sartre seems to experience his own freedom to choose himself, and even if we were to grant (1), that is, concede, that God's existence was thereby contradicted, this still would be negligible evidence against the existence of God compared to the relatively massive evidence that God is experienced, and so exists. Sartre's reasoning would be successful only if the number of person's allegedly experiencing themselves as free to choose themselves in Sartre's sense, a sense that implies God's nonexistence, and the variability of conditions in which these occurred, were impressive relative to the evidential value of alleged experiences of God. But this hardly seems to be the case. The evidence for Sartre's first premise is negligible at best.

A Sartre supporter might reply that in fact every person has an experience of his own freedom to choose himself, but that many are prone to deny this out of self-deception or "bad faith." But this reply would render Sartre's argument less a matter of having discovered evidence against God's existence and more a matter of combatting God's existence by way of a theory or world-view in which it has no place. The theory would have to be argued for in a convincing way, and it is a controversial matter whether this has ever been done.

Even granting (2), however, Sartre's argument does not establish the nonexistence of God, because (1) cannot be granted. And that is because our lack of freedom, in Sartre's sense, would follow, if at all, not from the very existence of God, but from that together with certain auxiliary premises taken from religious teachings about why God has created us, how God regards us, and that He has plans for us. These religious doctrines aside, we see no difficulty in supposing that God creates each of us, to borrow Sartre's phrase, as a "hole in the heart of being," each of us having to choose, in some important sense, our own "project." If there is a contradiction between God's existence and agency to choose oneself it has to be argued for in a much more convincing way than Sartre or others have ever done.

We submit that the major causes of alienation from religion in this century are, with the possible exception of the "problem of evil," scientific, moral, and existential. But none of these amount to so much as a prima facie argument that God does not exist. In this connection the words of John Baillie, written more than half a century ago, are relevant:

> Our conviction of the reality of God first forms itself in our minds in close
> association with a wide context of other beliefs. In the course of our later

intellectual development, however, many of these beliefs are seen by us to be false and are quite rightly surrendered. The effort of dissociation that is then required in order to separate our deep-seated belief in God from that part of its original context which we have now been forced to reject, is an effort to which our mental powers are not always equal, so that we are faced with the difficult alternative of either keeping our belief in God and keeping it with certain other beliefs the falsity of which seems quite obvious to us, or else surrendering these false beliefs and surrendering with them our belief in God also.[6]

Baillie is here noting a phenomenon which has accelerated since his words were written: the phenomenon of the dismissal of God's existence for reasons that do not really support the conclusion that there is no God. The reasons are thought to count against the existence of God only because they count against ideas and doctrines often closely associated with belief in God. In considering here the counterevidence to God's existence, therefore, we are not to include such reasons in our reckoning.

IV

Philosophers have advanced assorted arguments designed to show that God does not exist. As said previously, we cannot attend here to all of them. There are, however, two arguments which we will examine, these being the arguments which seem to pose the most serious challenge to belief in God's existence. The first consists of the argument that the "concept of God" is logically self-inconsistent, (the "Argument from Self-Inconsistency") and the second consists of the argument that the existence of evil is incompatible with or counts against God's existence (the "Argument from Evil"). We will show that neither of these gives us any reason for thinking that God does not exist.

The Argument from Self-Inconsistency actually includes a number of arguments put forward by philosophers in recent years.[7] These include: (1) claims of logical self-inconsistency within the concept of a particular perfection attributed to God, and (2) claims of logical inconsistencies *between* different perfections attributed to God. In (1) is to be included, for exam-

---

[6] John Baillie, *Our Knowledge of God* (London: Oxford University Press, 1939), pp. 59–60.
[7] We are not including under the heading of the Argument from Self-Inconsistency J. N. Findlay's famous negative ontological argument that the concept of God is self-contradictory. That argument has a somewhat different logic from the ones we mean to include in the present category. See J. N. Findlay, "Can God's Existence be Disproved?" in *New Essays in Philosophical Theology*, ed. Alasdair MacIntyre and Antony Flew (London: SCM Press, 1961), pp. 47–56. For a cogent reply to Findlay, see Alvin Plantinga, *God and Other Minds* (Ithaca: Cornell University Press, 1967), pp. 173–83.

ple, the charge that the concept of omnipotence is internally inconsistent, based on considerations such as whether God could create a stone too heavy for Him to lift; also included is the charge that there is something logically incoherent about omniscience, because it involves the notion of someone knowing the "set of all truths." In (2) is included, for example, the charge that God's impeccability, entailed by His goodness, is inconsistent with God's omnipotence, since if God cannot sin there is something He cannot do; also included is the claim that God's being timeless is inconsistent with His omniscience, since if God is timeless He cannot know what is transpiring *now*.[8]

The Argument from Evil comes in two forms, the logical argument and the probabilistic argument. The logical argument says that it is logically impossible for both evil and God, conceived of as an omnipotent, omniscient, and wholly good being, to exist. But evil exists. So God, so conceived, doesn't. The probabilistic argument is that since evil exists it is probable that God, conceived of as an omnipotent, omniscient, and wholly good being, does not, or else that evil makes God's existence less likely than it would be otherwise.

The logical and probabilistic arguments each break up into three arguments, depending on whether the argument bases itself on (1) the existence of any evil at all, (2) the existence of particularly horrendous evils, such as the torture of innocent children, or (3) the amount of evil in the world. We get, then, six different arguments from evil against the existence of God, three logical, (LE1)—(LE3), and three probabilistic, (PE1)—(PE3), plus possible combinations between these.

The first point we want to make is that *strictly speaking*, even if they were correct neither the Argument from Self-Inconsistency nor the Argument from Evil would show that God does not exist. And that follows from the logic of the name "God," as used in the religious life.

As we argued in Chapter 1, "God," in the religious life is typically a proper name, which:

(1) either has no semantic meaning or has only the meaning ascribed to it on the Nominal Description Theory;

(2) is a rigid designator intended to refer to a particular being allegedly known in experience by the person using the name or

[8] These problems are discussed in detail by, among others, Edward R. Wierenga, *The Nature of God: An Inquiry into Divine Attributes* (Ithaca: Cornell University Press, 1989); Michael Martin, *Atheism: A Philosophical Justification* (Philadelphia: Temple University Press, 1990); and Richard R. La Croix, *What Is God? The Selected Essays of Richard R. La Croix* (Buffalo: Prometheus Books, 1993).

known in alleged experiences by others, the user of the name intending to tie in to a referential chain going back to the naming of that being in those (alleged) experiences;

(3)   succeeds in referring only if it refers to a "supremely valuable" being, as captured by (N);

(4)   (putatively) refers to a being often thought of (in a generic way) as an absolutely perfect being;

(5)   (putatively) refers to a being often thought of as omnipotent, omniscient, and wholly good, in a secondary elaboration of either the concept of an absolutely perfect being or of a (putative) experience of God as an absolutely perfect being.

(N), referred to in (3), went like this:

(N) God is:

(1)   the most perfect actual being,

(2)   who is very high on the scale of perfection,

(3)   whose perfection is vastly greater than that of the second most perfect actual being, and

(4)   upon whom other beings in some important way are dependent.

Now it follows from this understanding of "God," that if it were to be proved that no being could be absolutely perfect, we would not thereby come to know that "our" God, *the very being who is purportedly known by experience*, did not exist. What would have been proven about God is only that "our" God was not an absolutely perfect being.

This understanding of the term "God" has direct implications for whether the Argument from Self-Inconsistency or the Argument from Evil presents us with an argument against the existence of God. As for the Argument from Self-Inconsistency, from the fact that it could be proven, if it can be proven, that no being can possibly be omnipotent, for example, it would not yet follow that we had reason to believe that God really did not exist. We cannot know just by the truth of the statement "God exists" that an omnipotent being exists. And the reason for that is that while it is a presupposition or implication of "God" naming that it name a *supreme* being, it is not a presupposition or implication of its naming that it name a being who is omnipotent. And no component of what it means to be a "supreme being," as per (N), entails that a supreme being is omnipotent. The same line of reasoning applies to other attributes involved in the self-inconsistency charge when taken one by one or when taken together.

Even if no being could be omnipotent, and omniscient, and a wholly good being, etc., that would not yet require of us to conclude that God did not exist.

At the same time, there is every reason to believe that there is no successful analogue of the Argument from Self-Inconsistency against the existence of a "supreme being," as characterized by (N). In particular there is every reason to believe that the concept of being "very high on the scale of perfection" is perfectly coherent. Hence, even were it be shown that the various alleged inconsistencies between perfections did really exist, this would not show that *God* did not exist.

With regard to the Argument from Evil, too, even if it were successful, in one or another of its forms, that would not show that *God* did not exist. And that is because that argument is formulated to show that no omnipotent, omniscient, and wholly good being existed. But even if no such being existed, it would not require us to conclude that *God* could not exist. It would only require the conclusion that the being experienced all along, God, was not omnipotent, omniscient, and wholly good, even though thought to have been so.

In addition, there is every reason to believe that there is no successful analogue of any of the forms of the Argument from Evil against the existence of a "supreme being," as characterized by (N). There is no good reason to think that if a (merely) supreme being, who was not perfect, existed then the world would not have the evils it does have. It might be the case that there exists a being who is very high on the scale of perfection and upon which all other beings depend, and who, let's suppose, is constantly fighting the world's evils with great success. This being has managed to prevent enormous amounts of suffering and has engineered immense amounts of good. But it has achieved all of this within the limitations of its own power and knowledge, which, unfortunately, are not able to eliminate a lot of the worst evils and not able to get evil down to less than it in fact is.

We conclude that *strictly speaking* neither the argument from alleged self-inconsistencies in the concept of God nor the Argument from Evil is an argument even directed against the existence of *God*, the very being known by experience to exist.

V

We have said that "strictly speaking" neither the Argument from Self-Inconsistency nor the Argument from Evil could show that God does not exist. But we will not rest content with that as a reply to the Argument from Self-Inconsistency and to the Argument from Evil. For one thing, were these arguments successful against the existence of an absolutely perfect being, many people would simply lose interest in the whole topic of whether or not God exists, since for them God holds interest only if an absolutely perfect being. But directly to the point of our enterprise, either of these arguments, if successful, might be thought to cause damage to our argument from alleged experiences of God on BEE and STING. Apparent experiences in which God is perceived to be absolutely perfect appear to make up a significant part of the total of alleged experiences of God. Were there to be proof that no omnipotent, omniscient, wholly good being existed, that might be thought to cast some doubt on the authenticity of experiences in which God seemed to be perfect. Thus, an important subgroup of alleged experiences of God might be compromised. We might have to conclude that alleged experiences of God as absolutely perfect were either entirely illusory or seriously untrustworthy. And this in turn would threaten the support our argument gains from the principle STING, the number of alleged experiences we can count on severely curtailed or impugned. Hence in the name of our argument for the existence of God (whether as absolutely perfect or only as a supreme being) we should be willing to consider directly the arguments against the existence of an omnipotent, omniscient, wholly good being.[9]

In addition, on the basis of apparent experiences of God in which He is perceived to be absolutely perfect, an argument can be constructed from BEE and STING to the conclusion that God is a perfect being. This argument might not be as strong as our argument to the very existence of God, since we may safely assume that the number of alleged experiences of God is larger than the number of alleged experiences of God as perfect. Nonetheless, it does make God's being perfect probable, everything else being equal. If there would be good evidence that no omnipotent, omniscient, wholly good being existed this would seem to be damaging to the conclusion of that argument. And so here is another reason to address directly the Argument from Self-Inconsistency and the Argument from Evil.

We turn, therefore, to these two arguments as arguments against the existence of an omnipotent, omniscient, wholly good being. In the re-

---

[9] Strictly speaking, an apparent experience of God being wrong about God's being perfect does not yet give reason for thinking that it is not nevertheless an experience of *God*. The perception might be reliable as to its being God who is experienced, and only unreliable about details. Rather than pursue this line of thought, however, we prefer to respond here in a more sweeping and elegant manner.

mainder of this chapter we examine the Argument from Self-Inconsistency, and in the next chapter we turn to the Argument from Evil.

Fortunately, in order to reply to the Argument from Self-Inconsistency we need not address ourselves to each and every argument that has been proposed to show that some "omni-attribute" or other is self-inconsistent and to every claim of mutual contradiction between the omni-attributes. Our reply will consist of general considerations showing that even were these arguments to be sound they would not have a deleterious effect on the belief that God is absolutely perfect or on our argument from BEE and STING.

In displaying these general considerations, we will divide our treatment of the Argument from Self-Inconsistency into two parts, treating first the charge of self-inconsistency within single omni-attributes, and later treating the charge of contradictions between omni-attributes.

We begin our first task by expanding on our discussion in Chapter 1 of how the omni-attributes—omnipotence, omniscience, and omni-goodness—enter into discourse on God. As noted there, a person might very well be able to experience God as possessed of some or all of the omniattributes. Or, God might reveal to a person that He was omnipotent, omniscient, and wholly good. But it seems plausible to think that typically the omni-attributes enter into discourse on God in a secondary elaboration upon the *generic* concept of an absolutely perfect being, a being possessed of maximal possible value.[10]

The secondary elaboration may be of a *theologically* generic conception or of a *perceptually* generic disclosure. In the former, the omni-attributes are invoked in order to explicate the *concept* of a perfect being or to provide a list of perfect-making attributes relative to that concept. The adequacy of these attributions would then be judged by their ability to successfully explicate the prior *concept* of an absolutely perfect being.

If the secondary elaboration is referred back to (alleged) perceptual disclosures of God, the omni-attributes would be invoked in order to explicate what is *experienced* as God's perfection in the generic sense, quite plausibly along with experiences of God's goodness, power, or wisdom (whether or not "omni"). The adequacy of the omni-attributes should then be judged by how true they were to the experiences. Judgments upon the

---

[10] Precedents for this way of looking at the omni-attributes can be found in Jerome I. Gellman, "The Paradox of Omnipotence, and Perfection," *Sophia* 14 (1975): 14, 31–39; and Gellman, "Omnipotence and Impeccability," *The New Scholasticism* 51 (1977): 151–61; and in George N. Schlesinger, "Divine Perfection," *Religious Studies* 21 (1985): 147–58; and Schlesinger, *New Perspectives on Old-Time Religion* (Oxford: Clarendon Press, 1988), pp. 4–34.

adequacy of these attributes would be made in reference to those experiences. And those who actually had such perceptions of God would be in a favored position to judge.

We suggest that whether the secondary elaboration is theologically or perceptually motivated, there are five tiers involved in the logic of God's perfection in relation to the attribution to God of the omni-attributes.[11]

In the first tier we have the generic concept of God's absolute perfection, i.e., of God's being possessed of maximal possible value.

In the second tier either the generic *concept* determines that God must have power, knowledge, and goodness, or God's having power, knowledge, and goodness, per se, is (allegedly) known through experience of God, and is linked to His perfection.

The third tier consists of attributing to God power, knowledge, and goodness, each individually and in a perfect way or to a perfect degree. The idea is that since God has power, for instance, and God is perfect, God's power must be maximal-value conferring.

The fourth tier consists of the assertion that God, therefore, must be able to "do everything," i.e., be omnipotent; and "know everything," i.e., be omniscient; and "do everything for the good," i.e., be wholly good; in order for His power, knowledge, and goodness to be possessed by Him (each individually) to a perfect degree or be maximal-value conferring.

Finally, in the fifth tier we get proposed detailed definitions or explications of each of the omni-attributes, of what exactly it might mean to say, for example, that God is omnipotent or "can do everything."

Some philosophers claim to have shown, against what is really the fourth tier, that one omni-attribute or another, or each of them in turn, is self-inconsistent. This they allegedly have done in some direct, general way for each attribute, or by having revealed particular, proposed explications to be self-inconsistent and thus showing that probably there are no self-consistent explications. Now let us suppose, which we do not in fact concede, that they have succeeded in this endeavor. From this it does not follow that there is a self-inconsistency at any of the tiers higher than the fourth. Take the third tier concept that God is perfect in power. This concept seems to be perfectly coherent and self-consistent. God's being perfect in power means God's having a level of power such that no level of power could confer more value on God than *it* does. And the higher tiered concept of God's being absolutely perfect means that God possesses the maximal positive value that any possible being could possess in any possible world.

[11] The present scheme is an expansion of the four-tiered scheme presented in Chapter 1.

These *generic* concepts are untouched by the disproving of the fourth tier claims.

But suppose, it might be said in reply, that as a result of the disproof of the claims of the fourth tier, we could no longer say any more about God's power, etc. and about God's perfection than what is already contained in the generic concepts themselves. Would this not show that these concepts were at best hopelessly vague? Actually, it would not. The generic idea of a power which confers the maximal value that power can confer and the generic idea of a being possessed of a value than which no greater can be possessed can be perfectly intelligible even if we are not able to explicate them any further. Perhaps they require no further analysis. Or, perhaps our human brainpower is great enough to be able to grasp clearly the generic idea of maximal possible power and maximal possible value but not great enough for us to be capable of *explicating* them any further. Could there not be a limit to our intellectual powers? If any of these suggestions were correct, we would have no reason for thinking the generic concepts to be "hopelessly vague," and certainly no reason for thinking them incoherent or self-inconsistent.

Surely the mere fact that you cannot explain in detail what you mean by a term does not show that the term has no meaning for you or that it is hopelessly vague. The inclination to think otherwise is no doubt a malady that torments some professional philosophers in particular. We can readily understand how this should happen. After all, in their professional lives philosophers often try to define, analyze, explicate, or give an "account" of various concepts which interest them. This task is venerable and to be applauded. But what is admirable turns into professional haughtiness and intellectual caprice when the legitimacy of a concept is judged by whether or not it allows philosophers to do to it what interests them. We have to have some other reason for thinking a term incoherent or hopelessly vague. And until we are given some other reason for thinking our generic concepts about God to be defective, we have every reason to think that they are coherent and are sufficiently clear to have application.

Hence we conclude that even were it found that one or another, or even all of the omni-attributes were each singly self-inconsistent that would not show that the notions of absolute perfection or of perfection in power, knowledge, or goodness were defective ideas.

We have made this excursion into the logic of God's perfection in relation to God's being thought of as an omnipotent, omniscient, and wholly good being in order to defend against the charge that alleged self-inconsistencies in omni-attributes, taken singly, threaten the evidential base of our argument from alleged experiences of God. The alleged threat comes from the fact that putative experiences of God as perfect can be assumed to be a significant portion of the total of alleged experiences of God. But if it could be shown that it was self-inconsistent for God to be omnipotent, omniscient, or wholly good, then that significant part of the alleged evidence might be thrown into doubt, and our evidential base might to that extent be seriously weakened.

We now see that this charge is incorrect. And this is because when God is experienced as perfect He is not necessarily being experienced as omnipotent, omniscient, and wholly good. He is, we propose, more often being known as possessed of a value that cannot be exceeded. And even were it to be the case that God simply *could* not be omnipotent, omniscient, or wholly good, that would not contradict the experiences in which God was allegedly experienced as generically perfect. And so the evidential base of our argument would not be diminished even were any or all of the concepts of omnipotence, omniscience, and omni-goodness to be exposed as each self-inconsistent. And God's being absolutely perfect in the generic sense would not have been affected.[12]

Consider now the other prong of the Argument from Self-Inconsistency, that the concept of God is self-inconsistent because of contradictions *between* omni-attributes, where these contradictions allegedly follow from the attempt to harmonize the attributes of power, knowledge, and goodness each to its maximal degree. We can reply to this charge just the way we did to the previous attack from the alleged self-inconsistency of individual omni-attributes. This involves repeating the point that even if it were to be established that it was logically impossible for God to be omnipotent, om-

---

[12] That there is an experience of God as "perfect" in the generic sense apart from what might be considered experiences of God as omnipotent, omniscient, and perfectly good distinguishes the case of God from cases where the experiences of an object or kind of object are themselves identifiable only by means of theories. In such cases were all available theories found to be inconsistent that would have grave consequences for the belief that the object or that kind of object existed. For example, suppose all available theories about electrons were found to be self-inconsistent. In that case, this would have grave consequences for the belief in the existence of "electrons," since putative observations of electrons count as such only within a theoretical framework. In the case of God, however, even if we wished to think of experiences of God as omnipotent, omniscient, and perfectly good as theory-laden, this would not have grave consequences for basing belief in God on experience. Since there are experiences of God as "perfect" in the generic sense, putative observations of God cannot be said to count as such only within a theoretical framework. Of course, one might want to say that the generic sense of perfect is also theory-laden. But even if so, that theory would be independent of the level of theory involved in the more detailed experiences of God, and thus remain intact even in case the latter doesn't remain intact.

niscient, and wholly good, that would not show that God was not absolutely perfect or was not perfect in power, knowledge, or goodness.

But there is a second reply available to us at this juncture.[13] The alleged discovery that the omni-attributes were mutually inconsistent needn't force the conclusion that the notion of God's perfection was internally contradictory. There is another way out. For what we might learn instead from the realization that different omni-attributes were not in logical harmony with one another is that we should discard the third tier's way of explicating God's perfection. Recall that the third tier consists in attributing to God power, knowledge, and goodness, *each individually*, to a perfect degree or in a maximal-value conferring way. Since God has power, for instance, and God is perfect, God's power, the thinking of this tier goes, must be maximal-value conferring. And the same for knowledge and goodness. Instead of adopting this understanding, however, we might define a *perfection set* as a consistent set of attributes which confers absolute perfection on a being who possesses that set (where to possess a set is to possess each of its members). And then we could maintain that the members of a perfection set need only be arranged together and exist in the set in individual degrees in such a way that *as a set* they confer absolute perfection on whoever possesses that set. This may not require that every member in a perfection set be such that each individually confers the maximal-value of a category of value which it confers on whoever possesses it. In fact it may not require it of *any* member of a perfection set. Whether every or any member of a perfection set does or does not confer maximal-value of a category of value which it confers on whoever possesses it is a matter which depends entirely upon the metaphysical facts about what makes for absolute perfection.

On this alternative understanding, then, the first tier consists of the generic concept of God's absolute perfection, the second tier consists of attributes such as power, knowledge, and goodness, and the third tier consists of the attribution to God of a perfection set made up, among others, of power, knowledge, and goodness, upon which God's perfection is supervenient.

But one might be moved to ask: does anything guarantee that there is not more than *one* perfection set which could confer absolute perfection upon God? Even fixing what the members of a perfection set must be, identified as "power", and so on, independent of their degrees, cannot

---

[13] With certain adjustments, this reply applies as well to the argument from individual self-inconsistencies in the omni-attributes.

different combinations of different degrees of them, respectively, give alternate perfection sets, each equally conferring absolute perfection? The simple reply is that the metaphysical facts will be what they will be, whether we know them or not. If there is only one perfection set the absolutely perfect being will have it. If there are more than one, the absolutely perfect being will have one of them. But, the protest might continue, which one? The answer again is that the metaphysical facts will be what they will be, whether we know them or not. How could there possibly be a basis for one perfection set being instantiated rather than another? We confess that we have no knowledge about this matter. At the same time we see no problem in its being a bare, brute metaphysical fact that one perfection set out of many, if many there be, be instantiated in an existing absolutely perfect being. Or maybe it is a broadly logically necessary truth that one particular perfection set be instantiated. We may not know or even be capable of knowing about any of this. But that hardly counts as evidence that an absolutely perfect being does not exist. Neither does it give any reason whatsoever for thinking the concept of an absolutely perfect being to be unclear or vague. There is nothing vague in the least about the idea of some perfection set or other conferring maximal possible value upon a being which possesses it.

Our second reply to the argument that the omni-attributes are mutually contradictory is, then, that even were this shown to be true this would not require the conclusion that the idea of God's absolute perfection was internally contradictory. For it may be maintained that all such a finding would prove is that the explication of God's perfection had been wrong and now must be revised. Indeed, that finding together with the experiences of God as absolutely perfect would provide the motivation for understanding the explication of God's perfection anew.

So we conclude again, now for a second reason, that even were the arguments correct that the omni-attributes were mutually contradictory, that would not diminish the evidential base of our argument for God's being experienced and thus existing.

We have now offered two replies to the cluster of charges included in the Argument from Self-Inconsistency. We conclude that even were all of the charges correct, they would not disprove the existence of an absolutely perfect being, although they would be a disproof of extant proposed ways of explicating the notion of God's absolute perfection. Since when God is experienced as perfect He is typically experienced as perfect in the generic sense, and, no doubt, experienced as powerful, knowledgeable, or good, it follows that even were the Argument from Self-Inconsistency correct, it would not affect our evidential base of experiences of God. This argument is therefore not a threat to our argument from BEE and STING, and not a threat either to an argument from BEE and STING to God's absolute perfection.

Evidence against
God's Existence II

I

We turn to the Argument from Evil. It is our contention that the argument provides no reason for thinking that an omnipotent, omniscient, wholly good being does not exist, and so provides no reason for thinking that God does not exist.

As noted in the preceding chapter, the Argument from Evil comes in two forms, the logical argument and the probabilistic argument. In turn, each breaks up into three arguments, one each from: (1) the existence of any evil at all, (2) the existence of particularly horrendous evils, and (3) the amount of evil in the world. We get, then, six different arguments from evil, three logical, (LE1)–(LE3), and three probabilistic, (PE1)–(PE3), as well as arguments resulting from merging premisses together from different arguments.

It is pretty widely held by philosophers today that the logical argument from evil is not successful, the main debate toward the close of the twentieth century being over the probabilistic argument. For that reason we will deal but briefly with the logical argument and devote ourself mainly to the probabilistic argument.

Argument (LE1) asserts that from

(1) An omnipotent, omniscient, and wholly good being exists.

it follows logically that:

(2) There exists no evil.

Some, such as David Hume, seem to have held that (1) by itself entails (2).[1] Others have offered auxiliary premises which together with (1) are supposed to entail (2). For example, J. L. Mackie offers this auxiliary premiss: "Good is opposed to evil in such a way that a being who is wholly good eliminates evil as far as he can, and there are no limits to what an omnipotent being can do."[2] But, the argument continues, (2) is obviously false, and, so, therefore is (1).

However, contrary to (LE1), (1) (either by itself or with Mackie's added premise) does not entail (2), but only:

(3) If evil exists, there is a morally justified reason for its existence.

(1), (3), and the falsity of (2) entail:

(4) The evil that exists is morally justified.

In order to show that the conjunction of (1) and (4) is logically impossible it would have to be shown that an omnipotent, omniscient, and wholly good being logically could not have a morally justifiable reason for allowing any evil. This has never been shown. And it would be difficult to show, because in order to do so one would have to know that of all of the logically possible ways in which morally justified results could be produced none of them logically required the existence of evil. Only in that way could it be shown that the logical constraints upon an omnipotent, omniscient, and wholly good being were not such as to permit the existence of evil for morally justified reasons.[3]

Corresponding replies apply to (LE2) and (LE3). (LE2) replaces (2) with a proposition of the form:

(2a) There exists no horrendous evil.

and (LE3) replaces (2) with a proposition of the form:

(2b) There does not exist N amount of evil.

[1] See David Hume, *Dialogues Concerning Natural Religion*, ed. Norman Kemp Smith (New York: Macmillan, 1947), part X.

[2] See J. L. Mackie, *The Miracle of Theism* (Oxford: Clarendon Press, 1982), p. 150. See Alvin Plantinga's discussion of an earlier version of Mackie's argument, in Alvin Plantinga, *God and Other Minds* (Ithaca: Cornell University Press, 1967), chapter 5.

[3] For more on the logical problem of evil see Nelson Pike, "Hume on Evil," *Philosophical Review* 72 (1963): 180–97, and Plantinga, *God and Other Minds*.

"N" numbering the amount of evil actually in the world. As before, however, (1) (either by itself or with Mackie's added premiss) does not entail either (2a) or (2b), but only, respectively:

(3a) If horrendous evil exists, there is a morally justified reason for its existence.

and:

(3b) If N amount of evil exists, there is a morally justified reason for its existence.

Once again, it would have to be shown that if an omnipotent, omniscient, and wholly good being existed it logically could not have a morally justifiable reason for allowing horrendous evil or N amount of evil in the world. This has never been shown. And an analogous reply is in place for the attempt to argue from the conjunction of the falsity of both (2a) and (2b) together.

We acknowledge that there might be persons for whom the existence of evils of particularly horrendous kinds or the amount of evil that besets our world constitutes a successful logical argument against the existence of an omnipotent, omniscient, and wholly good being. These would be people whose moral convictions included the belief that it was logically impossible for there to be any state of affairs that morally justified horrendous evils, or the amount of evil we know.

The idea is not that they would have disconfirmation of the existence of an omnipotent, omniscient, wholly good being because they could not *imagine* any moral justification, but rather that they possessed logically necessary moral principles on which it was sheerly impossible for there to be moral justification for the evils in question. And we acknowledge that in that case their evidence against the existence of an omnipotent, omniscient, and wholly good being might very well be stronger than the evidence for the existence of such a being from facts about experience of God.

At the same time, we doubt that there are many people who actually do believe that it is logically impossible for *horrendous evils* to be morally justified. And that is because there apparently are few people for whom there seems to be any moral problem or dilemma in having children. We should expect that a person who did think on moral principle alone that it was logically impossible for horrendous evils to be morally justified would find a problem in morally justifying having his own children, or at least would have some moral qualms about it. After all, given any randomly chosen individual there is some less than negligible chance that at some time or other in her life she will suffer a horrendous evil or else inflict a horrendous evil on others, or both.[4] But if it were logically impossible to morally justify such evils there would seem to be a moral problem in bringing more people into the world, because of thereby quite possibly being instrumental in increasing morally unjustifiable states of affairs in the universe.

Hereafter, in any case, our defense of our argument from the alleged experience of God is intended to be limited to those devoid of said moral sensibilities and so to those for whom the logical form of the Argument of Evil does not provide disproof of an omnipotent, omniscient, wholly good being.

II

The proponent of the probabilistic argument from evil can argue either that it is most improbable that an omnipotent, omniscient, wholly good being exists, or only that the existence of such a being is less probable on the facts about evil than it otherwise would be. There does not seem to be much chance of showing either of these from the mere existence of just any evil. Intuitively, if there is going to be a successful probabilistic argument it will have to be based on the distribution of evils in the world or on particularly horrendous evils, or both. An argument from both has been stated and defended in slightly different forms on different occasions by William Rowe.[5] Rowe argues that in light of the number of instances of

[4] For example, to name a few horrendous evils possibly awaiting her: people suffer from extreme poverty, are totally thwarted and defeated in their life's goals, live in misery from debilitating physical and psychological diseases, are tortured, terrorized, and subjugated by others, are wrongly jailed for many years, and die painful deaths.

[5] See William L. Rowe, "The Problem of Evil and Some Varieties of Atheism," *American Philosophical Quarterly* 16 (1979): 335–41, reprinted in *Contemporary Perspectives on Religious Epistemology*, ed. R. Douglas Geivett and Brendan Sweetman (Oxford: Oxford University Press, 1992), 33–42 (references to this article will be to the Geivett and Sweetman book); Rowe, "Evil and the Theistic Hypothesis: A Response to Wykstra," *International Journal for the Philosophy of Religion* 16 (1984): 95–100; Rowe "Evil and Theodicy," *Philosophical Topics* 16 (1988): 119–32; and Rowe, "Ruminations about Evil," *Philosophical Perspectives 5: Philosophy of Religion*, ed. James E. Tomberlin (Altascadero, Calif.: Ridgeview, 1991), pp. 69–88.

We have been helped in understanding the issues in Rowe's argument by Paul Draper, "Probabilistic Arguments from Evil," *Religious Studies* 28 (1992): 303–17.

intense suffering in the world it is most improbable that an omnipotent, omniscient, wholly good being exists. We take Rowe's argument to be the best attempt at a probabilistic argument against the existence of an omnipotent, omniscient, wholly good being, and so turn to an examination of it. Rowe argues that:

(R1) There exist instances of intense suffering which an omnipotent, omniscient being could have prevented without thereby losing some greater good or permitting some evil equally bad or worse.

(R2) An omnipotent, omniscient, wholly good being would prevent the occurrence of any intense suffering it could, unless it could not do so without thereby losing some greater good or permitting some evil equally bad or worse.

Therefore:

(R3) There does not exist an omnipotent, omniscient, wholly good being.[6]

Rowe defends (R1) by first focusing on a particular case of intense suffering, such as the agonizing death of a fawn from a forest fire or the rape and murder of a child, and then asserting that *so far as we can see* this particular evil is pointless. There does not seem to be any moral justification for it, based on "our understanding of the goods that do exist and that we can imagine coming into existence."[7] From this, concedes Rowe, it has not been *proven* that the evil in question is pointless. He notes that "perhaps, for all we know, there is some familiar good outweighing the fawn's suffering to which that suffering is connected in a way we do not see. Furthermore, there may well be unfamiliar goods, goods we haven't dreamed of, to which the fawn's suffering is inextricably connected."[8]

Nonetheless, continues Rowe, it would be *unreasonable* to believe this. And even if it were somehow to be shown to be reasonable in this *particular* instance, "in light of our experience and knowledge of the variety and

[6] Rowe, "The Problem of Evil and Some Varieties of Atheism," p. 34. Although Rowe puts his argument in terms of an "omnipotent, omniscient, wholly good being," he writes at the outset that his argument is meant to refute what he calls "narrow theism," which he characterizes as the belief in "the existence of an omnipotent, omniscient, *eternal*, supremely good being *who created the world*" (p. 33). Emphasis added. We will assume throughout our discussion that any being who is omnipotent, omniscient, and wholly good is also eternal and sufficiently in control of the world for Rowe's argument to go through.

[7] Rowe, "Evil and the Theistic Hypothesis," p. 96.

[8] Rowe, "The Problem of Evil and Some Varieties of Atheism," p. 36.

scale of human and animal suffering in our world, the idea that none of the suffering could have been [justifiably] prevented by an omnipotent being . . . seems an extraordinarily absurd idea, quite beyond our belief."[9] Rowe concludes that (R1) is probably true and that we have "rational support" for it. Hence, given the truth of (R2), the conclusion (R3) is probably true and we have rational support for believing that there does not exist an omnipotent, omniscient, wholly good being.

It will be useful for the ensuing discussion to represent Rowe as arguing in essence that since:

(A) It appears to us that there are no justifying goods for so much suffering.

it is therefore probable or most reasonable that:

(R) There really are no justifying goods for so much suffering.

and from (R), with auxiliary premises, that therefore it is probable or most reasonable that:

(O) No omnipotent, omniscient, wholly good being exists.

In replying to Rowe, Paul Draper argues that we are entitled to infer (R) from (A) only if we have good reason to believe that the sample of goods we have examined and found to have the property of not justifying the evils in question is "representative of all goods."[10] For Draper this condition is an instance of a general requirement that when projecting from a known sample to a general population, we have good reason to think that our sample is representative.

Draper continues by claiming that Rowe has no good reason to think that his sample of surveyed goods *is* representative of all goods.

In the first place, goods beyond our ken have no chance of belonging to Rowe's sample; so the sample is not random. Nor do we have any other good reasons for thinking that his sample is representative. Our information about the population in question—the class of all goods—is simply too limited to justify believing that the goods with which we are familiar are representative of all goods.[11]

[9] Ibid., p. 37.
[10] See Draper, "Probabilistic Arguments from Evil," p. 311.
[11] Ibid., p. 312.

Had Rowe's sample been random that would have counted in favor of its being representative. But it isn't, claims Draper. And we have no other good reason for thinking it representative. Hence, Rowe's inference fails to fulfill a necessary condition of its acceptability.

In order to clarify what we presume to be Draper's condition on probabilistic arguments, let's define the "projection class" of a probabilistic argument to be the class of objects about which the sample is being used to make a projection. If our sample is made up of ravens, and we wish to make a projection about the class of ravens, then ravens are our projection class. Our sample of ravens is also a collection of birds. However, if we wish to make a projection about the class of ravens, then birds are not our projection class, even though our sample is made up entirely of birds. Our sample of ravens may be representative of all ravens, but not of all birds.

Given this terminology, we believe Draper is requiring that there be good reason to believe that a sample is representative of the projection class of a probabilistic inference.[12] Let us say that a sample is *unbiased* when representative of the projection class with regard to those features which would negatively influence the warrant for our inference were the sample not to be representative in those ways. Otherwise it is *biased*. We are now in a position to formulate Draper's principle as follows:

(D) We are entitled to argue from our sample to our projection class only if we have good reason to believe that our sample is unbiased.

Prior to Draper's article Rowe had written that he was justified in arguing from much intense suffering that *appears* to us to be pointless, to the conclusion that in all probability it really *was* pointless, from (A) to (R) that is, as we regularly argue from the known to the unknown:

[12] There is an ambiguity here as to whether we must have good reason to believe that the sample is representative *per se* of the projection class or only that the sample is representative of the projection class with regard to those features which would negatively influence the warrant for our inference were the sample not to be representative in those ways. On the first alternative if our projection class were pit bulls, we would have to have a good reason for believing that our sample of pit bulls was representative of all the different ways pit bulls could be. On the second alternative we would have to have a good reason for believing our sample representative only of all the ways pit bulls could be which were such that its not being representative in those ways would negatively affect the warrant of our inference. Of the two, the second is the more plausible reading, and so we will adopt it as the interpretation of Draper's principle. In cases where we don't know what features would be relevant to our inference to our projection class and which not, the second reading will give way to the first.

All of us are constantly inferring from the A's we know of to the A's we don't know of. If we observe many A's and all of them are B's we are justified in believing that the A's we haven't observed are also B's. If I encounter a fair number of pit bulls and all of them are vicious, I have reason to believe that all pit bulls are vicious. Of course, there are all sorts of considerations that may defeat this inference. I may discover that all the pit bulls I've encountered have been trained for dog-fighting, a training that engenders viciousness. I may also come to know that there are pit bulls that are not so trained. If so, then this additional information, along with my initial information, may *not justify* me in believing that the pit bulls I haven't encountered are also vicious.[13]

Rowe's point is that until he learns of reasons for thinking his sample to *be* biased he is perfectly justified in inferring from the pit bulls he has known (if only from a distance, presumably) to those he has never seen.

This suggests that in place of (D) Rowe would endorse as a principle for projecting from a sample, something along the following lines:

(DR)   We are entitled to argue from our sample to our projection class only if we have no good reason to believe that our sample is biased.[14]

In the pit bull case we have no good reason to believe that our initial sample is biased, and so we are perfectly within our rights to proceed with our inductive generalization. Likewise, Rowe would presumably wish to say that in the case of seeking justifying goods for intense sufferings it may be that, for all we know, his particular sample of goods is biased; however we *have no good reason to believe* that it is. Hence Rowe is perfectly within his rights to infer that probably there are no justifying goods to be found.

For his part, Draper, using (D), would insist that to start with, Rowe must have good reason to think his sample of pit bulls was not biased, and similarly for Rowe's sample of justifying goods.

We believe that between the two, (DR), and not (D), is what we want. Were (D) true, we would always have to have good reason to believe that our sample was not biased. However, if we always had to have good reason for *that*, then such inferences would in fact never be warranted by inspection of our sample. And that is because then we could never have a good reason for thinking we had discovered a sample to be unbiased. And the reason for saying that begins with the fact that in any given case, for all we know, the number of ways in which a sample could possibly be biased is in

[13] Rowe, "Evil and Theodicy," pp. 123–24.
[14] See Draper, "Probabilistic Arguments from Evil," p. 312.

principle endless. At the very least there may be more ways than we can ever dream of for a sample to be biased. As many potential biases as there are that have been successfully eliminated, there may be more or even more than we have ever thought of. Hence, there is no way of knowing by mere enumeration that a sample is not biased in some way or other relevant to our inference.

The only way we could ever get a good reason for believing we had discovered a sample not to be biased, then, is by way of inductive, probabilistic support. However, were (D) true, that a sample was known to be unbiased in certain respects would not be a reason, let alone a good reason, for thinking it was unbiased per se.

Consider the structure of the inference from known ways in which a sample is not biased to the sample's probably being unbiased per se. Let the sample whose bias or lack of it we are judging be the "base sample." Then we are to envision a sample of potential biases which, in principle, the base sample could have had but which are found upon investigation to be absent in the case of the base sample. Let us call our sample of potential biases our "PB sample." We project from the base sample's lack of these biases to the population of potential biases at large, wishing to infer that probably the base sample does not have other potential biases either. From this we would conclude that the base sample was probably unbiased per se. But if (D) were true, we could not project from the PB sample to the general population of potential biases unless we had good reason to believe that our PB sample itself was unbiased. If we did not have a good reason to believe this, we would be barred, on the view we are challenging, from making any projection from the PB sample to the PB population. Since we cannot know all of the potential biases of the PB sample by enumeration, we must resort to an inductive or probabilistic inference from its *known* absences of biases to its absence of biases in general. Let us call our sample of biases known to be absent in the case of our PB sample the "PBPB sample." But of course if (D) were true, our PBPB sample itself would be worthless unless we had good reason to think that it, our PBPB sample, was unbiased. For that purpose we would have to construct for ourselves a PBPBPB sample. And of course, if it were true that (D), we would have to go on constructing higher and higher-ordered PB samples without end. We would have to go on indefinitely in the process of finding good reasons to think our samples were unbiased.[15]

---

[15] There may be some point in the chain of justifications at which the belief that a sample is unbiased is supported by a theory. However, the theory will have to be a well confirmed

We conclude that if (D) were true, in no case would we ever have a good reason for thinking that we had discovered our sample to be unbiased, because we could never get to the point of *having* the good reason. In fact we could never discover *any* reason for thinking this.

(D), therefore, turns out to be a skeptical constraint upon inductive reasoning. Since we recognize the validity of inductive reasoning we should reject the notion that (D) is true.

On the other hand, (DR) is implementable. For (DR) requires only that we have no good reason for thinking that our sample *is* biased. We see no difficulty in its coming about that we have no good reason of this sort. And (DR) does seem to be a necessary condition of the acceptability of inferences from a sample. So we accept (DR) as a condition of inductive inferences, and reject (D).

We contend, that is, that a probabilistic inference is disqualified if we have good reason for believing our sample to be biased. But it is not disqualified if we do not have a good reason for believing that our sample is *un*biased.

This is not to say that an inference would not merit more confidence the more reason we had for thinking our sample unbiased. We may be aware of a property, P (aside from the property of being an undersized sample), such that, for all we knew, P possibly belonged to our sample and was such that it would be a good thing for our sample not to have P rather than have it. If our sample lacked P, our argument would be more commanding then than it is now.

There are at least two reasons why it would be better for a sample not to have P than to have it, aside from the obvious instances where we want to project the lack of P onto the projection class. One would be that were our sample to have P that would be cause to suspect (or expect, or have good reason to believe) that our sample would be a biased sample with regard to the present inference. So it would be a good thing to be able to show that our sample did not have P. Let us call such a property a "Potential Bias Suspect," or "PBS." For example, suppose we have no good reason to believe our sample of pit bulls to be biased. This includes, let's say, our having no good reason for believing that all of the animals in our sample all belonged to the same strain of pit bulls. We then infer, and rightly so, from the viciousness of the pit bulls in our sample to their viciousness *at large*. At the same time suppose that, for all we know, possi-

---

one, and so supported, at least in part, by inductive inferences which confirm it. In that case, the infinite regress will not have been terminated at the theory.

bly our sample *is* comprised entirely of pit bulls of only one strain, whereas we know that there are many strains of pit bulls in the world. And suppose further, we realized that *were* this to be true of our sample this would be a reason to suspect that our sample was biased with regard to the present inference. It would be a good thing to be able to show in the first place that our sample of pit bulls was not biased in this way.

Note that we are not talking about a reason for believing that our sample *was* biased. What we are talking about is a reason for suspecting or believing that *were* our sample to be unrepresentative of our projection class in a certain way, that would raise a justifiable suspicion or more that our sample was biased for purposes of our present inference. The suspicions we are talking about are not real suspicions *that* our sample is biased. Not at all. They are suspicions about *properties* that our sample might or might not have, but which *were* it to have them would justify the suspicion that our sample was biased for present purposes.

In each case our suspicion would be based on an analogy between our present inference from our sample class, pit bulls, say, and other cases where we actually know or have good reason to think that an unrepresentativeness of this sort constitutes a bias. We have independent, positive reasons to think, for example, that different strains within the same species of animal would or might very well affect the character of the individuals in the species. By analogy, were our sample of pit bulls to be biased with respect to the strain of its members within the species, this would create a suspicion that our inference would to that extent be negatively affected.

Getting back to our example, suppose, as we have said, we have no good reason to believe our sample of pit bulls to be biased. This includes our having no good reason for thinking all of the animals in our sample to be of one strain. At the same time, for all we know, possibly our sample *is* comprised entirely of pit bulls of only one strain, whereas we know that there are many strains of pit bulls in the world. And, further, we realize that *were* this to be true of our sample this would be a reason to suspect, at least, that our sample was biased with regard to the present inference. The property of being a sample of only one strain of pit bulls is a PBS. Were we able to show that our sample was not unrepresentative in this way that would increase the strength of our inference. And in general, the more PBS's we find not to be possessed by our sample, the better is our inductive inference.

A second reason why it would be a good thing for our sample not to have a property, P, would arise when we were utilizing an inductive argument to disprove or weaken a belief or hypothesis, B. Suppose that were B to be true, it would follow that our sample would (have to) be ineffective against B were it to have P. In that case, even though our inductive inference would be fine and would be warranted even if we did not have a good reason for believing our sample *not* to have P, nevertheless in the context of combatting B our argument would be stronger were we able to show good reason for believing that our sample did *not* have P. If we were wishing to give a good proof against B, it would be helpful to have a good reason to believe that our sample did not have P. Let us call such a property a "Potential Bias Culprit," or "PBC".

For example, suppose that there was an entrenched belief, B, that of all pit bulls only one strain was vicious. Also suppose we collected a sample of pit bulls all of whom were found to be vicious. We have no good reason, suppose further, to believe that our sample is biased. Condition (DR) is fulfilled. We then are fine in inferring that all pit bulls are vicious, based on our sample. We have no reason to disqualify our inference. However, even though we would be justified in making that very inference, were it to be the case that *only* pit bulls of one strain were vicious it would follow that our sample "had" to be comprised only of animals from that strain. Hence, in the interest of disproving or weakening B it would be a good thing to be able to show that our sample was not comprised only of one strain of pit bulls. Were we unable to come up with a good reason for thinking our sample unbiased in the relevant way, our argument would be weaker against B than it could be.

The more PBS's and PBC's we can show our sample not to possess, the better is our argument. But the failure to eliminate them does not *disqualify* our argument as a proper probabilistic argument. The elimination of PBS's and PBC's gives ways of making such inferences better than they otherwise would be.

We suspect that any impression there might be that it is true that:

> (D) We are entitled to argue from our sample to our projection class only if we have good reason to believe that our sample is unbiased.

arises from a confusion between (D) and the very different claim that the more PBS's and PBC's we can show our sample not to possess, the better is our argument. And the reason for this confusion is that when reading (D), one is liable to implicitly be thinking *not* of finding a good reason for thinking our sample to be unbiased per se, but instead is liable to be wondering whether our sample is free of certain well known PBS's or PBC's, thus supplying an implicit context not provided for in (D); and one is liable to confuse what would make our inferences *better* with what is a necessary condition of their being warranted at all. Once these distinctions are made, the impression that (D) is a necessary condition of inductive inferences would hopefully dissipate itself.

Our conclusion is that Draper cannot judge Rowe's argument to be disqualified as a proper inference on the grounds that (D) is true. (D) is not acceptable. The most Draper can say against Rowe is that his argument would be stronger than it is were Rowe able to show that various relevant Potential Bias Suspects and various relevant Potential Bias Culprits were not possessed by his sample of goods. And this may very well be true. Deciding whether this is so and if so, deciding just how strong Rowe's argument is and how it compares when put up against our argument from the experience of God would be a complicated task indeed. Fortunately, however, we need not enter into it in order to be able to show good reason for thinking that Rowe's probabilistic argument from evil does not adversely affect our argument from experience of God. The reason for that is that we believe there to be good reason on other grounds for rejecting Rowe's argument. We will develop and present this reason by way of an examination of a critique of Rowe's argument given by Stephen Wykstra.

III

Stephen Wykstra has challenged Rowe's argument by means of a principle which he calls "the Condition of Reasonable Epistemic Access," or, "CORNEA." We reformulate CORNEA and call it "(W)" (the reformulation intended to avoid minor objections that can be raised against the original):

(W) It is reasonable for S to believe that solely on the basis of S's cognition of a situation C, she is entitled to claim that it appears to be true that p, only if it is reasonable for S to believe that if p were not the case, C would likely be appropriately different in a way discernable by S.[16]

where the reasonableness at issue in (W) has to do with external rationality, and not with the internal rationality of S.

[16] Stephen J. Wykstra, "The Humean Obstacle to Evidential Arguments from Suffering: On Avoiding the Evils of 'Appearance'," *International Journal for Philosophy of Religion* 16 (1984): 85. (See also Wykstra and Bruce Russell, "The 'Inductive' Argument from Evil: A Dialogue," *Philosophical Topics* 16 [1988]: 133–60.)

As applied to Rowe's defence of (R1), (W) yields:

(WR) It is reasonable for us to believe that solely on the basis of our
      observing no justifying goods we are entitled to claim that it ap-
      pears to be true that there are no justifying goods provided for by
      an omnipotent, omniscient, wholly good being only if it is reason-
      able for us to believe that if there were such goods our present
      observation would likely be appropriately different in a way dis-
      cernable by us.[17]

However, argues Wykstra, if an omnipotent, omniscient, wholly good
being exists then "there is good reason to think that if there is an outweighing good of the sort at issue connected to it, we would not have
epistemic access to this."[18] We have "epistemic access" to a state of affairs S,
just in case we can discern S to be the case. According to Wykstra, because
such an omnipotent, omniscient, wholly good being is so vastly superior to
us in vision and wisdom:

> It is entirely expectable—given what we know of our cognitive limits—that
> the goods by virtue of which this Being allows known suffering should very
> often be beyond our ken. Since this state of affairs is just what one should
> expect if theism were true, how can its obtaining be evidence *against* theism?[19]

Hence, concludes Wykstra, it is wholly *un*reasonable to believe that if there
were to exist justifying goods for the evils in question brought about by an
omnipotent, omniscient, wholly good being, we would have epistemic access to them. Hence it could not be reasonable to believe that we *would*
have epistemic access to them.[20] Hence, (W) is not fulfilled, and Rowe's
defence of (R1) collapses.

Rowe has replied to Wykstra's objection by saying that the mere fact
that an omnipotent, omniscient, wholly good being existed would not be a
reason to expect that if there were justifying goods for the evils in question
we would not have epistemic access to them. This is because the "mere
assumption" that such a being exists "gives us no reason whatever to suppose *either* that the greater goods in virtue of which he permits most suffering are goods that come into existence far in the future of the sufferings we
are aware of, or that once they obtain we continue to be ignorant of them

[17] See S. Wykstra, "The Humean Obstacle," p. 89.
[18] Ibid., p. 88. Emphasis in original.
[19] Ibid., p. 91.
[20] Ibid., p. 87.

and their relation to the sufferings."[21] Rowe's point seems to be that given the existence of such a being, it is true that there is reason to believe that the justifying goods *could* be undiscernible by us, but that is no reason yet to expect that they *would* be undiscernible by us. There is nothing strange or otherwise suspicious about the idea of an omnipotent, omniscient, wholly good being who decides to act only in ways that are perfectly perspicuous to his creatures. And so it follows that the hypothesis of an omnipotent, omniscient, wholly good being gives us no reason to believe that we would *not* have epistemic access to the justifying goods that such a being allows or brings about.[22]

We begin our assessment of this exchange between Rowe and Wykstra by considering (W). (W) is an acceptable principle to us if understood as:

(W1)   It is reasonable for S to believe that solely on the basis of S's cognition of a situation C, she is entitled to claim that it appears to be true that p, only if S has no good reason to believe that if p were not the case, C would not likely be appropriately different in a way discernable by S.[23]

But (W) is not acceptable if it means the same as:

(W2)   It is reasonable for S to believe that solely on the basis of S's cognition of a situation C, she is entitled to claim that it appears to be true that p, only if S has good reason to believe that if p were not the case, C would likely be appropriately different in a way discernable by S.

[21] Rowe, "Evil and the Theistic Hypothesis," p. 98.

[22] Rowe's reply to Wykstra actually differs slightly from what we have attributed to him, this having to do with Rowe's interpretation of Wykstra's principle. We are putting what we take to be the best face on Rowe's reply, and so will connect Rowe's reply to (W1), a principle we take to be true.

[23] In truth, (W1) stands in need of supplementation for at least two reasons:

(1) It is reasonable for S to believe that S exists, solely on the basis of cognizing her own existence, even though it is false that S has no good reason to believe that were she not to exist she would not discern that fact. We trust that (W1) can be stated so as to skirt this objection. I owe this point to David Widerker.

(2) A stronger principle than (W1) is needed for the modes of cognition themselves. With regard to them, S must have good reason to believe that they grant her epistemic access to the present situation. It's not enough to require that S have no reason for believing that they do not. After all, S must have a good reason in the first place for thinking that she can tell whether the milk is sour or not by *smelling* it. It's not enough to require that S simply have no reason for thinking that she can't detect whether the milk is sour by smelling out. We exclude the modes of cognition from the purview of (W1) and trust that an appropriate principle can be formulated for them.

(W1) bears an affinity to what appears in Chapter 5 as the "E-Reductionist Principle."

Our objection to (W2) is as follows. Suppose you smell the milk to determine whether or not it is sour. On the basis of the way it smells you conclude that the milk is not sour. On (W2) it is reasonable for you to believe that you are entitled to make this inference only if you have good reason to believe that if the milk were sour you would not have smelled it to be fresh. But consider the possibility that the milk really is sour but that it emits invisible smell-blockers, small particles or whatever, which mask the sour smell. Let's call this hypothesis (B). If (B) were true, you would not have epistemic access by smell to the milk's being sour even if it were. So it is reasonable for you to believe that you do have epistemic access to the milk's sour smell only if you have good reason to believe that the milk does not emit smell-blockers. But on (W2) you could not have good reason on the basis of observation to believe that there were no smell-blockers. For on (W2), you would have such a reason only if you had good reason to believe that if there were smell-blockers present you would have epistemic access to their being present. But suppose there existed smell-blocker blockers, invisible particles or whatever which blocked one's ability to discern the presence of smell-blockers. On (W2) you would have a good reason to believe that there were no smell-blockers only if you had a good reason to believe that there were no smell-blocker blockers. But on (W2) you would have a good reason to believe that there were no smell-blocker blockers only if you had a good reason to believe that there were no smell-blocker blocker blockers, and so on, until the end of all generations.

At some point, of course, you might have a good reason for any of the beliefs in question on the basis of some well confirmed theory on which it followed that there did not exist blockers of the requisite level. But presumably any such theory will have been confirmed at least in part by an inductive inference of some sort. Concerning that inductive inference you would have to have a good reason to believe that there existed no blockers of a type which blocked epistemic access to a negative result. And with regard to the theory itself, on (W2) you would have good reason to adopt the theory only if you had good reason to believe that there were no theory-blockers, invisible particles or whatever, which when they attack us prevent us from seeing that this theory is false when it is. So once again the infinite regress is in place. Hence, were (W2) acceptable, you could never have a good reason based on observation to believe that the milk was not sour on the grounds that it smelled fresh. But surely you do have good reason to believe that on the basis of observation. And the reason why it is reasonable is because you do not have to have a reason for thinking that you have epistemic access to the smell of the milk if it is sour (aside from your reason for thinking that smell is a sensory mode for detecting the sourness).[24] It is only necessary that you have no reason for thinking that you do not have epistemic access to it. So (W2) must be rejected.

Wykstra does not need (W) in the form of (W2), though, to make his protest against Rowe. For since Wykstra wishes to argue only that if an omnipotent, omniscient, wholly good being existed we would have a good reason to believe that we would *not* have epistemic access to justifying goods, he could make this argument with the application of (W1) as:

(WR1) It is reasonable for us to believe that solely on the basis of our observing no justifying goods we are entitled to claim that it appears to be true that there are no justifying goods provided for by an omnipotent, omniscient, wholly good being, only if we have no good reason to believe that if there were such goods our present observation would not likely be appropriately different in a way discernable by us.

Wykstra could then proceed as before to argue that we *do* have good reason to believe that if there were to exist justifying goods for the evils in question, goods brought about by an omnipotent, omniscient, wholly good being, we would *not* have epistemic access to them.

Accepting (W1) and (WR1), then, we proceed to an evaluation of Wykstra's argument construed as arguing from (WR1) and from the claim that were an omnipotent, omniscient, wholly good being to exist we should expect that we would not have epistemic access to justifying goods.

Rowe is right, against Wykstra, in insisting that in itself the existence of an omnipotent, omniscient, wholly good being does not give us any reason to believe we would *not* have epistemic access to justifying goods were they to exist. As we have said, there is nothing odd a priori about the supposition that such a being should create a world transparent to human creatures. However, this having been said, Rowe's argument does not afford a reason to believe that an omnipotent, omniscient, wholly good being probably does not exist.

To see why Rowe's argument fails, we must distinguish between two quite different claims that Rowe might want to make. One is that:

(J1) Prior to consideration of the world's suffering and our continuing inability to discover justifying goods, we have no good reason to think that *if* there existed an omnipotent, omniscient, wholly good being, then if there existed justifying goods we would not have epistemic access to them.

[24] See item (2) in note 23.

and the other:

> (J2) In a situation with as much intense suffering as we know the
> world to have and in which we are continually unable to discover
> justifying goods, we have no good reason to think that *if* there
> (then) existed an omnipotent, omniscient, wholly good being,
> then if there existed justifying goods we would not have epistemic
> access to them.

(J1) is true. In the "a priori position" there is no reason to believe that an
omnipotent, omniscient, wholly good being would *not* govern the world
in a way quite transparent to human experience and reason. Hence there is
no a priori reason to *expect* that justifying goods would escape our understanding if they existed. But (J2) is simply false. And (J2) is false because in
the face of the frequency of suffering and our continuing inability to discover justifying goods, we *do* have good reason to believe that *if* an omnipotent, omniscient, wholly good being (then) existed then we would not
have epistemic access to the justifying goods, if they existed. And the reason for thinking that is that in light of the way the world appears to us it
would be incompatible with the existence of such a being to suppose that
there were no justifying goods, given the infinite power and unlimited
good intentions and knowledge of that being. But since we know of no
such goods, after considering the matter at length, it must therefore be the
case that *if* an omnipotent, omniscient, wholly good being (now) exists,
the justifying goods exist and are not epistemically accessible to us.[25]
    In effect, Rowe wishes to argue from:

> (A) It appears to us that there are no justifying goods for so much
> suffering.

with the auxiliary premise:

> (J) We have no good reason to think that if there existed an omnipo-
> tent, omniscient, wholly good being then justifying evils would
> not be epistemically accessible to us.

to the conclusion that we have good reason to conclude that

> (O) No omnipotent, omniscient, wholly good being exists.

[25] This reply to Rowe should not be confused with what he calls the "G. E. Moore shift,"
which says that *since* an omnipotent, omniscient, wholly good being exists, therefore all of
the world's suffering is justified. Our reply does not depend on asserting that an omnipotent,
omniscient, wholly good being exists.

We now see that this is a mistake, for (J) is true only as (J1), only a priori to our experience of the world's inexplicable (to us) suffering. But given our experience of the world, acknowledged in (A), (J) is no longer true. It is not true that we *now* have no good reason to think that if there existed an omnipotent, omniscient, wholly good being then justifying goods would be epistemically inaccessible to us. It is now reasonable, given the way the world is, to believe that *if* there were to exist justifying goods for the evils in question brought about by an omnipotent, omniscient, wholly good being we would *not* have epistemic access to them. Hence (WR1) is violated, and the inference from (A) to (O) fails. What we should infer from (A), instead, is that we have good reason to believe that *if* an omnipotent, omniscient, wholly good being exists, the justifying goods of the world's suffering are hidden from us. We should not infer that no omnipotent, omniscient, wholly good being exists.

To better bring out the logic of the situation here, consider an illustration having a somewhat similar logic. Consider the hypothesis: The British will attack. From what we know of the capabilities of the British, a priori, as it were, there are two equal possibilities: the British can attack by land or by sea. Hence from the a priori situation,

(SB) We have no good reason to believe that if the British attack, they will attack by sea.

since there is the equal possibility they will attack by land.

Similarly,

(LB) We have no good reason to believe that if the British attack, they will attack by land.

since there is the equal possibility they will attack by sea.

Subsequently, we learn that the British will not attack by land. Then, of course, it would be folly to continue to affirm (SB). For we are then not in the a priori position any longer. We would then have good reason to believe that *if* the British attack, they *will* attack by sea. And we would have no reason whatsoever for believing that the British will *not* attack at all.

The only instance in which our learning that the British will not attack by land would give us good reason to believe they will not attack at all would be if at the outset in the a priori position instead of (LB) it were true that: We have good reason to believe that if the British attack at all, they will attack by land. Only in that case does the information that they will not attack by land give us a good reason for believing they will not attack at all. But given (LB)'s truth at the start, we have no good reason for believing the British will not attack at all just because we know they will not attack by land. Similarly we have no reason to believe that if the British do not attack by land, it is then less probable than it would be otherwise that they will attack at all.

This is similar to Rowe's argument. Consider the hypothesis that an omnipotent, omniscient, wholly good being exists. This entails that all of the world's suffering is justified. While it is true that we have no good reason to *expect* that the justifying goods would be hidden from us, nevertheless, given the vast amount of power, knowledge, and good will of this higher being we have good reason *to take into account* the *possibility* that the justifying goods, or at least a good portion of them, would be hidden from us. The fact that this being's options are so vastly greatly than ours—are infinite—should make us alive to the (not just logical, but actual) possibility that some or many or all of the justifying goods would be beyond our ken. (This is a different claim from Wykstra's that we should *expect* the justifying goods to be hidden.) So, in the a priori position we have reason to entertain in a serious way two kinds of justifications of the evils: revealed justifications that we know about or can find out about, and justifications beyond our ken.

In the a priori position we can assert both that:

(KR) We have no good reason to believe that if there exists an omnipotent, omniscient, wholly good being, then the justifying goods will be known to us.

and:

(UR) We have no good reason to believe that if there exists an omnipotent, omniscient, wholly good being, then the justifying goods will be *un*known to us.

Now, it is true that people experience the world to be full of suffering not justified by goods known to them. What we should conclude is not that no omnipotent, omniscient, wholly good being exists, but rather that we now have a good reason to conclude that *if* there exists an omnipotent, omniscient, wholly good being the justifying goods are *un*known to us.

There is one instance in which our coming to know that the sufferings of the world were not justified by goods known to us *would* give good reason for believing that an omnipotent, omniscient, wholly good being did not at all exist. That would be if instead of (KR) being true at the outset, it were true that: We *have* good reason to believe that if there exists an omnipotent, omniscient, wholly good being, then the justifying goods *will* be known to us. But that would be just clearly false. At the outset, in the a priori position, there is absolutely no reason whatever to believe either that the justifying goods *would* be known to us or that they would *not* be known to us, were an omnipotent, omniscient, wholly good being to exist.

And at the outset there is also no reason to believe that if an omnipotent, omniscient, wholly good being existed it would be more *likely* that justifying goods would be known to us than that they would not be known to us. If anything, the opposite is the case. Hence, Rowe's argument could not be used even to show that the world's evils make the existence of an omnipotent, omniscient, wholly good being less likely than it would be otherwise.

Common to the British example and to the problem of evil is that at the outset there are two alternatives worthy of consideration, and there is no good reason to believe that either alternative is more likely than the other. This is what separates these two cases from, say, considering the hypothesis that there is a chair in the room, then finding no chair, and thus concluding that there is a chair there but it is invisible. We all take it that the hypothesis that an invisible chair is in the room is not worthy of consideration. It need not be taken into account. Hence, this case is different from either the example of the British or of the problem of evil. That the British will attack by sea is a real possibility, as it is that an omnipotent, omniscient, wholly good being will bring about goods beyond our ken.

A difference between the British case and the problem of evil might be that our having to take into account both an attack by land and an attack by sea has to do with prior experience by armies, or by the British army itself, of attacks by land and by sea. We have familiarity with both kinds of attacks, and that's why each alternative is *worthy* of consideration. In the problem of evil, on the other hand, our having to take into account both open and hidden justifying goods does not derive from any past familiarity with the ways of an omnipotent, omniscient, wholly good being. This does not change the fact, however, that we have good reason to take into account that an omnipotent, omniscient, wholly good being *might* bring about goods beyond our ken. But if that is not a satisfying answer, we can invent an exactly parallel case to the problem of evil by pretending that there has never been a military attack in the world before this, but that we do know that the British *have* both land and sea forces, and we are considering the hypothesis that the British will attack.[26] This case is similar to the situation with the probability argument from evil. In each case both alternatives are worthy of consideration because both present themselves as real possibilities.

To sharpen our reply to the probabilistic argument from evil, return to the milk and the smell-blockers. You smell the milk and it smells nonsour. You conclude that in all probability it is not sour. Now the fact is that there is good reason to believe that *if* the milk is sour but emits smell-blockers then you would not detect the sourness by smell. But it would be absurd to refuse to believe the milk was not sour just because of that. Yet we are claiming that just because there seems to us to be no justifying goods is not a good reason for believing that there simply *are* no such goods, in the face of the hypothesis that *if* there exists an omnipotent, omniscient, wholly good being the goods are unknown to us. Why shouldn't unknown goods provided for by an omnipotent, omniscient, wholly good being be like sour milk whose sourness is masked by smell-blockers? Why shouldn't hidden goods be like blocked smells?

Our reply is that in the milk example we are simply not prepared to entertain the hypothesis that the milk is sour and emits smell-blockers. We refuse to take this hypothesis seriously. We believe, for whatever reason, that it is plainly false. The case of Rowe's argument would be similar only if we were not prepared to take seriously the very idea that an omnipotent, omniscient, wholly good being existed who provided justifying goods beyond our ken. But it is hardly justified to invoke this refusal as a reason for rejecting our reply to Rowe. After all, the whole point of Rowe's argument is to show that it is improbable to think that an omnipotent, omniscient, wholly good being exists who provides justifying goods beyond our ken. It would not be enough to have shown only that such an idea was improbable after we had refused to entertain that possibility. It would not be enough because in the context of our inquiry we would have to be given a reason for refusing to entertain that hypothesis. And so Rowe's argument would be incomplete because no such reason has been given, and of course were it to be given Rowe's argument would become superfluous.

One way to show that the hypothesis was not worthy of being entertained would be to show that to begin with the belief that an omnipotent, omniscient, wholly good being existed was improbable. Another way would be to show that even if such a being did exist it would be improb-

---

[26] We ask the reader to ignore the impact on the example of the unlikelihood that an attack will take place since no army has ever attacked in the past. Pretend that the British have the first army that has ever been formed.

able that it provided justifying goods beyond our ken. As for the first alternative, were it to be invoked here, it would make Rowe's argument utterly
dependent upon other good reasons for believing that an omnipotent, omniscient, wholly good being did not exist. Rowe's argument would no
longer be an independent reason for thinking that.

As for the second alternative—that it is improbable to suppose that even
were such a being to exist it would provide (not: *have* to provide) justifying
goods beyond our ken for suffering in the world—it fares no better. As we
have already remarked, this is a clearly false proposition. Why should anybody think in advance that an omnipotent, omniscient, wholly good being
would not (not: would not *have* to) provide justifying goods beyond our
ken? What would an argument that explains this look like? Is the idea
perhaps that it might be likely that such a being would provide justification
beyond our ken for a *few* evils or for less horrendous evils than there are,
but not for those we know to exist? But what would make it improbable?
It's hard to see on what grounds one could even begin to argue this for an
omnipotent, omniscient, wholly good being.

Indeed, we suspect that the probabilistic argument from evil is thought
to show that an omnipotent, omniscient, wholly good being probably
doesn't exist only by those who in any case are not prepared to entertain
the hypothesis that one does exist, for those to whom the idea of an omnipotent, omniscient, wholly good being who justifies evils is as about
inviting as the idea of smell-blockers. They then think that they have
found in the argument a *reason* for their unwillingness. If we are right,
Rowe's argument would work for such persons only as a kind of "coherentist" device, showing that *if* we reject the idea of the existence of a
omnipotent, omniscient, wholly good being who provides justifying
goods that rejection will find confirmation by what we know of the
world's evils. That use of the argument does not show, however, that it is
in any way or form improbable on the basis of the evidence that an
omnipotent, omniscient, wholly good being does not exist. In fact, the
world's intense sufferings are not a reason for believing it improbable that
such a being exists.

We therefore conclude that Rowe's probabilistic argument gives us no
reason to believe that an omnipotent, omniscient, wholly good being does
not exist. And by reasoning that is partially already noted and similar to the
above it also follows that the existence of the numerous instances of intense
suffering in the world does not even make the existence of an omnipotent,
omniscient, wholly good being *less probable* than it would be otherwise. For
it to do so, it would have to be the case in the a priori position that we

have good reason to believe that if there existed an omnipotent, omniscient, wholly good being, then there would be *more likelihood* that justifying goods would be known to us than that they would not be known to us. But while we might have no reason to believe that were such a being to exist the justifying goods would more likely than *not* be unknown to us, we equally have no reason at all for believing it more likely than not that they *would* be known to us.

We conclude that the probabilistic argument from evil, incarnated in Rowe's argument, fails to give any reason for thinking that an omnipotent, omniscient, wholly good being does not exist, because

(A) It appears to us that there are no justifying goods for so much suffering.

fails to provide a good reason for:

(O) No omnipotent, omniscient, wholly good being exists.

IV

In this section we want to consider what the implications would be for our argument from putative experiences of God as perfect, based on BEE and STING, were we to suppose, contrary to fact, that (A) did show that (O) was probable.[27] Supposing that the world's evils did show that it was improbable that an omnipotent, omniscient, wholly good being existed, what would the repercussions of this finding be on our argument from experience of God?

The evidence in favor of God's being perfect involves putative *perceptions* of God, whereas the evidence from evil against the existence of an omnipotent, omniscient, wholly good being would be, relative to that, perceptually *indirect* evidence. In general, everything else being equal, evidence in favor of the existence of an object O which consists of putative perceptions of O is to be favored over perceptually indirect evidence against the presence of O. The putative experience of the presence of an object enjoys evidential priority over indirect evidence that the object is not present. For example, suppose it were highly unlikely that anybody could be present in a small, empty room, because the room had been locked and the keys were

[27] In this section we will be ignoring the conceptual distinction we argued for in the previous chapter between God's being perfect in a generic sense, and God's being omnipotent, omniscient, and wholly good. We will pretend for the sake of this section that being perfect is conceptually the same as being omnipotent, omniscient, and wholly good.

in your pocket, and because before locking it you verified that no one was in there. Upon opening the room, however, you *seem* to encounter there a human being who walks and talks before your very eyes. Your apparent direct perception of the person has evidential priority over the perceptually indirect evidence you have that no one could be there. Everything else being equal, it would be more reasonable to believe that the person was there than not, against the perceptually indirect evidence that no one could be there. Everything else being equal, it would be more reasonable to believe that there must be a good explanation for the person being there than to believe that you were having a delusory experience.

In order for perceptually indirect evidence to outweigh direct perceptual evidence it has to be so strong as to make it reasonable to think that the subject had an hallucination of O, or at the least had a misperception of an object other than O. Our rational commitment to the value of perception requires very strong indirect evidence for such a move.

It follows that even were Rowe's argument correct it might not be sufficient to force a retreat from our argument from experience of God to the conclusion that God exists or that a perfect being exists. At the outset, each perceptually direct episode in favor of the presence of God may have more internal evidential strength than does each instance of perceptually indirect evidence, (provided by a case of suffering) against the existence of such a being. It would have to be the case that the total negative evidence from the world's suffering was stronger than that of the total number of episodes of experiences of the requisite sort, in order for it to follow that God or an absolutely perfect being was not really experienced, and that the alleged experiences were mere apparitions or misperceptions. It is not entirely clear, therefore, that Rowe's argument would succeed against our argument from experience of God even if its premises warranted accepting its conclusion. (It is also not entirely clear, however, that it would *not* ultimately succeed.)

This means we have a reason for thinking that Rowe's argument, even if successful, *might* not be ultimately decisive against our argument from experience of God. We have, though, in addition, a good reason to believe that Rowe's argument, even if successful in showing the improbability of an omnipotent, omniscient, wholly good being, would *not* be successful in weakening in the least our argument from BEE and STING. In order to set out this reason we attend to a distinction Rowe himself makes between "restricted standard theism," and "expanded standard theism," and to Rowe's correct observation that his argument, if correct, counts only against the former and not against the latter.

Rowe calls "standard theism" any view which holds or entails that there exists an omnipotent, omniscient, wholly good being.[28] "Expanded standard theism" is, for Rowe, the view that an omnipotent, omniscient, wholly good being exists "conjoined with other religious claims about sin, redemption, a future life, a last judgment, and the like." "Restricted standard theism," "RST," on the other hand, is the view that there exists an omnipotent, omniscient, wholly good being, "unaccompanied by other, independent religious claims."

Rowe claims that his probabilistic argument from evil shows that RST is probably false, because that it appears to us that there are no justifying goods for much suffering, shows, with auxiliary premises, that it is improbable that an omnipotent, omniscient, wholly good being exists. Rowe correctly sees that even if this is true, there are versions of expanded theism for which this is clearly not the case. In particular, says Rowe, suppose we added to RST the hypothesis that the justifying goods for vast amounts of suffering will be realized only at the end of days, getting what Rowe calls, "EST." The fact that it appears to us that there do not exist justifying goods would not render EST unlikely or more unlikely than it would be otherwise. And that is because it is what we all would agree we should *expect* were EST's added hypothesis true. Hence, Rowe avers, EST is not damaged by Rowe's argument. And of course there could be other versions of expanded standard theism besides EST which Rowe's argument would not touch.

Now, if alleged experiences of God supported RST alone, and did not support a version of expanded theism, then the evidence provided by such experiences, on BEE and STING, would have to contend with the counterevidence of Rowe's argument from evil against RST, were the latter to be a successful argument. It would be of no help to us if the conclusion that God exists could be augmented by auxiliary hypotheses *not supported by putative experiences of God* to create a version of expanded standard theism which escaped from Rowe's argument. After all, the thesis of this entire book has been that the facts about apparent experiences of God were sufficient all *by themselves* to make belief in God strongly rational. That thesis could not be made immune from Rowe's argument by adding on independent auxiliary hypotheses.

[28] Rowe, "Evil and the Theistic Hypothesis," p. 95. Actually, Rowe includes that this being "created the world." For simplicity, and since Rowe himself omits this clause in the statement of his argument, we omit this and assume simply that any omnipotent, omniscient, wholly good being would be sufficiently in control of the world for Rowe's argument to function.

In our defense, then, we wish to argue for the thesis that not only do putative experiences of God support RST, they support as well a version of expanded standard theism which is clearly immune from Rowe's evidential argument, as Rowe himself would be the first to admit. Hence, even were we to suppose Rowe's argument from evil to be correct against RST, we would have been given no reason to think that it damaged our argument from experience of God.

The way in which Rowe's argument might damage our argument from BEE and STING is by casting doubt on those experiences in which God is allegedly known as a perfect being. And if for that reason those alleged experiences of God were to be subtracted from the total experiential evidence for God's existence, this would appreciably weaken our argument's evidential base. However, and this is our claim, if those very alleged experiences of God in which God is perceived as an absolutely perfect being also support a version of expanded theism not touched by Rowe's argument, then even if Rowe's argument were successful, it would do nothing to weaken the evidential base of our argument.

The reason we believe that putative experiences of God as perfect support a version of expanded standard theism immune to Rowe's argument has to do, first, with the fact that such experiences also support the belief that God is an inscrutable mystery, as noted in this work. When God is *revealed* in experience He is covered up as well as revealed and known. God "dwells in thick darkness." This does not refer merely to someone's sense of failing to know God, but refers to the disclosure of an actual positive quality of God's. God, even when revealed, is discerned (in a positive way) to be largely mysterious and inscrutable. God is perceived to be massively uncomprehended and unintelligible. Rudolf Otto noted, in a particularly strong version of the present point that:

> The truly "mysterious" object is beyond our apprehension and comprehension, not only because our knowledge has certain irremovable limits, but because in it we come upon something inherently "wholly other," whose kind and character are incommensurable with our own, and before which we therefore recoil in a wonder that strikes us chill and numb.[29]

An experience of God as absolutely perfect is often not an experience of a "transparent" object, which as far as the experience goes might just as well proceed to act in ways perfectly clear to us as not. Rather, to experi-

[29] Rudolf Otto, *The Idea of the Holy*, trans. John W. Harvey (London: Oxford University Press, 1957), p. 28.

ence God as absolutely perfect is often enough a matter of perceiving an object that—no matter what is revealed about it—is also perceived to be otherwise positively impenetrable, and therefore about which we have every right to believe that its ways will *not* be transparent to us.

Those very experiences in which God is allegedly known as perfect, therefore, themselves present us with a good reason to believe that God is perfect *and* that His ways are inscrutable.

Furthermore, experiences of God as perfect disclose to their subjects the glimpse of a good to be valued beyond all other goods. This is the good of being in God's presence, of beholding the Divine Beatitude. This glimpse in its partial nature is already so precious that together with the revealed nature of God as absolutely perfect it points to a fullness of actualization which, if only known, would be seen to be incommensurable with the preciousness of all else. And so this glimpse provides reason for thinking that *somehow*, we know not how, beholding the Divine Beatitude will make all of the suffering and sorrow of the world worthwhile. The perfection and mystery and inscrutability of God taken all together hold out the promise that God's sovereign good will be realized in its true glory, and give reason to believe that while we cannot know how this will come about or how the evils of this world are required to bring it, nonetheless it will come about and the evils of this world will be justified, somehow, thereby.

Hence, experiences of God as perfect support not only restricted standard theism, but also the following version of expanded standard theism, which we shall call "perceptual theism," or "PT":

> There exists an absolutely perfect being, God, who is mysterious and inscrutable, who will bring about the sovereign good of knowing Him, in its fullness, which good has the power to justify (we know not how) all of the world's suffering and sorrow.

Experiences of God as perfect, we wish to claim, support PT without benefit of attached auxiliary hypotheses. But then the premise in Rowe's argument:

> (A) It appears to us that there are no justifying goods for so much suffering.

is not true. Or to put it more carefully, (A) could appear to be true only to a person who was not taking into consideration all of the available evidence. Were we to take into consideration all of the available evidence, including experiences of God as perfect and what they disclosed, it would then indeed appear to us that there were or will be or must be justifying goods for so much suffering.

In any event, Rowe's argument fails to show that PT is false. It fails to show, that is, that in light of (A) it is improbable that there exists an absolutely perfect being, mysterious and inscrutable, who will bring about the sovereign good of knowing Him, in its fullness, which good has the power to justify (we know not how) all of the world's suffering and sorrow. And neither does it show that PT is less probable that it would otherwise have been.

We can now summarize our discussion of the Argument from Evil. We briefly considered and dismissed the charge that the existence of evil in itself or in particularly horrendous forms or in the quantity we find in the world is logically incompatible with the existence of an omnipotent, omniscient, wholly good being. We then examined the probabilistic argument from evil in the form of Rowe's argument. We found that it does not give any reason to believe that standard theism:

> There exists an omnipotent, omniscient, wholly good being.

is probably false. And we also found that even had it shown this, it would not have given us any reason for thinking that perceptual theism:

> There exists an absolutely perfect being, God, who is mysterious and inscrutable, who will bring about the sovereign good of knowing Him, in its fullness, which good has the power to justify (we know not how) all of the world's suffering and sorrow.

was probably false, where perceptual theism is supported by putative perceptions of God as perfect.

Neither does the probabilistic argument from evil give us any reason to believe that standard or perceptual theism is less likely on the facts about evil than it would be otherwise.

Therefore, we are not even called upon to weigh the evidence from the experience of God on *behalf* of the existence of an absolutely perfect being opposite the evidence from evil *against* the existence of such a being. Neither the logical nor the probabilistic forms of the Argument from Evil pose any counter-evidential threat whatsoever to the existence of a perfect being as disclosed in experiences of God.

Prior to discussing the Argument from Evil, we examined and turned back the charge that the very concept of an absolutely perfect being was self-inconsistent or logically defective.

In addition, there is every reason to believe that there is no successful analogue of the Argument from Self-Inconsistency or of the Argument from Evil against the existence of a "supreme being," as characterized in this work. The idea of a being "very high on the scale of perfection" is surely a logically coherent one. And just as surely there is no logical contradiction between evil, any evil, and the existence of a being very high on the scale of perfection upon whom the world depends in some important way.

Neither does the probabilistic argument from evil count against the existence of a supreme being, since the analogue of (R1), in Rowe's argument:

(R1)′ There exist instances of intense suffering which a supreme being could have prevented without thereby losing some greater good or permitting some evil equally bad or worse.

is wholly unsupported. As we have noted earlier, for all we know, given the world's evils, there might very well exist a being who is very high on the scale of perfection and upon which all other beings depend, who is constantly fighting the world's evils with great success; this being has managed to prevent enormous amounts of suffering and has engineered immense amounts of good; there isn't a person whom this being has not saved from catastrophe. But all of this has been achieved within the limitations of the supreme being's own power and knowledge, which, unfortunately, are not able to eliminate a lot of the worst evils and not able to bring evil down to less than it in fact is.

We conclude that neither the Argument from Self-Inconsistency nor the Argument from Evil provide any evidence against the existence of a supreme being or a perfect being. We conclude, therefore, that they provide no evidence against the existence of God.[30]

V

It follows from what was shown in this work prior to our examination of the Argument from Self-Inconsistency and the Argument from Evil, that:

[30] This conclusion applies with the exception, as noted earlier, of a person who holds a rock-bottom moral principle on which it follows that horrendous evil cannot be morally justified.

(1) If there is no evidence against the existence of God, then it is strongly rational to believe that God is experienced and thus exists.[31]

On the face of it, the Argument from Self-Inconsistency and the Argument from Evil are the most serious challenges to the existence of God. By having shown that neither of them count in the least against the existence of God, therefore, we have disposed of what seem to be, on the face of it, the best reasons around for thinking that God does not exist. Of course, by having shown that neither of these argument-clusters provides any evidence against God's existence, we cannot be said to have shown that there *is* no evidence against the existence of God. We have not considered all the arguments there are against God's existence. Hence we cannot be said to have established that:

(2) There is no evidence against the existence of God.

However, in accordance with the dual task we set ourselves in these last two chapters, we have done whatever we can to make (2) seem plausible. We have done so first by pointing out that at least most major intellectual reasons for the lack of religious faith in this day and age are not relevant to the question of whether God exists. We hope thereby to have placed the potential evidential threat against God's existence into its proper perspective. We hope that enough was said to weaken the impression that our argument from experience of God faces a vast array of types of counterevidence. And, second, we have shown that the two most dangerous looking arguments against God's existence pose no danger at all.

So we have gone as far as we can go here in supporting the truth of (2). Anything more we leave for others or for another time. In the meantime, we can only say that as far as we have considered the question, (2) is true.

Hence, we conclude that as far as we have considered the question it is strongly rational to believe that God is experienced and thus that God exists.

---

[31] This is not the same as saying that *only if* there is no evidence then it is strongly rational to believe that God exists. We do not endorse that, since even if there were evidence against the existence of God the evidence from experience of God might still be stronger, and so it would still be strongly rational to believe.

We remind the reader that we recognize that there can be persons for whom (1) may be false, such as persons who rationally hold religious or anti-religious world-views which affect adversely our argument. As pointed out in the Introduction such views are bracketed in this study.

Bibliography

Alston, William P. "Externalist Theories of Perception." *Philosophy and Phenomenological Research* 51 (1990): 73–97.

——. "The Fulfillment of Promises as Evidence for Religious Belief." In *Faith in Theory and Practice: Essays on Justifying Religious Belief*, ed. Elizabeth S. Radcliffe and Carol J. White. Chicago: Open Court, 1993.

——. "Ineffability." *Philosophical Review* 65 (1956).

——. *Perceiving God: The Epistemology of Religious Experience*. Ithaca: Cornell University Press, 1991.

——. "Referring to God." *International Journal for Philosophy of Religion* 24 (1988): 113–28.

Bach, Kent. *Thought and Reference*. Oxford: Clarendon Press, 1987.

Baillie, John. *Our Knowledge of God*. London: Oxford University Press, 1939.

——. *The Sense of the Presence of God*. New York: Scribner's, 1962.

Beardsworth, Timothy. *A Sense of Presence*. Oxford: Oxford University Press, 1977.

The Brahma Sutra: The Philosophy of Spiritual Life, ed. and trans. S. Radhakrishnan. London: Allen and Unwin, 1971.

Broad, C. D. "Arguments for the Existence of God: II." *Journal of Theological Studies* 40 (1939).

——. *Religion, Philosophy, and Psychical Research*. London: Routledge and Kegan Paul, 1953.

Buber, Martin. *I and Thou*, ed. and trans. Walter Kaufmann. New York: Charles Scribner's, 1970.

Carman, John B. *Majesty and Meekness: A Comparative Study of Contrast and Harmony in the Concept of God*. Grand Rapids, Mich.: Eerdmans, 1994.

Davis, Caroline Franks. *The Evidential Force of Religious Experience*. Oxford: Clarendon Press, 1989.

Douglas-Smith, Basil. *The Mystics Come to Harley Street*. London: Regency Press, 1983.

Draper, Paul. "Probabilistic Arguments from Evil." *Religious Studies* 28 (1992): 303–17.

Durkheim, Emile. *The Elementary Forms of the Religious Life*, trans. J. W. Swain. New York: Free Press, 1965.

Edwards, Jonathan. *Selected Writings of Jonathan Edwards*, ed. Harold P. Simonson. New York: Ungar, 1970.

Evans, Donald. "Can Philosophers Limit What Mystics Can Do? A Critique of Steven Katz." *Religious Studies* 25 (1989): 53–60.

Findlay, J. N. "Can God's Existence Be Disproved?" In *New Essays in Philosophical Theology*, ed. Alasdair MacIntyre and Antony Flew. London: SCM Press, 1961.

Flew, Antony. *God and Philosophy*. London: Hutchinson, 1966.

Freud, Sigmund. *The Future of an Illusion*, trans. W. D. Robinson-Scott. London: Hogarth Press, 1962.

Gellman, Jerome I. "Experiencing God's Infinity," *American Philosophical Quarterly* 31 (1994): 53–61.

———. *The Fear, the Trembling, and the Fire: Kierkegaard and Hasidic Masters on the Binding of Isaac*. Lanham, Md.: University Press of America, 1994.

———. "The Name of God." *Noûs* 29 (1995): 536–43.

———. "Naming, and Naming God." *Religious Studies* 29 (1993): 193–216.

———. "A New Look at the Problem of Evil." *Faith and Philosophy* 9 (1992): 210–16.

———. "Omnipotence and Impeccability." *The New Scholasticism* 51 (1977): 151–61.

———. "The Paradox of Omnipotence, and Perfection." *Sophia* 14 (1975): 14, 31–39.

———. "Religious Diversity and the Epistemic Justification of Religious Belief." *Faith and Philosophy* 10 (1993): 345–64.

Gilson, Etienne. *The Mystical Theology of St. Bernard*, trans. A. H. C. Downes. London: Sheed and Ward, 1955.

Godin, André and Monique Hallez. "Parental Images and Divine Paternity." In *From Religious Experience to a Religious Attitude*, ed. André Godin. Brussels: Lumen Vitae Press, 1964.

Grover, Stephen. "Religious Experiences: Skepticism, Gullibility, or Credulity?" In *Faith in Theory and Practice: Essays on Justifying Religious Belief*, ed. Elizabeth S. Radcliffe and Carol J. White. Chicago: Open Court, 1993.

Gutting, Gary. *Religious Belief and Religious Skepticism*. Notre Dame: University of Notre Dame Press, 1983.

Hestevold, H. Scott. "The Anselmian 'Single-Divine-Attribute Doctrine'." *Religious Studies* 29 (1993): 63–77.

Hick, John. *Faith and Knowledge*, 2nd ed. Ithaca: Cornell University Press, 1966.

———. *An Interpretation of Religion: Human Responses to the Transcendent*. London: Macmillan, 1989.

Hood, Ralph W., Jr. "Psychological Strength and the Report of Intense Religious Experience." *Journal for the Scientific Study of Religion* 13 (1974): 65–71.

Horton, Robin. *Patterns of Thought in Africa and the West*. Cambridge: Cambridge University Press, 1993.

Hume, David. *Dialogues Concerning Natural Religion*, ed. Norman Kemp Smith. New York: Macmillan, 1947.

James, William. *The Varieties of Religious Experience*. New York: Mentor, 1958.

Katz, Jerrold J. "Names without Bearers." *Philosophical Review* 103 (1994): 1–39.

Katz, Steven. "The 'Conservative' Character of Mysticism." In *Mysticism and Religious Traditions*, ed. Steven Katz. New York: Oxford University, 1983.

——. "Language, Epistemology, and Mysticism." In *Mysticism and Philosophical Analysis*, ed. Steven Katz. New York: Oxford University, 1978.

King, Sallie B. "Two Epistemological Models for the Interpretation of Mysticism." *Journal of the American Academy of Religion* 56 (1988): 257–79.

Kook, Abraham Isaac. *The Essential Writings of Abraham Isaac Kook*, ed. and trans. Ben Zion Bokser. Amity N.Y.: Amity House, 1988.

——. *Kook, A. Y.: Selected Letters*, trans. Tzvi Feldman. Ma'aleh Adumim, Israel: Ma'aliot, 1986.

Kripke, Saul. *Naming and Necessity*. Oxford: Basil Blackwell, 1980.

La Croix, Richard R. *What Is God? The Selected Essays of Richard R. La Croix*. Buffalo: Prometheus Books, 1993.

Lindbeck, George. *The Nature of Doctrine: Religion and Theology in a Postliberal Age*. Philadelphia: Westminster Press, 1984.

Lipton, Peter. *Inference to the Best Explanation*. New York: Routledge and Kegan Paul, 1991.

Mackie, J. L. *The Miracle of Theism*. Oxford: Clarendon Press, 1982.

Martin, Michael. *Atheism: A Philosophical Justification*. Philadelphia: Temple University Press, 1990.

Mavrodes, George. *Belief in God: The Epistemology of Religious Experience*. New York: Random House, 1970.

——. *Revelation in Religious Belief*. Philadelphia: Temple University Press, 1988.

Miller, Richard B. "The Reference of 'God'." *Faith and Philosophy* 3 (1986): 3–15.

Nozick, Robert. *The Examined Life: Philosophical Meditations*. New York: Simon and Schuster, 1989.

Organ, Troy Wilson. *Hinduism: Its Historical Development*. Woodbury, N.Y.: Barron's, 1974.

Otto, Rudolf. *The Idea of the Holy*, trans. John W. Harvey. London: Oxford University Press, 1957.

——. *Mysticism East and West*. New York: Macmillan, 1932.

Perovich, Anthony N., Jr. "Mysticism and the Philosophy of Science." *Journal of Religion* 65 (1985): 63–82.

Pike, Nelson. "Hume on Evil." *Philosophical Review* 72 (1963): 180–97.

Plantinga, Alvin. *Does God Have a Nature?* Milwaukee: Marquette University Press, 1980.

——. *God and Other Minds*. Ithaca: Cornell University Press, 1967.

——. "Is Belief in God Properly Basic?" *Noûs* 15 (1981): 41–53.

——. "Is Belief in God Rational?" In *Rationality and Religious Belief*, ed. C. F. Delaney. Notre Dame: University of Notre Dame Press, 1979.

Pollock, John L. *Knowledge and Justification*. Princeton: Princeton University Press, 1974.

Proudfoot, Wayne. *Religious Experience*. Berkeley: University of California Press, 1985.

Rahner, Karl. *Theological Investigations*, vol. 5. Baltimore: Helicon Press, 1966.

Ramakrishna, *The Gospel of Sri Ramakrishna*, trans. Swami Nikhilananda. Sri Ramakrishna Math: Mylapore, 1964.

Rowe, William L. "Evil and Theodicy." *Philosophical Topics* 16 (1988): 119–32.

——. "Evil and the Theistic Hypothesis: A Response to Wykstra." *International Journal for the Philosophy of Religion* 16 (1984): 95–100.;

——. "The Problem of Evil and Some Varieties of Atheism." *American Philosophical Quarterly* 16 (1979): 335–41. Reprinted in *Contemporary Perspectives on Religious Epistemology*, ed. R. Douglas Geivett and Brendan Sweetman. Oxford: Oxford University Press, 1992.

——. "Religious Experience and the Principle of Credulity." *International Journal for Philosophy of Religion* 13 (1982): 85–92.

——. "Ruminations about Evil." In *Philosophical Perspectives 5: Philosophy of Religion*, ed. James E. Tomberlin. Altascadero, Calif.: Ridgeview, 1991.

Russell, Bertrand. *Religion and Science*. London: Oxford University Press, 1935.

Sartre, Jean-Paul. *Existentialism and Humanism*, trans. Philip Mairet. London: Methuen, 1948.

Schimmel, Annemarie. *Mystical Dimensions of Islam*. Chapel Hill: University of North Carolina Press, 1975.

Schlesinger, George N. "Divine Perfection." *Religious Studies* 21 (1985): 147–58.

——. *New Perspectives on Old-Time Religion*. Oxford: Clarendon Press, 1988.

Scholem, Gershom. *Major Trends in Jewish Mysticism*. Jerusalem: Schocken, 1941.

Siegman, A. "An Empirical Investigation of the Psychoanalytic Theory of Religious Behavior." In *Psychology and Religion: Selected Readings*, ed. L. B. Brown. Harmondsworth: Penguin Education, 1973.

Smith, Huston. "Is There a Perennial Philosophy?" *Journal of the American Academy of Religion* 55 (1987): 553–66.

Snowdon, P. "Perception, Vision, and Causation." *Proceedings of the Aristotelian Society* 81 (1980–81): 175–92.

Swinburne, Richard. *The Existence of God*, rev. ed. Oxford: Clarendon Press, 1991.

Teresa of Avila, *The Life of Teresa of Jesus*, ed. and trans. E. Allison Peers. Garden City: Doubleday, 1960.

Uffenheimer, Rivka Schatz. *Hasidism as Mysticism*. Jerusalem: Magnes Press, 1993.

Underhill, Evelyn. *Mysticism: A Study in the Nature and Development of Man's Spiritual Consciousness*. London: Methuen, 1945.

Unger, Johan. *On Religious Experience: A Psychological Study*. Uppsala: Uppsala University Press, 1976.

Wainwright, William J. "Mysticism and Sense Perception." In *Contemporary Philosophy of Religion*, ed. Stephen M. Cahn and David Shatz. New York: Oxford University Press, 1982.

——. *Mysticism: A Study of Its Nature, Cognitive Value and Moral Implications*. Madison: University of Wisconsin Press, 1981.

Ward, Keith. *Religion and Revelation*. Oxford: Clarendon Press, 1994.

Weiss, Joseph. *Studies in East European Jewish Mysticism*, ed. David Goldstein. Oxford: Oxford University Press, 1985.

Westphal, Merold. *God, Guilt, and Death*. Bloomington: Indiana University Press, 1984.

Wierenga, Edward R. *The Nature of God: An Inquiry into Divine Attributes*. Ithaca: Cornell University Press, 1989.

Wykstra, Stephen J. "The Humean Obstacle to Evidential Arguments from Suffering: On Avoiding the Evils of 'Appearance'." *International Journal for Philosophy of Religion* 16 (1984): 73–93.

Wykstra, Stephen J., and Bruce Russell. "The 'Inductive' Argument from Evil: A Dialogue." *Philosophical Topics* 16 (1988): 133–60.

Yandell, Keith E. *The Epistemology of Religious Experience*. Madison: University of Wisconsin Press, 1993.
——. "Some Varieties of Ineffability." *International Journal for Philosophy of Religion* 6 (1975): 167–79.
Zaehner, R. C. *Hinduism*, 2nd ed. London: Oxford University Press, 1966.
——. *Mysticism Sacred and Profane*. New York: Oxford University Press, 1961.

Index

Index